Praise for *The Great Spiritual Migration*

"This is Brian McLaren's finest book: a beautiful exploration of a hopeful, joyful, mystical, and just faith that invites Christians to move from fear to love. On every page, he calls out to longing readers, 'Don't give up. A better world, a better way of belief is possible.' And he is right."

—Diana Butler Bass, author of
Grounded: Finding God in the World—A Spiritual Revolution

"Brian McLaren is refining the meaning of orthodoxy in our time. Read this and be assured that you are not crazy making in what you are seeing and suffering today."

—Richard Rohr, author of *Falling Upward*

"*The Great Spiritual Migration* puts into words what so many people of faith are experiencing, and in a way that is at once accessible and profound. This may be Brian's most important work yet."

—Rachel Held Evans, author of *Searching for Sunday*

"A refreshingly honest and enriching analysis of the spiritual moment that is changing all our lives."

—Joan Chittister, author of *Between the Dark and the Daylight*

"I have such respect for Brian McLaren; I would follow him anywhere, and so should you. This well-conceived, intelligent, warm, truthful book is our guide to a life of faith defined by love-in-action."

—Dr. Jacqui Lewis, senior minister,
Middle Collegiate Church, New York City

"McLaren continues to have his finger on the pulse of a new kind of Christianity. A prophetic and winsome invitation to join the work of the Spirit in transformation."

—Peter Enns, author of *The Sin of Certainty*

ALSO BY BRIAN D. McLAREN

THE
GREAT SPIRITUAL
MIGRATION

How the World's Largest Religion Is Seeking

a Better Way to Be Christian

BRIAN D. MCLAREN

CONVERGENT

NEW YORK

Copyright © 2016 by Brian D. McLaren

Published in the United States by Convergent Books, an imprint of the
Crown Publishing Group, a division of Penguin Random House LLC,
New York.
crownpublishing.com

CONVERGENT BOOKS is a registered trademark and the C colophon
is a trademark of Penguin Random House LLC.

Originally published in hardcover in the United States by Convergent Books,
an imprint of the Crown Publishing Group, a division of
Penguin Random House LLC, New York, in 2016.

Library of Congress Cataloging-in-Publication Data
Names: McLaren, Brian D., 1956– author.
Title: The great spiritual migration / Brian D. McLaren.
Description: First Edition. | New York: Convergent Books, 2016.
Identifiers: LCCN 2016008188 | ISBN 9781601427915 (hardcover) |
ISBN 9781601427922 (pbk.) | ISBN 9781601427939 (ebook)
Subjects: LCSH: Christianity—21st century.
Classification: LCC BR481 .M295 2016 | DDC 270.8/3—dc23
LC record available at https://lccn.loc.gov/2016008188

ISBN 978-1-60142-792-2
Ebook ISBN 978-1-60142-793-9

Printed in the United States of America

Book design by Lauren Dong
Cover design by Jessie Sayward Bright

10 9 8

First Paperback Edition

*This book is dedicated to my colleagues in
three wonderful organizations:
Convergence (convergenceus.org), the Auburn Senior
Fellows Program (auburnseminary.org/seniorfellows), and the
Wild Goose Festival (wildgoosefestival.org).
They are pioneers in the great spiritual migration.*

CONTENTS

SWALLOW-TAILED KITE

THE HUMAN STORY IS A TALE OF PEOPLE IN MOTION. Anthropologists tell us that our ancient ancestors lived in southern Africa some two hundred thousand years ago, but it didn't take long before many began migrating north, eventually crossing into the Middle East. Some then migrated west across Europe and others moved east across Asia. And that, we know, was just the beginning.

The Bible also tells a story of humans on the move, tracing the human journey from life as hunter-gatherers in a garden to nomadic pastoralists with their patriarchs to settled agriculturalists with tribal chiefs and warlords. From there, human beings transition to life in city-states and from there, we become uneasy citizens of jostling kingdoms and colonizing empires. Exodus and exile, two of the main story lines of the Hebrew Scriptures, are tales of a people in motion, and the biblical plot line seethes with the deeply human tension between settling down and moving on. Jesus himself was perpetually in motion, leading his disciples from town to town, their physical movements mirroring the spiritual odyssey on which he led them. "Foxes have holes and birds of the air have nests," he said, but he had no such home. He was always on the move, never settling down anywhere for long. His first words were "Follow me," and his final words were "Go into all the world." Jesus, we might say, was a migrant messiah, and the Bible is a book of migrations.

As a boy I was an avid reader of the Bible, and this sense of movement was deeply embedded in me. Then as a teenager, I began reading science fiction, and my adolescent imagination was soon expanding with grand dreams of traveling among the stars.

It's no wonder that *Homo sapiens* has also been called *Homo viator*. We are human wayfarers and pilgrims—always on the move.

Well, maybe not always. I grew up in a fundamentalist Christian tradition called the Plymouth Brethren. We didn't have an official motto, but if we did, it might have been "We shall not be moved." We contributed to the larger Christian community several of Christianity's worst ideas, including dispensationalism and the Rapture and the whole "left behind" last-days scenario. (You're welcome.) Our little sect was made slightly famous by the great American humorist Garrison Keillor. His stories about his childhood in "the Sanctified Brethren" often elicit from me a chuckle of familiarity—and sometimes a wince or groan.

My paternal and maternal grandparents were dedicated members of the Brethren—missionaries and elders, true loyalists.[1] As a faithful firstborn son, I was predisposed to join their ranks as a good Brethren boy, to stay put and play by the rules. But by my teenage years, it was clear that I simply didn't fit in the rigid Brethren box. My love for philosophy, evolution, and rock and roll were three spiritual strikes that counted me out. Providentially for me, the Jesus Movement came along in those years, and my experience in that movement made it possible for me to stay Christian, but in a new way, no longer as a fundamentalist, but as an *Evangelical*.

Although Evangelicals are seen by many as archconservatives, folks like me who were born fundamentalist often experience Evangelicalism as a big step into more freedom. Scratch an Evangelical, you might say, and underneath the paint you'll find a fundamentalist seeking a little room to grow.[2] As a young nondenominational Evangelical in my thirties, I became a church planter and pastor and felt very much at home. I had already come a long way, and I wasn't going anywhere.

But just as I was settling down, politically ambitious fundamentalists staged a decisive takeover of Evangelicalism in the United States, pulling it firmly into the orbit of the "religious right" and reclaiming it as a camouflaged form of fundamentalism. As a result, by the age of forty, I found that I had moved to the progressive margin of the Evangelical camp. I began writing books from that vantage point, but I quickly learned that zealous conservative gatekeepers were eager to purge anyone to their theological or cultural left. So my location even in Evangelicalism grew more tenuous.[3] Whether I emigrated or was deported is a question up for debate, but one way or the other, by fifty, I found myself on the move again.

Over the last ten years, something has changed for me. I haven't simply moved to a new location where I am now settling down—from, say, static fundamentalism to static Evangelicalism to static liberalism. Instead, I've come to see that what matters most is not our *status* but our *trajectory,* not where we are but where we're going, not where we stand but where we're headed. Christian faith for me is no longer a static location but a great spiritual journey. And that changes everything.

As I see it, religion is at its best when it leads us forward, when it guides us in our spiritual growth as individuals and in our cultural evolution as a species. Unfortunately, religion often becomes more of a cage than a guide, holding us back rather than summoning us onward, a buffer to constructive change rather than a catalyst for it. In times of rapid and ambiguous change, such a regressive turn in religion may be understandable, but it is even more tragic: when a culture needs wise spiritual guidance the most, all it gets from religious leaders is anxious condemnation and critique, along with a big dose of nostalgia for the lost golden age of the good old days. We see this regressive pull in many sectors of Christianity, along with sectors of Islam, Hinduism, Buddhism, Judaism, and other religions too.

In that light, it's no surprise that people by the millions are moving away from traditional religions entirely, often into secularism, often into experimental forms of spirituality that are not yet supported by religious traditions. But at this pivotal moment, something else is happening. Within each tradition, unsettling but needed voices are arising—prophetic voices, we might call them, voices of change, hope, imagination, and new beginnings. They say there's an alternative to static or rigid religion on the one hand and religion-free secularism on the other. They claim that the Spirit is calling us, not to dig in our heels, but rather to pack up our tents and get moving again. They invite us on a great spiritual migration—not *out of* our religions, but out of our cages and ruts, not as jaded ex-members, but *as hopeful pilgrims moving forward in the journey of faith.*

It took me almost five decades to understand that the call to Christian discipleship is a call to get going, to move forward. That's why I've written this book. This isn't just a report of what's going on. It's an invitation for you to get involved, to come along, to help create a better future for our faith and for our world.

Since childhood, I've been interested in birds. As a little boy in upstate New York, I was taught by my mother to notice the arrival of the robins as an early sign of spring. I have a primal childhood memory of walking along a trail in a meadow and noticing a sparrow sitting on a fencepost, singing a song I had never heard a sparrow sing before: three high notes followed by a liquid trill. I begged my mom to take me to the library, where I scoured books until I could identify what I had heard—a song sparrow—and my lifelong love for birds had begun.[4]

I spent most of my life in Maryland and by the time I moved away, I could identify nearly every bird I encountered by both sight and song. For about seven years, I have lived along the Gulf Coast in Florida, and I am getting acquainted with a whole new array of bird species. Now, the harbinger of spring is not the robin, but the swallow-tailed kite that flies in from South America in February and March. Any day now, I will again see it, sleek white body, black wing bars, black forked tail, diving and gliding, soaring and hovering with perfect grace just over the treetops. And I will again be moved by the wonder of migration, written not only into the human heart, but into all of creation.

What must it be like to be a young bird, happily spending winter or summer in some comfortable location, and then suddenly to feel the irresistible summons to migrate? I don't know what it feels like to be a bird, but I do know what it feels like to be a human being who feels the call to rise and move. I think you do too.

Although I'm writing as a Christian primarily for my fellow Christians, I would hope that people of other faiths could learn lessons from our experience that are applicable to their own, just as we will learn from theirs. Like flocks of geese migrating in our distinct V's from different starting points, I believe we will discover that we are being called in the same direction, and if we heed that call, we will discover one another in new ways.

I would even dare to hope that many who have left Christian faith—often for very good reasons—will find in these pages even better reasons for hope, along with an invitation to reengage, to join in this epic project, this transforming quest, this great spiritual migration toward a better way of being Christian, and a better way of being human.

COKE AND THE CAN

IMAGINE THAT YOU JUST BOUGHT A TWELVE-PACK OF COKE. Each virgin can sits before you, bubbling with the promise of caffeinated, carbonated, carbohydrate-rich pleasure. You remove the first can from the cardboard box and pop it open.

Fizz.

You lift the can to your lips, but the liquid tastes salty and foul. Shocked, you throw it away and open the second can. You take a sip and immediately—*phhhhht!*—spit it out: it tastes like spoiled milk. You open a third can and lift it cautiously to your lips but don't drink: the smell of carbonated sewage disgusts you. If the fourth and fifth cans greet you with the scent of gasoline and vinegar, how likely is it that you'll open the sixth through twelfth cans, each of which has the classic, sweet, velvety, tongue-tingling taste you were expecting?

Now imagine you call Coca-Cola customer service and share with them your experience.

CUSTOMER SERVICE: Coca-Cola World Headquarters. How may I help you?

YOU: I just bought a twelve-pack of Coke that tasted terrible.

CUSTOMER SERVICE: I'm sorry to hear that. What color were the cans?

YOU: The cans were normal—bright red with white lettering.

CUSTOMER SERVICE: Well, that's the most important thing. Was the cardboard box sound—the box that contained the twelve cans?

YOU: Yes. The cardboard box was fine. It was the taste that was the prob—

CUSTOMER SERVICE: Thanks for calling! I'm glad the cans were red and the box was sturdy. Enjoy Coke and have a nice day![1]

A brand like Coke only has meaning because it is linked to an essential quality or qualities for a soft drink: taste—not the can. With a politician, policies, effectiveness, and character count—not hairstyle or skin color. With a bicycle, speed, weight, and comfort are paramount, but not saddle color.

And what are the qualities of Christian faith that really matter, regardless of the packaging?

Therein lies the trouble. Therein lies our need for migration.[2]

FOR CENTURIES, Christianity has been presented as a system of beliefs.[3] That system of beliefs has supported a wide range of unintended consequences, from colonialism to environmental destruction, subordination of women to stigmatization of LGBT people, anti-Semitism to Islamophobia, clergy pedophilia to white privilege. What would it mean for Christians to rediscover their faith not as a problematic system of beliefs, but as a just and generous way of life, rooted in contemplation and expressed in compassion, that makes amends for its mistakes and is dedicated to beloved community for all? Could Christians migrate from defining their faith as a system of beliefs to expressing it as a loving way of life? Could Christian faith lose the bitter taste of colonialism, exclusion, judgment, hypocrisy, and oppression, and regain the sweet and nourishing flavor of justice, joy, and peace?

For centuries, Christians have presented God as a Supreme Being who showers blessings upon insiders who share certain beliefs and proper institutional affiliation, but who punishes outsiders with eternal conscious torment. Yet Jesus revealed God as one who "eats with sinners," welcomes outsiders in, and forgives even while being rejected, tortured, and killed. Jesus associated God more with gracious parental tenderness than strict authoritarian toughness.[4] He preached that God was to be found in self-giving service rather than self-asserting domination. What would it mean for Christians to let Jesus and his message lead them to a new vision of God? What would it mean for Christians to understand, experience, and embody God as the loving, healing, reconciling Spirit in whom all creatures live, move, and have their being?

For centuries, Christianity has presented itself as an "organized religion"—a change-averse institution or set of institutions that protects and promotes a timeless system of beliefs that were handed down fully formed in the past. Yet Christianity's actual history is a story of change and adaptation. We Christians have repeatedly adapted our message, methods, and mission to the contours of our time. What might happen if we understand the core Christian ethos as creative, constructive, and forward-leaning—as an "organizing religion" that challenges all institutions (including its own) to learn, grow, and mature toward a deepening, enduring vision of reconciliation with God, self, neighbor, enemy, and creation?

A SHARED FRUSTRATION

Today, millions of us—Catholics, Evangelicals, mainline Protestants, and Orthodox Christians—share something that we seldom verbalize: we're worried that the "brand" of Christianity has been so compromised that many of us are barely able to use the label anymore. Whether we lean conservative, progressive, or moderate, whether we're clergy or laypeople, old or young, more and more of us feel that there must be a better way to be Christian.

We all love Jesus. To us, he is the best thing about Christianity. We all think he was right, and we all want to follow the way of life he modeled and taught. We all believe there are many wonderful and unique treasures in our Christian faith. But we are coming to realize that many sectors of our faith need something more radical than renewal, revival, or even reform. We need migration.

Of course, we all know many people who are happily Christian in the conventional sense, their only complaint being that people like us won't leave them to their relative bliss in the spiritual status quo.

But we also know that for a lot of people Christianity is malfunctioning, seriously so, and it's not pretty.

I've traveled to more than forty countries in the last twenty years, interacting with people from dozens of denominations, and everywhere I turn, I hear alarming reports. A Latin American Pentecostal pastor tells me his experience of Christianity "from the inside" has led him out of faith and into atheism; he no longer believes what he preaches and feels like a fraud, but has no other way to support his family. A young mom in the United States laments that she can't bring her kids to church for fear that Christianity will instill the same sense of inferiority and shame in them that it did in her. An African Christian college student tells me that prosperity-gospel preachers in his country have turned Christianity into a financial scam, a form of theft—"religious organized crime," he called it—enriching pastors at the expense of parishioners.[5] An Asian Catholic activist tells me that he hasn't attended Mass in decades because it feels like a way of pacifying victims of injustice rather than organizing and empowering them as protagonists in their own liberation. A European pastor tells me that he thinks it is already too late: the best thing that can happen is for the Christian religion to collapse under its own weight so something new can arise from the rubble. He sees himself as doing hospice work for his religion. These stories of frustration, turmoil, and discouragement can break your heart.

We've all seen the statistics. Nearly all sectors of Christian faith in the West are experiencing numerical decline, especially among their younger generations.[6] Some of our colleagues comfort themselves in the face of these downward trends: *the half-hearted and superficial are dropping out,* they say, *so only the true believers (like us!) remain.* More of us, however, are beginning to realize that a sea change is under way, and the causes of decline go deeper than supposed spiritual flaws in those who've left.

To make matters worse, it seems like every day some of our fellow Christians are reaching new lows in making Christian faith look ugly, dull, ridiculous, dangerous, or dim-witted. (And each of us, of course, has made his or her own contributions in this category.) It's not just us Christians who feel this way about our faith. Jews, Muslims, and others are coming to the same conclusion: *our religions often stand for the very opposite of what their founders stood for.*

The pattern is predictable. Founders are typically generous, visionary, bold, and creative, but the religions that ostensibly carry on their work often become the opposite: constricted, change-averse, nostalgic, fearful, obsessed with boundary maintenance, turf battles, and money. Instead of greeting the world with open arms as their founders did, their successors stand guard with clenched fists. Instead of empowering others as their founders did, they hoard power. Instead of defying tradition and unleashing moral imagination as their founders did, they impose tradition and refuse to think outside the lines. A religion that cuts itself off from the example of its founder while still bearing the founder's name often becomes little more than a chaplaincy for other ideologies, offering its services to the highest bidder. No wonder so many religious folks today wear down, burn out, and opt out.

JESUS, KIDNAPPED

And no wonder more and more of us who are Christians by birth, by choice, or both find ourselves shaking our heads and asking, "What happened to Christianity? What happened to Jesus and his beautiful message?" We feel as if our founder has been kidnapped and held hostage by extremists. His captors parade him in front of cameras to say, under duress, things he obviously doesn't believe. As their blank-faced puppet, he often comes across as antipoor, antienvironment, antigay, anti-intellectual, anti-immigrant, and antiscience (not to mention protorture, proinequality, proviolence, pro–death penalty, and prowar). That's not the Jesus we met in the Gospels! That's not the Jesus who won our hearts!

Meanwhile, we notice a sizable minority of Christians who quietly but firmly resist this ideological project. Too often, though, this minority can only speak convincingly about what they're against and what they no longer believe. They struggle to define in positive terms what faith means for them after it has been scrubbed of overconfident myth, superstition, and ideology. If their counterparts seem angry and closed, these folks often seem smart but lost. Preoccupied with formalities, committees, and tradition, they remain strangely silent about spiritual experience. If their counterparts check their minds at the front door of the church, these folks sometimes seem to have checked their hearts.

People like you and me feel we are offered endless pairs of unacceptable alternatives: ignorance on fire or intelligence on ice;[7] excessive certainty or insufficient confidence; updated styles and structures with an outdated message or an updated message with outdated styles and structures; a regressive movement or a progressive bureaucracy. Again and again we are offered two ways of being irrelevant. Neither option works long term, neither compels, and neither offers a good way to live.

For many of us, this tension has been building for decades. I seriously considered dropping out of the pastorate, and even the faith, on several occasions. At those junctures, I imagined that I would continue to love Jesus—what he stood for, what he taught, and how he lived—but I would slip out the back door of the religion and no longer wear the Christian T-shirt. The discredited brand just didn't seem worth the stress and hassle anymore. You could call me "spiritual but not religious." You could call me post-Evangelical or even post-Christian. You could call me whatever you want. But I was tired of bailing out a ship that seemed full of leaks and whose captains seemed intent on steering straight into yesterday's sunset. I was ready to swim for shore.

But there was one problem. Whenever I quieted my heart, never once did I hear the Spirit whispering, "Give up. Turn back. Drop out." Instead, again and again, I heard, *"Go farther!* Don't be afraid! Hang in there! *Go forward!"* So I strove to do so, and the titles of my books tell the story of a restlessness, a quest, a spiritual journey or migration.[8]

CAN CHRISTIANITY BE SAVED?

A lot of us have heard a lot of sermons about the need for "sinners" to be saved, born again, or converted. Now we're daring to wonder: *Can Christianity experience for itself the things it has preached for others? Can Christianity be saved? Can Christian faith be born anew?*

I know some of you aren't sure, but I'll bet you at least hope the answer is *yes*.

Those of us who have been on this spiritual migration for many years often forget that each day there is another fourteen-year-old coming of age and asking questions for the first time, afraid she's the only one, afraid she'll be kicked out of her church and even her family for questioning what she was taught. Across town from her, there's a pastor whose inherited theological high heels have gone way beyond causing blisters to making it hard to take another step. And not far from her, there's an old grandfather whose kids and grandkids are far from God and far from the church, and he's having second thoughts about the whole thing himself. And just down the street, there's a young mother putting her kids to bed at night, wishing she could teach them to pray and maybe tell them a Bible story, but not wanting to infect them with the shame, fear, and guilt that her religious upbringing instilled in her.

It is tempting to leave Christian faith altogether, I know. But there is a treasure hidden in its field, and I want to assure you that you have permission to shovel away the distractions and rediscover the precious gift that has for too long been buried. That's my good news: you don't have to give up on Christian faith. Nor do you have to accept it as it is. Christian faith can be saved, and you are invited to participate in its conversion. If just a dozen of us here and a handful of us there begin migrating in the right direction, that's enough to start something. Changing hearts moving together—soon the center of gravity shifts, and soon a migration is under way.

What are we moving toward? My most direct answer would be that we are migrating toward a profound *conversion* in Christian faith. We're seeking a change in the content, not just the can; in substance, not just in style or structure.

The word *conversion* can be scary, I know, especially if Christian faith as you've understood it has done you more good than harm. It's a little like the word *surgery* or *chemotherapy;* a doctor utters one of those words, and you whisper to yourself, "I didn't think the diagnosis was *that* serious!" But you'll see in the coming chapters why I believe our beloved faith's diagnosis is, indeed, serious, and the need for migration and conversion are real.[9]

The word *conversion* is scary for other reasons as well. In the hands of the religious ambassadors of colonizing powers (Spanish, Portuguese, English, Dutch, American, and others), *conversion* meant a process of co-opting and domesticating those they were occupying and exploiting by force. In other words, from 1492 to well into the twentieth century, *conversion* came to mean a kind of cultural genocide, supposedly "saving souls" by eradicating their original religion and culture so they could be assimilated into the religion, culture, and economy of their conquerors.

Perhaps the only way to redeem such a term is to turn it on the religion that abused it.

That's why, when I use the word *conversion,* I'm thinking of how we Christians typically use the word for everybody except ourselves.

As we all know, conversion involves repentance—a radical rethinking. It includes remorse—for harm done in the name of our faith. But conversion means more than being sorry; it means becoming different. That difference won't change our essential identity; it's not about erasing our hard drive and starting from scratch. But it will mean learning to live life in a new way: seeking a deeper aliveness, a better version of life, a truer expression of Christian faith.

Consider how people use *conversion* in reference to energy: "We live in a consumptive and unsustainable fossil-fuel economy," they say, "and we need to be *converted* to a sustainable economy based on solar energy, wind power, and other renewable sources." To be converted from a dirty-energy way of life to a clean-energy way of life won't change who we are in our essence, but it will change a lot about us: our values, our behavior, our priorities, our definitions of success. We might say that an energy conversion will allow us to become a better, more responsible, wiser, and more sustainable version of ourselves.

Similarly, the spiritual conversion we need won't change the true essence, heart, or treasure of Christian faith. Christianity will still be rooted deeply in Jesus and his good news. It will still draw sustenance, as Jesus did, from the Bible as a rich library full of wisdom, warning, challenge, travail, and inspiration. It will still be informed by the Christian tradition with all its inspiration and ambiguity, its tragedy and comedy, its irony, paradox, and restless hope. It will still engage in the core spiritual practices that have sustained Christians for centuries—prayer, contemplation, fellowship, worship, service, lifelong learning from our texts and traditions. Yes, it will differ in significant ways from conventional Christianity, especially in its modern Anglo-American form. But it will still be *Christian* in the best sense of the word: a better, more responsible, wiser, and more sustainable way to be human . . . in the way of Jesus.

Imagine that your home has fallen into disrepair. Its roof leaks, its walls lack insulation, its floor joists have been colonized by termites, its plumbing and electricity weren't properly installed. Another coat of paint or a new carpet won't solve its problems. You could sell it and move elsewhere, or you could just burn the whole thing down and start over. But if you value the memories and character contained in the old house, if you love it and want to save as much of it as possible, you have to engage in some careful demolition. It's not demolition for destruction, but demolition for salvation.

Over the years, many of us have done a lot of demolition: exposing leaky spirituality, ripping up shaky ecclesiology, pulling out dangerous theological wiring, knocking down poorly installed missiology. Eventually the time comes when we must move beyond demolition and focus instead on construction. We have to identify not just what we're moving from and leaving behind, but what we're moving toward and what we want to build.

Your Little Inner Fundamentalist

I know a lot of us have a little inner fundamentalist perched on our right shoulder, and he is scolding us right now. "Just a minute!" he's whisper-shouting into our ear. "You're not allowed to do that. Christian faith was defined once and for all by Jesus and the apostles. It is encoded in the creeds and preserved by religious leaders and institutions. It's already fully constructed, and there's nothing to deconstruct or reconstruct. Our generation's duty is to hand it down faithfully, without change. Here we stand, without apology, accommodation, or migration. Christianity must always be what it has always been. Anything else is unorthodox, heretical, apostate, and wrong."

My inner fundamentalist intimidated me with this kind of talk for much of my early life. He (my inner fundamentalist always seems to be male) loved to quote Jude 1:3, which urges people to "contend" for the faith "once delivered to the saints."[10] The little guy had a point: the message of and about Jesus is in fact a given—it is Christianity's pearl, our treasure, our gift, and it must never be lost. The meaning-rich stories of what Jesus said and did form the unique heart of Christian faith that must always pulse within us.

But my inner fundamentalist also misled me. He assumed that what our grandparents and parents gave us was exactly the same treasure given by Jesus and the apostles. He didn't realize how often through history we Christians have tampered with that original gift, how often we've weighed it down with baggage or suppressed some parts of it and exaggerated others, how often we've said the words but missed the point. He mistook "the old-time religion" that was "good enough for my father" for the original good news that Jesus embodied and proclaimed. My well-meaning little inner fundamentalist "misunderestimated" how often Christianity has found itself in need of spiritual migration and conversion.

To see how needful repeated and ongoing migration has been in Christian history, just imagine if church leaders today allowed political leaders to preside over church affairs as Constantine did in the fourth century.[11] Imagine if popes or pastors today had the power to launch armed attacks on Jews and Muslims in their neighborhoods, or organize new rounds of Crusades as they did in the twelfth and thirteenth centuries.[12] Imagine if church officials today imprisoned, tortured, banished, and executed those they considered heretics the way they did in the medieval era of Inquisition.[13] Imagine if a pope or other religious leader today legitimized land theft against non-Christians, or called for their enslavement, as was done in *Terra Nullius* in 1095 and *Romanus Pontifex* in 1455.[14] Imagine if the majority of Christians today still used the Bible to defend anti-Semitism, slavery, segregation, the inferiority of women, or the earth-centered universe.[15]

Thank God that Christianity has a rich tradition of changing course!

The Catholic theologian Gustavo Gutiérrez agreed: "Conversion is a permanent process," he said, "in which very often the obstacles we meet make us lose all we had gained and start anew."[16] Or as Martin Luther said in the first of his oft-mentioned but seldom-read ninety-five theses, repentance, rethinking, and, yes, experiencing ongoing migration and conversion are absolute necessities, not just at the beginning of one's faith journey but at every step of the way.[17] Without continuing conversion, our traditions grow proud and corrupt, self-seeking and ingrown, rigid and constricting. Without continuing conversion, we can be faithful neither to Christ nor to ourselves and the world around us.

Not long ago, a former Islamist extremist helped me see this more clearly. During a radio interview, he was asked if he saw Islam as a warrior religion or a peaceful religion.[18] He replied that Islam, like Christianity and Judaism and Hinduism and almost every other religion, has at times in the past been both peaceful and warlike, and in the future can be either. And then he added ten words that are both unsettling and empowering in their import: *A religion will be what its adherents make of it.*

A Threefold Migration

Christian faith, we might say, was born on a weekend, between Good Friday and Easter Sunday. Those three days represent three essential movements that we must experience, as individuals and as communities, so our faith can be born anew.

First, on Good Friday, there is a painful death, a letting go. For us today, this represents the collapse of what I call "belief-system Christianity."[19] Such a death is traumatic and must be faced with courage and resolve. Our little inner fundamentalists will be chattering constantly, threatening us with hellfire and damnation for even daring to consider that the essence of Christian faith might not be our beliefs. If we are willing to endure the trauma of Good Friday and experience this *spiritual migration,* we will discover that our faith can be reborn, not simply as a stronger or purer system of beliefs, but as something bigger, deeper, and richer: a way of life, which is the way of love. That will be our work in part I of this book.

Saturday represents a silence, a contemplative pause in the aftermath of Friday's loss, a coming to terms with what Friday's traumas meant and will mean. If Friday represents a letting go, Saturday represents a letting be, a sinking to the depths, a descent to a deeper vantage point. In part II, we'll face some tough truths about the great damage that conventional, unconverted understandings of God have caused and are causing. Then we'll see how a positive shift in our basic understanding of God—a *theological migration*—can unleash Christianity's unseized potential for healing and transformation in our world.

Part III corresponds to Easter Sunday. Having let go of so much on Friday and Saturday, we can now travel lighter, rising up in a *practical, ecclesial,* or *missional migration.* We'll develop a fresh understanding of communities, institutions, and movements so we can migrate from *organized* religion to *organizing* religion—that is, *religion organizing for the common good.* This movement orientation, we will see, is sustained and empowered by a joyful spirituality that produces ongoing, lifelong, multigenerational transformation.

Some readers will gravitate strongly to one of these migrations and will wonder why I included the other two. My reply would be that because I travel widely across Christian traditions, I see how all three are needed in various sectors of the Christian community, and, ultimately, I believe all three are inextricably related. Be that as it may, I hope readers will feel free to concentrate on the parts of the book that they are ready for now, and come back to the other parts later (later, but as soon as possible, I would hope, for reasons that will be clear in part III). The same goes for the material in the appendices.

As you read, be aware that others at all levels of church life and in all sectors of the Christian community are considering the same challenges and opportunities as you. Open yourself to the possibility that you and they are being orchestrated in a genuine movement of the Spirit, that together we are being led and called together into a better way of being Christian, and a better way of being human.

"Stop!" some people have told you. "You've gone far enough."

"Go back!" others have said. "You've already gone too far."

"Go farther!" the Spirit is saying. *Move forward!*

CONTEMPLATION, CONVERSATION, AND ACTION: INTRODUCTION

Contemplation: In stillness, ask yourself this simple question: what emotion or emotions do I feel most strongly after reading this introduction?

Conversation:

1. What one sentence, paragraph, image, or idea from this introduction do you most want to talk about?
2. Do you know any people who have left Christian faith or are close to doing so? What has driven them away?
3. "Our religions often stand for the very opposite of what our founders stood for." Do you agree? Disagree? Respond.
4. What treasures do you feel are to be found deep in the heart of Christianity?
5. Respond to the word *conversion* as explained in this introduction.
6. Do you have a "little inner fundamentalist"? If so, what is he or she like?
7. "A religion will be what its adherents make of it." Respond.

Action: Tell a few friends who aren't part of a faith community that you're reading this book. Share your impressions so far, and ask them what they think about Christianity being in need of change. Consider inviting a few Christian friends to read this book with you, recalling that the best conversions happen through conversations.

PART I

THE SPIRITUAL MIGRATION

{ *From a System of Beliefs* *to a Way of Life* }

1

CRISIS BY THE PALO VERDE TREE

OH, I GET IT," SHE SAID, NODDING. THIS GREGARIOUS young mom was sitting across from me in an airport waiting area. Her little boy was asleep in a stroller, and she, noticing how intensely I was pecking away on my laptop, had asked me what I was writing about. When I did my best to summarize the main idea of this book, she said, "So you're saying that Christianity isn't very Christian anymore. You want Christianity to become more Christian. Is that it?"

When I said yes, she responded, "Good luck with that! By the looks of things, it won't be easy. Try to get it worked out in time for my little boy, okay?"

FOR BILLIONS OF people, for Christianity to be Christian, only one thing matters: *correct beliefs*. Based on the priorities of many Christian leaders and institutions, we might conclude that Jesus said, "By their beliefs you shall know them," or "This is my command, that you believe the right doctrines," or "Behold, a new systematic theology I give unto you."[1]

Or that Paul said, "Though I speak in the tongues of men and of angels, but have not the right theory of atonement, I am a noisy gong or clanging cymbal."[2]

Or that James said, "True religion is this: to have the right concept of spiritual authority."[3]

Or that John said, "God is a doctrine, and those who have the correct beliefs know God and abide in God."[4]

In spite of the fact that no such statements can be found in the Scriptures, you can take this to the bank: when it comes to Christianity in many of its forms, have the right beliefs and you are *in*. Orthodox. Certified. Bona fide. Legit.

But as important as beliefs are, they are not the essential, unchanging, defining feature of Christianity.[5]

FEELING DIZZY?

The Jesus we encounter in the Gospels wasn't at all impressed by people who said the correct words ("Lord, Lord!") or engaged in impressive religious behaviors (prophesying, exorcising, even performing miracles). In the Sermon on the Mount, for example, he employed vivid imagery—wolves and sheep, fruit and thorns—to make the point that religious labels, displays, or words aren't the point:

> *Beware of false prophets, who come to you in sheep's clothing but inwardly are ravenous wolves. You will know them by their fruits. Are grapes gathered from thorns, or figs from thistles? In the same way, every good tree bears good fruit, but the bad tree bears bad fruit. A good tree cannot bear bad fruit, nor can a bad tree bear good fruit. Every tree that does not bear good fruit is cut down and thrown into the fire. Thus you will know them by their fruits. (Matthew 7:15–20)*

Jesus's original hearers could have heard these words as a simple call for genuineness, applicable to others, but maybe not to themselves. But Jesus's next words would have confronted them more directly as the people who call Jesus "Lord":

> *Not everyone who says to me, "Lord, Lord," will enter the*
> *kingdom of heaven, but only the one who does the will of my*
> *Father in heaven. On that day many will say to me, "Lord,*
> *Lord, did we not prophesy in your name, and cast out demons*
> *in your name, and do many deeds of power in your name?"*
> *Then I will declare to them, "I never knew you; go away from*
> *me, you evildoers." (Matthew 7:21–23)*

To feel the full effect of these words, we can imagine Jesus speaking to a denominational assembly today: "Not everyone who believes the Nicene Creed will enter the kingdom of God . . . not everyone who has said the 'sinner's prayer' or believes in being born again and Spirit-filled . . . not everyone who believes in papal infallibility or biblical inerrancy . . . not everyone who believes in transubstantiation or baptism . . ."[6] He followed these challenging words with another image, equally challenging, from the construction industry, something he would have known well from his father Joseph, who was a builder. The "not everyone" of his previous statement contrasts with the first word he utters now:

> *Everyone then who hears these words of mine and acts on*
> *them will be like a wise man who built his house on rock. The*
> *rain fell, the floods came, and the winds blew and beat on that*
> *house, but it did not fall, because it had been founded on rock.*
> *And everyone who hears these words of mine and does not*
> *act on them will be like a foolish man who built his house on*
> *sand. The rain fell, and the floods came, and the winds blew*
> *and beat against that house, and it fell—and great was its fall!*
> *(Matthew 7:24–27)*

His hearers immediately realized how radically this teaching differed from that of standard religious leaders of the day. They obsessed over outward appearances (observing purity codes, avoiding taboos, answering questions in conventional ways). They obsessed over outward observances (fastidious fasting and tithing, circumcision, public charitable contributions). They obsessed over dramatic religious demonstrations (casting out demons, performing miracles). In short, they obsessed over the Coke can, just as we do today.

But Jesus focused on the contents, not the container—on the wine, not the wineskin, on what was inside the cup, not outside (Matthew 9:17, 23:25).

That's why, if we think Jesus was right, we have to stop obsessing over beliefs. Our opinions, our conceptual formulations, our doctrinal statements may be interesting. They may even be important. But they aren't the point, and they can easily distract us from the point. Our problem isn't simply a matter of having the wrong beliefs. It's a matter of believing that right beliefs are what matters most. In a previous book, I said that what we need is not simply a new set of beliefs, but a new way of believing, and this is true.[7] But we must go even further. We must understand the essence of our faith to be something other than a list of opinions, propositions, or statements that our group holds but cannot prove.[8]

If you are already feeling a little queasy or dizzy, I understand: just reading those words can be scary, much less saying them out loud. Knowing how dangerous and easily misunderstood those words are, I wouldn't risk saying them if it weren't for a come-to-Jesus moment I had in front of a palo verde tree in San Antonio, Texas, about fifteen years ago.

CRUMBLING IN A DESERT GARDEN

I was a pastor at the time, spending a few days with some colleagues at a Catholic retreat center. Deep within me, a concern had been growing that something was wrong with my faith—the Coke tasted flat, a little soapy, a little fake, even though the can looked shiny and bright. On this particular day, I woke up at dawn and knew I wouldn't get back to sleep. So I slipped into my clothes and went outside.

Behind the retreat center, I found a beautiful desert garden through which gravel pathways curved. I started walking the paths in the early morning light, circling this way and that. I can still picture the cacti, the trees, the clumps of desert grasses, and I can still hear the sound of the gravel under my feet.

I was standing in front of a palo verde tree in the amber sunlight when suddenly my thinking cracked open and I fell through the crack into a deeper level of reflection. At least, that's the best way I can describe the experience now, looking back.[9]

A succession of thoughts dropped into my mind, blunt and heavy: *My faith is a system of beliefs, and it's not working. The system is crumbling. I can't save it. I can't save it. It's over.*

This was an especially serious matter for me because as a pastor my vocation was, in a sense, a belief-systems job: hold the right beliefs, organize them in the right system, and pass that system on to the congregation. But I was encountering all kinds of problems with my beliefs. Some of them I didn't actually *believe* anymore. And others were being challenged by a whole array of information, questions, theories, experiences, and, yes, new beliefs that wouldn't fit in with the old ones. On the one hand, if I went public with my predicament, I feared I would be punished or expelled by my local congregation and the larger religious systems to which we belonged. On the other hand, if I refused to acknowledge what was happening to me, I would be saying things I didn't actually believe.

Why would I pretend to believe things I don't actually believe? I asked myself. *For money. For comfort. For lack of courage,* I answered.

What's the word for people who say one thing publicly but secretly think another? I asked myself. *Hypocrite,* I answered.

I suddenly realized it was the danger of being a hypocrite that wouldn't let me sleep, that kept my thoughts running laps in my head, that kept me walking laps around that garden.

I realized the game was indeed over. I would have to let go of my system of beliefs. I would have to stop trying to patch it, prop it up, and pretend everything was fine. I would have to let it collapse under its own weight. Only then would I discover if anything of value would rise from the ruins.[10]

That insight was followed by a rush of fear. *Would there be anything left? After all, what is my faith apart from my concepts about God, Jesus, church, and life after death?*

MOMENTS PASSED AS I stood, motionless and shaken, in the desert morning. I gradually noticed that my fear was tinged with something else. Was it hope? Maybe, just maybe, I thought, beliefs were never the point. Maybe they're like leaves that come and go, not like the roots and trunk that abide. Maybe instead of constantly trying to perfect my system of beliefs, it's time to find something deeper. Maybe I am being called at this moment, here on this path in front of this palo verde tree, to sift through the shards of my shattered system of beliefs to find something better. *Maybe God is in this.*

Around this time, I heard someone walk up behind me. It was another early riser, a member of our retreat group. I didn't tell him what had just happened to me. It was too fresh, too raw. But I knew he was struggling with the same issues I was, and as we began walking the loops of the desert garden together, I found myself thinking out loud with him, pouring out my heart.

Maybe what really matters, maybe what always mattered, I said, isn't *the beliefs* we're told to proclaim, but *the stories* from which the beliefs have been abstracted and derived through various processes of interpretation. (I think my exact words—somewhat pedantic, I know—were "Maybe narrative precedes system.") Maybe the "truths" and "principles" that have so preoccupied so many of us aren't the only treasure hidden in those stories. Maybe they aren't even the primary treasure. Maybe those ancient stories have far more precious treasures to offer. I don't know if any of this made sense to my walking companion that morning, but it helped me to have his listening ear.

BOTTOMLESS WELLS OF MEANING

That morning walk didn't solve all my theological problems. It was more like the first of a series of earthquakes that eventually would alter the landscape of my faith and life.

Many years later, for example, I was retelling my palo verde story to a friend who is a rabbi. "That's something about you Christians that never made much sense to me as a Jew," she said. "We don't read stories in the Bible looking for beliefs. We read them for *meaning*. Most of us aren't literalists, and we aren't looking for some timeless, abstract statements about reality. We're looking for meaning to guide us in the predicaments of life, to help us know who we are, why we're here, where we're going, to help us be better people, so we can heal the world. And we never let one interpretation end the conversation. We see our sacred stories as bottomless wells of meaning."

"Bottomless wells of meaning"—the phrase stayed with me a few weeks later when I was invited to preach at a church that uses the Revised Common Lectionary. In the Gospel reading that week, Jesus staged a dramatic public protest in the Temple (John 2:13–22). While Matthew, Mark, and Luke locate the story at the very end of Jesus's ministry, John locates it at the beginning. While for Matthew, Mark, and Luke, the story functions climactically as the last straw that leads to Jesus's arrest, torture, and execution, for John, the story seems to set the stage for everything that will follow.[11] As I prepared that sermon and preached it with my rabbi friend's words in mind, I saw in a fresh way how John's telling of the story offers deep meaning for all of us who are sifting through the rubble of collapsed systems of belief, wondering if anything of value will remain.

Picture this: as the Passover holiday approaches, Jesus comes to Jerusalem (2:13), center of religious and political life. He moves directly to the Temple where he finds cattle, sheep, and doves being sold in preparation for the annual Passover sacrifice, just as one would expect. He braids some ropes into a whip and drives the animal sellers and their animals out of the Temple, along with those who exchange currency, turning over their tables and scattering their coins.

According to a traditional interpretation of the story, Jesus is upset by the Temple market's high cost of animal blood. Jesus drives the sellers and money changers out of the Temple because of his concern for poor people who can't afford their merchandise. If the animal merchants and money changers weren't so greedy, if only sacrificial blood were cheaper, the traditional interpretation implies, Jesus wouldn't have been upset.

But if that were the case, Jesus should have driven out the cattle and sheep and left the doves, since they were the bargain-priced sacrifice. But John clearly emphasizes that Jesus wants the cheap doves out of the Temple right along with the costly cattle and sheep. Perhaps the conventional interpretation is right about Jesus's antipathy to greed and his compassion for the poor. But perhaps it actually misses the deeper meaning in this story.

As I pondered the story in light of my palo verde tree experience, with my rabbi friend's observations in mind, another possible meaning emerged. Perhaps it is not merely *the cost* of sacrifice that Jesus protests. Perhaps it is the whole *belief system* associated with sacrifice, based on the fundamental, long-held belief that God is angry and needs to be appeased with blood. Perhaps Jesus is overturning that belief right along with the cashiers' tables, right along with the whole religious system built upon it.

The story leads us in exactly this direction. The religious leaders ask Jesus for a sign, presumably a miracle that would prove he has the God-given authority to interrupt the annual ritual of Passover sacrifice—a ritual that God, they believe, mandated through Moses. If in God's name Jesus is upstaging a tradition that goes back to Moses, God better demonstrate the proper credentials! Jesus offers not a sign, but an enigmatic yet highly meaningful answer about destroying and raising the Temple in three days.

Seen in this light, Jesus is making a revolutionary proposal: the Temple could crumble. It could pass away, and its collapse wouldn't be the end of the world. If the Temple and the whole sacrifice-appeasement industrial complex that it represented came to an end, something better would rise from the rubble: a system of extravagant and generous grace, open to all people, devoid of appeasement in any form. A more human, loving, embodied way of relating to God, self, one another, and all creation.

Of course, the Temple police weren't ready for a proposal like that. And neither was I that morning as I stood motionless on the gravel path, staring into that palo verde tree in the garden. I could no more imagine my Christianity surviving a collapse of my belief system than Jesus's contemporaries could have imagined their religion surviving a collapse of their Temple.

Now, many years later, it's all so clear: like a seedling taken out of a greenhouse, my faith has not only survived the collapse of my old belief system—it has grown and thrived as it never could have under the glass.

John's Temple protest story tells the truth: even if the worst imaginable thing happens, even if our traditional religious architecture crumbles—physically or conceptually—*even then* God can raise something beautiful from the rubble. The end is not the end. It's actually the doorway to a new beginning.

COMPETING TRADITIONS

It turns out that Jesus wasn't the first to dare to question the architecture of appeasement. More than seven hundred years before Jesus, Hosea dared to say that God desired compassion, not sacrifice. (This, by the way, is the only Scripture about which Jesus said, "Go and learn what this means"; see Matthew 9:13 and Hosea 6:6.)[12] Around the same time, Isaiah dared to say that God found sacrifices disgusting when people weren't seeking justice for the oppressed (Isaiah 1–2). And centuries earlier, the poet-king David made the audacious claim that God takes no pleasure in sacrifice, but desires a "contrite spirit" and "truth in the innermost being" (Psalms 51). In other words, Jesus wasn't abandoning Jewish tradition when he said sacrifice wasn't necessary. He was siding with the prophetic[13] and mystical/poetic traditions within Judaism, even though that set him against the traditions of the priests and scholars.[14]

Similarly, when I say that beliefs are not the essential and unchanging essence of Christian faith, I'm not rejecting Christian tradition. Rather, I'm siding with the prophetic and mystical/poetic wings of the Christian tradition—even though that may put me in tension with sectors of the scholastic and priestly wings for whom beliefs often matter most.

It is true that the scholastic and priestly wings seem to own most of the religious real estate and often act as if the larger Christian tradition is theirs and theirs alone. And it's true that they often presume to be the sole proprietors of orthodoxy and pronounce those who differ as heretics. But we must grapple with this uncomfortable question: if Jesus dared to side with the prophetic tradition and suffer the wrath of the scholastic/priestly establishment, shouldn't his followers do the same when necessary?[15]

The scholastic/priestly tradition does indeed have its version of orthodoxy, but we must realize that the mystical and prophetic traditions do too.[16] My friend Richard Rohr speaks of the "alternative orthodoxy" of Saint Clare and Saint Francis, of John Duns Scotus and Saint Bonaventure.[17] This alternative orthodoxy doesn't spend a lot of time quarreling about or denying traditional beliefs, as Richard explains:

> *The Franciscan School found a way to be both very traditional and very revolutionary at the same time by emphasizing practice over theory. At the heart of their orthopraxy was the practice of* paying attention to different things *(nature, the poor, humility, itinerancy, the outsider, mendicancy, and mission instead of shoring up home base and "churchiness").*[18]

So alternative orthodoxy is willing to be a minority report within the tradition, simply proceeding with other emphases and practicing the wisdom articulated well by Buckminster Fuller: *You never change things by fighting the existing reality. To change something, build a new model that makes the existing model obsolete.*

THE SOCIAL AND POLITICAL FUNCTIONS OF BELIEFS

The existing belief-based model of Christianity has a long pedigree. The Harvard theologian Harvey Cox associates the rise of beliefs with the era of Constantine in the fourth century.[19] But to really understand the important role beliefs play in human societies, we can reach even further back, to our tribal history as hunter-gatherers, when distinctive tattoos, language, or dress distinguished the *us* to trust and defend from the *them* to fear and fight.[20] As societies became more complex and multicultural, distinctive tattoos, language, and dress became less effective as markers of belonging. Beliefs could easily be substituted for those outward markers. Instead of showing the expected tattoo or dialect, you could prove your status simply by affirming that you believe this or that doctrine.

When beliefs become a primary marker for belonging, religious gatekeepers gain one of humanity's greatest powers: to excommunicate or expel. In this way, belief-based systems centralize power and provide an easy way to test compliance with authorities: *will you recite the required beliefs?*[21] Belief systems perform practical survival and political functions that are completely independent of the truth of their component beliefs. Believing, it turns out, is more about belonging and behaving—and more about politics and sociology—than we typically realize.

MANY OF US feel on a visceral level that faith should not be reduced to a tool of social control or political manipulation. We believe faith has a more important and creative role to play in human life and evolution.

For this reason, more and more of us who identify as Christians have reached the conclusion that Christian faith—or, at least, willing sectors of it—must migrate from where it has been to a new place. Just as our dirty-energy fossil-fuel economy needs to be radically converted to a clean and sustainable alternative energy source, Christian faith needs to be radically converted to a new fuel. We need to be energized by something other than beliefs, because beliefs are not the point.

Not the point. That's not to say beliefs are insignificant. They are powerfully significant, for better or worse. For example, if you believe that Jesus is coming soon to beam you and your friends up to heaven, you'll find plenty of reasons not to protect the environment or address deep-seated structural racism. If you believe God has given you the right to take the lands of other people and subordinate their rights to your own, then your belief will lead to action, significant and tragic. Conversely, if you believe that every human being matters and bears the holy image of God, from my friends with mental illness to my precious relatives on the autism spectrum, from the urine-perfumed bag lady whose eyes met mine at the bus stop yesterday to the little boys and girls who are being conscripted as child soldiers in Africa right at this moment, then your belief can be significant indeed, a beautiful belief for you and for others, if it leads you to action.

But wait a minute, you might be thinking. Is such a radical and systemic shift really necessary? Couldn't we just fix the specific beliefs that are broken?

That's exactly what I tried to do for many years. When I saw problems with my inherited "eschatology/end times module," I unscrewed it and installed a new one with slightly different beliefs. When my "creation versus evolution module" stopped working, I upgraded it with new belief components. When my "inerrancy module" failed, I replaced it with a new model with enhanced beliefs. But eventually I realized that this approach was analogous to solving the problem of global warming merely by exchanging incandescent for compact fluorescent lightbulbs, or by shifting from "dirty coal" to "clean natural gas." These exchanges may be steps in the right direction, and they may lessen one's carbon footprint a bit, but they won't solve the problem of climate change long term. Similarly, we will not resolve the deep tensions in our Christian faith with quick and shallow fixes. Thankfully, our search for deep solutions is well under way.

CONTEMPLATION, CONVERSATION, AND ACTION: CHAPTER 1

Contemplation: Let the dramatic story of Jesus's Temple protest play out in your imagination. Imagine a moment of silence after the animals and cashiers have been ejected. In that silence, let your heart respond to God.

Conversation:

1. What one sentence, paragraph, image, or idea from this chapter do you most want to talk about?
2. "For billions of people, Christianity boils down to one thing, practically speaking, and one thing only: *a system of beliefs.*" Do you agree? Disagree? Respond.
3. "Suddenly my thinking cracked open and I fell through the crack into a deeper level of reflection." Have you ever had an experience like this?
4. Describe the difference between focusing on stories and focusing on beliefs.
5. Retell the "protest in the Temple" story in your own words.
6. Do a little research on the palo verde tree. How might it become a metaphor for you . . . for religion in general, for Christianity in particular, or for something in your own life?
7. Reflect on the idea that beliefs have a social and political function apart from their truth.

Action: Alternative orthodoxy, Richard Rohr says, involves "paying attention to different things." In the days to come, think of something you usually pay attention to and practice "paying attention to different things" instead. For example, rather than noticing what clothes people wear, pay attention to the looks on their faces. If you usually focus on traffic delays or other annoyances, try paying attention to displays of beauty instead.

2

A DEEPER LOYALTY

GRACE AND I MARRIED IN 1979, AND BY LATE 1980 Grace was pregnant with our wonderful daughter Rachel. A friend of ours, maybe twenty years our senior and the mother of a teenager, came to us one day with a gift. "This is the book that helped me through my pregnancy. I'm done having kids now, so I wanted to pass it on to you," she said. "It was written by a doctor, and it contains of lot of interesting facts about the physical and emotional aspects of pregnancy." We felt her emotion as she gave it to us, a sign that the gift was indeed a precious one.

A few nights later, Grace and I were reading in bed. Grace started to laugh. "Can you believe this?" she said, handing me the pregnancy book and pointing to a paragraph at the bottom of a page: "Even if you don't normally smoke cigarettes, we recommend you smoke at least one cigarette a day during your pregnancy. Nicotine has been scientifically proven to relax smooth muscles and help pregnant women."

How much can change in fifteen years! What was "scientifically proven" in the 1960s was found to be scientifically ridiculous, not to mention dangerous, by the 1980s. And that realization—that science routinely gets its cherished facts wrong—can help us imagine a new approach for Christians regarding our cherished beliefs.

WHAT RELIGION CAN LEARN FROM SCIENCE

Science is deeply interested in facts—in determining them, organizing them, presenting them in an orderly way, and using them in practical ways. Religion, we might say, does the same thing with beliefs: it determines what beliefs are acceptable, organizes and presents them, and uses them in practical ways.

But here's a key difference: science's primary loyalty is not to the facts it currently proclaims. Rather, it pledges its deepest loyalty to a method or practice.[1] The scientific method—of experiment, observation, and measurement—claims priority over any statement today considered to be a fact.

When scientists employ the scientific method, they begin with a mystery, a set of data or observations without a satisfying explanation. They then develop a hypothesis: a possible explanation for this mystery. They subject the hypothesis to repeated experimentation, and if they confirm it, they consider it a tested scientific theory. If, over a long period of time, the theory is never refuted and is repeatedly confirmed, it is considered a scientific fact. It and other similarly tested facts are presented to students in lectures and textbooks, and those students depend on these facts in their daily life and work.

But sometimes new evidence arises that calls long-held scientific facts into question. The facts are, in a sense, demoted to the status of a theory or a hypothesis, and they are again tested. When scientists, working in fidelity to the scientific method, produce results that undermine long-established facts, they break up with their old facts out of loyalty to their method. They are, in other words, more in love with their method than with their facts.

Breaking up with old facts is hard to do and often takes a lot of time and argument. But that process doesn't discredit science

as being unfaithful to its tradition or essence: it enhances the credibility of the scientific community because of its relentless pursuit
of truth, using a consistent and transparent method or practice,
even to the point of overturning previously proclaimed certitudes.
The continuity of science, then, grows out of a consistent practice of seeking truth, the method by which it constantly upgrades
what it says.

This pattern of behavior in the scientific community raises
obvious questions for people of faith. To what do we owe our
deeper loyalty? Is there a deeper method or practice to which we
are so passionately loyal that because of it we are willing—no,
more than willing—we are *committed* to call into question long-
accepted beliefs? Is there a deeper loyalty that requires us to constantly upgrade our beliefs?

Roman Catholics have traditionally entrusted the regulation
of beliefs to the *magisterium,* meaning the pope and his loyal bishops. If the magisterium calls into question a long-held belief, the
belief can be changed. But once the magisterium has established
a belief, it can never be questioned again, even (so far, at least) by
future magisteria.[2] For this reason, Catholic argumentation typically involves quoting from the infallible magisterium. We might
call this the Catholic method.[3]

Protestants broke with this tradition and created a new
one. They dared claim that any Christian man was free to use
the Bible as a higher authority than the magisterium. (Back in
those days, Christian *women* were excluded from the theological game.)[4] The results among Protestants were predictable: new
denominations proliferated, each claiming that it alone had established the one *biblical* system of beliefs. Most denominations
tended to write down their beliefs in doctrinal statements, often
including copious references to the inerrant or infallible Bible as
proof. We might call this the Protestant method.[5]

The more Catholics and Protestants argued about their differing methods of determining correct beliefs, the more they rein-forced their deeper agreement that *beliefs were the point.*

Today, both the Catholic and Protestant methods face a real problem. Claims to infallibility and inerrancy in today's world are a liability, not an asset. The more you double down on infallibility or inerrancy, the smaller the corner you paint yourself into. If you want to earn people's *dis*trust today, there are few things more guaranteed to work than to claim, "What I'm about to tell you is absolutely true because an inerrant authority says so."[6] That kind of logic makes our beliefs seem *unbelievable,* because thoughtful people today trust corrigibility (which means *capable of being corrected*) and transparency (which means *openness about decision-making processes*) far more than claims of inerrancy or infallibility.

CORRIGIBILITY AND CREDIBILITY

Today, if a community is capable of learning and changing its mind (that's corrigibility) and if it "shows its work" by publicly demonstrating how and why it does so (that's transparency), then that community earns credibility. And this, in fact, is exactly what science does, at its best.[7] It is corrigible through the scientific method, and the methods and results of new research are trans-parently available. As a result, what the scientific community says is widely regarded as *believable.*[8]

That's why I say it's high time for religious communities to learn a lesson from science. Could we adopt a willingness to ques-tion even long-held beliefs when new evidence arises? Could we allow our beliefs to be open to testing and improvement? Could we say that our religious communities are held together not by forever subscribing to the same beliefs, but by forever upholding the same passion to learn, even if new learning requires regularly admitting we were previously wrong?

It would be dangerous for a Christian leader to say this, because even admitting the possibility that our beliefs might be wrong could set the heresy watchdogs growling and howling. But it would also be dangerous *not* to say this, because presuming to be error-free would send most thoughtful people looking for the door.

Interestingly, a Buddhist leader has led the way in saying what needs to be said. Secular Buddhism is widely known in the West—where it is typically seen as a kind of sanitized practice, free of beliefs. But in Asia, the birthplace of Buddhism, the religion is full of beliefs—about karma, about the cycle of rebirth and reincarnation, even about hells (some of which are hot and some cold). So it was quite a daring thing for the Dalai Lama, the leader of Tibetan Buddhism, to say, "If scientific analysis were conclusively to demonstrate certain claims in Buddhism to be false, then we must accept the findings of science and abandon those claims."[9]

This statement is not an abandonment of the truth, although one can imagine someone's inner Buddhist fundamentalist getting nervous about it. Nor is it a rejection of beliefs. It is a migration to a deeper loyalty. By admitting that Buddhist beliefs are corrigible, the Dalai Lama expresses a desire for Buddhist beliefs to be ever more in alignment with the truth. Instead of simply exchanging one set of beliefs for another, this is a new way of holding our beliefs altogether—holding them more lightly because we want to hold on to other things more tightly.

A CASE STUDY

We can see a specific example of this process unfolding before our eyes. In our lifetimes, few beliefs have been under more scrutiny than the long-standing and once-universal belief that homosexuality is a sin. That certainly is what I was taught to believe, and it is what the Catholic Church, the Orthodox Church, and the majority of Evangelicals currently require their people to believe.

I had no reason to question this belief until I was in high school, when one of my closest friends came out to me. I had led Bible studies with this friend. We had been counselors at summer camp together, taken road trips together, sang and prayed together, shared communion together. Our religious establishment said my friend was simply a pervert who had made a sinful choice in yielding to the abominable temptation of "the gay lifestyle." But I knew him: he was one of the finest people I knew, and so I knew the religious establishment's diagnosis of him was beyond false—it was ridiculous and vicious.

I wish I could say I became an outspoken ally of LGBT people back in 1974. I didn't. What I did become was a person who privately loosened my grip on the belief that homosexuality was a sin. My friend's coming out forced me to have second thoughts and gave me the gift of doubt. It presented me with evidence contrary to accepted belief and started me on a gradual migration.

Fast-forward ten years. I had become a pastor and had many more gay people come out to me in those intervening years. These people had fought hard against being gay, as if it were stage-four soul cancer. They had prayed fervently to be healed, with all their heart, soul, mind, and strength. Many of them, in hopes of being "cured," had undergone exorcisms and "reparative therapies" that had caused them deep self-loathing, cost them a lot of money and time, and left them worse off than they were before. Some of them had committed to a life of celibacy, and some even married, hoping that a spouse of the opposite sex would "reorient" them.[10]

I'll never forget a lunchtime conversation during those years with a woman who had been married to a gay man, a pastor, for over twenty years, but now was initiating a divorce. "Can you imagine," she asked me as tears fell into her salad, "what it feels like to know every single day for twenty years that the man you love is incapable of finding you attractive? That he has to pretend every time you are intimate? Can you imagine what that does to a woman? And can you imagine what this did to him?"

Stories like these made it increasingly impossible for me to remain silent. So I did what scientists do: I allowed new data to correct a long-standing belief. I wasn't simply "conforming to the world" or "accommodating to popular opinion," as my critics frequently asserted. No, I was conforming to reality, to the best current evidence, to a growing bank of experience. I was practicing corrigibility. I was seeking to conform to the way of Christ by being willing to rethink.

SYSTEM OF BELIEFS VERSUS WAY OF LIFE

You might also say it like this: I had a Christian belief system and a Christian ethic of love. Upholding my Christian belief about homosexuality put me in the position of repeatedly violating my Christian ethic of love. To stay faithful to the belief, I would have to harm real people I was getting to know. I had to decide to which element of my faith—my belief system or my ethic of love—I would be more deeply loyal. For me, my ethic, my way of life, my commitment to love my neighbor as myself subverted my inherited belief. Thousands of Christians have gone through a similar process in recent decades, and many of us have paid a high price for "coming out" as supportive of LGBT equality.

But remaining in hiding also has its costs. There are moral and spiritual costs when we publicly profess allegiance to beliefs we privately disbelieve. And there are social and relational costs when we throw our LGBT friends and their allies under the bus to protect ourselves. And there are very practical costs when we place ourselves outside of the sphere of sharing in the blessings and gifts our LGBT friends and their allies offer.

My migration to being supportive of LGBT equality happened more slowly and less decisively than I now wish in retrospect. But I am so glad I didn't delay any longer, because just three months after taking a final step in going public with a change in belief, one of my sons came out as gay. And not long after that, so did one of my daughters. I am so glad that when the time came for them to come out, they didn't have to wonder whether their father would reject them.

It will forever be true that for centuries Christianity taught people to believe that gay people were extraordinarily evil. Similarly, it will forever be true that for centuries Christianity taught people to believe that women were inferior to men and dark-skinned people were inferior to pale-skinned people; that the earth was in the center of the universe; that colonialism, slavery, and apartheid were justified; that kings had a divine right to rule; and that irrational behaviors were the result of demonic possession. And it will forever be true that eventually most Christians stopped teaching these things.

What is not yet true, but soon could be, is that Christianity migrated from its old way of defining itself as a system of beliefs, and embraced a new understanding of itself.

We could say that Christian faith (like many other faiths) was an engine of human cultural evolution when it came on the scene. It introduced new beliefs into human consciousness that liberated millions from older and less helpful beliefs. (Those beliefs themselves may have been liberating and helpful when they were first introduced, but having fulfilled their purpose became unhelpful and even imprisoning.) But eventually, by defining itself as a settled system of beliefs, Christianity froze itself, as it were. It rendered itself incapable of making ongoing contributions to human cultural evolution as conditions changed. In fact, it became the opposite of what it had originally been: it became a leash or a locked door impeding ongoing growth instead of a force for liberation and forward movement.

That's why members of the Christian faith (like members of many other faiths) now face this critical question: must we stay where we are, forever defining ourselves as a system of beliefs, or may we migrate to a new understanding of Christian faith as a way of life, a practice of ongoing personal growth and cultural evolution? If such a migration is possible, how would we describe that way of life toward which we are moving?

If we are to be truly Christian, it makes sense to turn to Jesus for the answer.

JESUS'S UNFLINCHING EMPHASIS

Of the many radical things said and done by Jesus, his unflinching emphasis on *love* was most radical of all. Love was the greatest commandment, he said. It was his new commandment, his prime directive—love for God, for self, for neighbor, for stranger, for alien, for outsider, for outcast, and even for enemy, as he himself modeled. The new commandment of love meant that neither beliefs nor words, neither taboos, systems, structures nor the labels that enshrined them mattered most. Love decentered everything else; love relativized everything else; love took priority over everything else—everything.

In the Sermon on the Mount (Matthew 5–7), for example, Jesus makes this audacious statement: God generously showers both the good and the evil with rain and sun. In other words, God's love is completely nondiscriminatory (or, in the words of Gustavo Gutiérrez, God's love is *gratuitous*): God loves us not because we are so deserving and lovable, but because God is so

loving, without limitation or discrimination. This nondiscriminatory love, Jesus says, is the true perfection, the true maturity
toward which we should aspire: to be perfect as God is perfect
is to love without discrimination because that is how God loves.
Luke makes the point even more clearly in his Sermon on the
Plain. Instead of Matthew's "Be perfect as your Father in heaven
is perfect" (5:48),[11] Luke says, "Be compassionate [or merciful, or
loving] as your Father is compassionate [or merciful, or loving]"
(6:36).

I'm glad we have a variety of words to use more or less inter-
changeably with *love,* since *love* is so easily turned into a cliché.
Along with *mercy* and *compassion,* we can speak of *peace,* a state
of relational wholeness and well-being in which love, not hostility,
reigns. Or we can speak of *reconciliation,* the process of bringing hostile parties into a state of peace and love. Today, we might
speak of *nonviolence,*[12] *kindness, community, solidarity, friendship,*
even *humanity* (as opposed to inhumanity). Whatever words we
use, we see this theme of the supremacy of love running like an
electric current through everything Jesus says and does.

On one occasion, when his critics challenge him for not observing Sabbath rules carefully enough, Jesus dares to say that the
rules aren't absolute; human well-being takes precedence (Mark
2:27–28). Immediately after that statement, he defiantly performs
a healing on a Sabbath day. Jesus's anger at the compassionless
hearts of his rule-obsessed critics stands in stark contrast to their
anger about their precious rules being broken (3:5). Luke tells of a
similar incident (13:10ff.). Jesus evokes the common human compassion of any farmer who gives his oxen and donkeys a drink on
the Sabbath day, suggesting that human compassion even for animals trumps rigid conformity to Sabbath rules.[13] Shortly there-
after, Jesus performs another healing on the Sabbath and again
evokes the compassion of any good father or farmer for a child
or an ox who falls into a ditch on the Sabbath (14:1ff.). No person

with an ounce of human compassion would wait until the next day to pull out the victim, again affirming that the rules aren't absolute; compassion holds a higher value.

Love was not only the heart of Jesus's teaching; it was also the heartbeat of his daily life. The disciples see a bunch of noisy children and try to send them away; Jesus welcomes them. The disciples see a crowd of hungry people and try to send them away; Jesus feeds them. The disciples see a woman of another culture and religion and ask Jesus to send her away; Jesus (eventually) listens to her and meets her need. A crowd refuses to show common courtesy to a social outcast named Zacchaeus; Jesus sees him up in a tree and treats him with dignity and respect. A group of prestigious people at a formal banquet look at a disreputable woman with disdain; Jesus sees her as someone who has loved much, and so must be forgiven much. His love even brings him to tears (John 11:5, 35). In story after story and without a single exception, we see that the driving motivation in Jesus's life is love.

Near the end of his life, at the time when leaders typically utter the farewell speech their followers will always remember, Jesus's final message was simple and direct (John 13–17): *You are my friends. Love one another as I have loved you.*

"THE ONLY THING THAT MATTERS"

Early in his life, Paul (then known as Saul) had no time for this kind of love talk. He was a religious-correctness man, not a love man.[14] To guard the purity of his code, he was even willing to kill (Acts 9:1). But Paul was converted, deeply converted, and he migrated from religious correctness to love.

In fact, in his writings he not only echoed Jesus's radical proposal but made it even more explicit. There were nearly nine hundred rules identified by his religion, but you could trade them all up for this one, he said: "The only thing that matters is faith expressing itself in love" (Galatians 5:6). I'm sure if a member of the scholastic/priestly establishment had been present, he would have asked, "Errr, excuse me. Did you mean to say *the only thing?* That seems a bit ... immoderate." And I'm sure Paul would have responded without equivocation, "Yes. I meant what I said. Exactly."

There is an important distinction to be made here—a distinction between faith and beliefs. Note that Paul did not say, "The only thing that matters is *correct beliefs* expressing themselves in love." He said *faith.* Faith and beliefs seem like the same thing to many people, but they actually differ in profound ways.[15]

Beliefs are commonly defined as opinions or judgments about which a person or group is fully persuaded.[16] Although beliefs generally can't be proven, they are treated among believers as certainties, perhaps not as absolute certainties, but as certain enough that they aren't up for questioning. (For this reason, we might define beliefs sociologically as *statements that a group requires members to affirm and not question or contradict.*) In contrast, faith is conviction, the deep and motivating sense that a course of action is right and worth doing. This conviction is lived out in the context of uncertainty. It involves a risk, an unknown. It proceeds not by certainty, but through confidence, the deep and motivating sense that a risk is worthwhile. This conviction (faith) and confidence (hope) are then expressed through love.[17] Seen in this light, you can have a lot of beliefs with very little faith, and you can have a lot of faith with very little in the way of beliefs.

If you doubt that, consider Abraham, the undisputed father of faith in the Bible. He was thick on faith but thin on beliefs. He had no scripture, no temple, no laws, no doctrines, no clergy, no atonement theories, no concept of heaven, no concept of hell, no vestments, no sacraments, no creed, no baptism, and no name for his religion. The beliefs he had were shaped by the polytheistic

Mesopotamian culture in which he lived, so his faith in God required him to exchange his established beliefs for something far less concrete but far more precious: a calling, a sense of beckoning promise, the hope of a new and different future—which led him to venture out in faith without even knowing where he was going.

Jesus and Paul were not denying their tradition in this emphasis on faith expressing itself in love; they were faithfully extending it, letting it grow and flow forward. In Jesus's words, they weren't "abolishing the law," but rather they were "fulfilling it"—fulfilling its intent, fulfilling its potential (Matthew 5:17). Love was already part of the tradition, as Deuteronomy 6:5 makes clear; they were saying it was *the most important* part of the tradition. They were decentering old things—religious rules, temples, sacrifice, hierarchies, and the like—and recentering the tradition on love. They called for a migration to love, and so must we.

THE WHOLE NEW TESTAMENT RESONATES

If we accept this revolutionary migration to love, any definition of God that doesn't lead us to a reconciling, harmonizing, all-embracing love is, from the start, misguided and false. Any form of religion, any system of beliefs, any hierarchy or institution that's not marked by love for our neighbor and love for the earth we share is, from the start, misguided and false.[18] Other writers in the New Testament resonate:

> *Whoever says, "I am in the light," while hating a brother or sister, is still in the darkness. Whoever loves a brother or sister lives in the light, and in such a person there is no cause for stumbling. But whoever hates [a brother or sister] is in the darkness, walks*

in the darkness, and does not know the way to go, because the
darkness has brought on blindness. (1 John 2:9–11)

How does God's love abide in anyone who has the world's
goods and sees a brother or sister in need and yet refuses help?
Little children, let us love, not in word or speech, but in truth
and action. (1 John 3:17–18)

Beloved, let us love one another, because love is from God;
everyone who loves is born of God and knows God. Whoever
does not love does not know God, for God is love. . . . No one
has ever seen God; if we love one another, God lives in us, and
[God's] love is perfected in us. (1 John 4:7–8, 12)

If a brother or sister is naked and lacks daily food, and one of
you says to them, "Go in peace; keep warm and eat your fill,"
and yet you do not supply their bodily needs, what is the good
of that? So faith by itself, if it has no works, is dead. (James
2:15–17)

In light of Scriptures like these, you might think that the primacy of love would be a settled matter in Christian faith. But
here we are two thousand years into this religion, and for many
beliefs still rule, and love too often waits out in the hallway, hoping to be invited in and taken more seriously. (Even Pope Francis
seems to be facing some resistance in this regard among his bishops, who fear that his emphasis on mercy and love violates the
tradition.) True, we may have decentered old behavior-correctness
codes, but in essence, many of us have merely exchanged them
for new belief-correctness codes. We couldn't handle the call to
faith expressing itself in love, so we reverted to beliefs expressing themselves in exclusion instead. Could it be that now is the
time, at long last, for Christians to migrate to the vision shared

by its original founder and his original followers? Are we ready to say that Christianity must no longer be defined by a list of un-changing beliefs, but rather by the dynamic pursuit of love, by the primacy of compassion—by a way of life centered in love, as embodied by Jesus?

If Christian faith can be redefined in this way, if our prime contribution to humanity can be shifted from teaching correct be-liefs to practicing the way of love as Jesus taught, then our whole understanding and experience of the church could be trans-formed. That's why I'd like us to take a fresh look at the church as a *school of love.*

CONTEMPLATION, CONVERSATION, AND ACTION: CHAPTER 2

Contemplation: Let this prayer form and rise from the deepest part of your heart: *Please help me, above all else, to become a compassionate, loving person.*

Conversation:

1. What one sentence, paragraph, image, or idea from this chapter do you most want to talk about?

2. Put into your own words what you think faith can learn from science.

3. Respond to the word *corrigibility,* and to the Dalai Lama's quotation included in this chapter. Do you think he gives too much power to science? Why or why not?

4. What has been your journey in response to the question of LGBT equality? How is it similar to and different from the author's?

5. Many words are given as synonyms or correlates for love: *mercy, compassion, peace, reconciliation, nonviolence, kindness, community, solidarity, friendship,* and *humanity.* Which words do you respond most positively to and why? What words would you add to the list?

6. "Faith and beliefs seem like the same thing to many people, but they actually differ in profound ways." How would you express the difference in your own words?

7. Choose one Scripture referenced in this chapter and explain why it feels important to you.

Action: Read 1 Corinthians 13 at least once per day. You may wish to record it and listen to it, or to write it on a card that you place on your mirror, car dashboard, or computer screen. See what parts of the chapter speak most strongly to you, and look for opportunities to put the chapter into practice.

3

Learning How to Love

Shortly after I left the pastorate, my wife and I moved to a new town in a new state. We didn't know anyone there. For the first time in my life, nobody would know whether I went to church or played hooky. I was a little curious myself: now, as a "civilian," after over twenty years in the pastorate, would I still go to church out of a sense of duty, would I stop going entirely, or would I actually feel a need for church—for the sake of my own soul?

To my surprise, I did indeed feel a need. But what I needed as a parishioner was very different from what had preoccupied me as a pastor. I wasn't looking for clever sermons or a certain style of music. I didn't need a church that was "cool" or "contemporary" or big or small. I certainly didn't need a church whose primary goal was to police the belief systems of its members.

Instead, I wanted and needed a church that would help me live a life of love, with as little distraction as possible. I needed sustenance, encouragement, and help in loving God, loving myself, loving my wife, loving my kids and grandkids and extended family, loving my neighbors, especially people I might struggle to love, and loving the earth. I felt that without a community and regular gatherings to help me, I could too easily drift, too easily shift into autopilot, too easily stagnate and sour.

Without intentional care and relevant practices, my soul could grow weary and cold, or go small and dark. I could lose my way. Easily.

I was so grateful to find a nearby church with a kind and good-hearted pastor and lay leaders who frequently put these words on its marquee: *God loves everyone. No exceptions.* That commitment expressed itself in many ways, including an extraordinary commitment to the diversely abled (often called, unhelpfully, the disabled).[1]

FINDING HOME

I know a lot of people who have tried and tried to find a church home centered in a loving way of life rather than a system of beliefs, but they can't. Just today, I received an e-mail from a woman who recently lost her son to cancer. "My husband has almost lost faith, and many beliefs I've held for life have changed too," she wrote. As a result, she and her husband no longer feel they can survive in their church. "How does one narrow the search for a new place of worship?" she asked. "The emotional energy to physically visit church after church in search of the right fit is just too much for us right now."

Many people share this frustration. When they check out church websites, all they see are detailed "statements of faith," which are actually just statements of beliefs. Or they read "All are welcome," but when they visit, they find that only those who hold the same beliefs really fit. They wish they could find a church that focused on the way of love and then practiced in reality what they posted online—like my friends at EastLake Community Church in Bothell, Washington. Here's how they described themselves on their website[2]:

It's probably important to start by making it clear that we're not the ones who "finally got the Bible right." Neither do we possess the secret to life, exclusive access to GOD or "Seven Steps to Satisfaction." We are, however, powerfully drawn to the person of Jesus, his teaching and even more so, his life. So we are experimenting, and failing, and building a community that collectively follows his Way; hoping, trusting and even doubting that it might seed something beautiful in the world. Namely; full and abundant life for all creation. We think the TRUTH about LIFE may just be LOVE and LOVE may just be the WAY.

If people find that kind of honesty and humility attractive, they can search a little deeper and they'll find a page called "What We (aspire to) Believe," which begins like this:

We think the world is tired of religious people who claim to believe a list of ideas when those very ideas don't translate into any kind of personal transformation. Plus, we see belief as a dynamic lived out in reality, which doesn't translate well into a few paragraphs on a website.

They then offer this articulation of what it means, for them, to be Christian:

The way of Jesus is a lifestyle of holistic healing for individuals, families, neighborhoods and nations. To follow this way is the countercultural road of limitless forgiveness, radical acceptance, nonviolent peacemaking, abundant generosity and sacrificial love. Salvation isn't a contractual relationship of filling in the right theological answers or behaving the correct way, but an ongoing covenantal relationship with our Creator. This understanding can move us away from religious systems as our pathway to God as we understand that union with God simply "is" because of Jesus. In this way, salvation is about your NOW life, not your afterlife. We mustn't confuse the Kingdom of God with the kingdoms of this world. God's Kingdom is power under, not power over; invitation, not coercion; service, not consumption. As a community of Jesus followers, we welcome all persons, regardless of gender, race, ethnicity, age, physical or mental capacity, education, sexual orientation, and socioeconomic or marital status. God doesn't cause suffering, but redeems it. And calls us to join in the work of renewing and reconciling and redeeming all things. The future is open and full of possibilities. We must embrace the awesome role we are invited to play in it.

Something deep and powerful is going on in those words. This church doesn't just have another set of beliefs; it is holding its beliefs differently. It has decentered beliefs and focused instead on "the way of Jesus," namely, the way of love.

EastLake isn't alone. More and more churches are moving in this direction.

What Will the Church of the Future Look Like?

In my travels, people repeatedly ask me what I think the church of the future will look like. I typically have two answers. First, I tell them I think this is a dangerous question. You can ask it in such a way as to mean "something is going to happen and I need to adjust to it." That approach, I say, is profoundly disempowering. It diminishes you from being a protagonist in your own story to being an observer and a responder. It's far better to ask, "What could and should happen with God's help, and how can we pray and work together to help that possibility become a reality?"

Then I tell them how I would answer that question. What I

believe can and should happen is that tens of thousands of congregations will become what I call "schools" or "studios" of love. That's the desired future to which I am passionately committed. I'm not concerned about a congregation's denomination, musical style, or liturgical tastes; I don't care if they meet weekly in a cathedral, monthly in a bar, annually at a retreat center, or daily online. I don't care whether they are big or small, formal or casual, hip or unhip, or whether their style of worship is traditional or contemporary or whatever. What I care about is whether they are teaching people to live a life of love, from the heart, for God, for all people (no exceptions), and for all creation.

These churches would aim to take people at every age and ability level and help them become the most loving version of themselves possible. They would help people face the challenges of life—challenges that could make them bitter, self-absorbed, callous, or hateful—with openness, courage, and generosity. They would help people recognize when they're straying from the way of love and help them get back on the path.

If our churches make this migration, if they make the way of love their highest aim, they will experience what Paul prayed for in his Epistle to the Ephesians: their members will be "strengthened in [their] inner being with power through [God's] Spirit, [so] that Christ may dwell in [their] hearts through faith, as [they] are being rooted and grounded in love" (Ephesians 3:16–17). They will employ every text, prayer, song, poem, work of visual and dramatic art, ritual, rite of passage, and other spiritual resource to help people comprehend "what is the breadth and length and height and depth, and to know the love of Christ that surpasses knowledge, so that [they] may be filled with all the fullness of God" (3:18–19).

Many churches, no doubt, are already seeking to fulfill this function, including, I hope, your congregation. But thousands of our churches are terribly busy doing lesser things. In their absence, who specializes in teaching people to love? Who develops, teaches, and refines a transformative curriculum of love? Who trains teachers and leaders who exemplify and teach the love that the world so needs? If our churches don't do these things, who will?

SCATTERSHOT PROGRAMS

A few years back, I was talking to a professor of math education. Although she loves math, her real specialty is not math, but the teaching of math. Professionals in math education study what math concepts human brains are capable of understanding at various ages, what skills and concepts must be taught first as a preparation for others to follow, how students learn and strengthen math skills, and what teaching methods most help students become fluent in mathematics. During our conversation about her profession, I remember thinking, The Christian religion has been around for two thousand years, and as far as I know, we have no well-conceived pedagogy of love, no love curriculum. All we have are scattershot sermons, songs, readings, and programs that we hope will teach people to love, if they consume enough of them. We test people's beliefs before we'll ordain them, but we don't assess whether they embody the skills and practices of love. In fact, we are pretty fuzzy on what those skills and practices would even be.

We need to ask ourselves a tough question: are we more serious about teaching math than we are about teaching love?

Thankfully, a growing number of churches are not only announcing their intention to put love first but also actually developing a curriculum of love to back up that intention.[3] The process begins, as we saw in the last chapter, with individuals like you and me defecting from the conventional system that preoccupies itself with correct beliefs. But we don't just drop out, pledging mushy allegiance to an undefined spirituality without religion. Rather, we passionately commit ourselves to make love our highest aim, and we get organized to turn that commitment into reality through practice—in a community of practice.

I first experienced such a community back in high school through a Jesus Movement group simply called "the Fellowship." We created a little alternative society in our school where everyone was welcome, including the kids others bullied, ignored, or ostracized. It was probably the only place in our school where high-status athletes mixed with what today would be called nerds and geeks, where the "cool" kids learned to be warm, where the "out of it" kids felt like insiders, and where squeaky-clean church kids actually became friends with pregnant teens and kids with drug problems and STDs. I discovered at a young age that although you can learn beliefs in isolation, you can't learn love apart from a community. And for us, the Fellowship in our school and the larger Jesus Movement with which we identified were, first and foremost, communities of love.

Today, it's about time for another Jesus Movement, a convergence of "just and generous communities" for whom love in the way of Jesus is the primary aim.[4] These communities may be traditional congregations, but they may also take other forms: urban abbeys, neo-monastic communities, home groups, prayer groups, mission groups, online groups, classes, alternative schools (like the Living School launched by the Center for Action and Contemplation), learning networks, or campus groups.[5] Whatever their form, they serve as studios, dojos, or schools of love, and they generally follow a four-part curriculum.[6]

START WITH YOUR NEIGHBORS

First, disciples in these communities learn to *love their neighbors*. You can think of neighbor love as Love 101 in our proposed curriculum. Putting love for neighbor first may sound strange, but it is actually the direction of the New Testament, and there is a good theological reason for it. Jesus, of course, said the greatest commandment was to love God with all our heart, soul, and mind (Matthew 22:37–38). That isn't terribly surprising. The surprise came when he added, "And a second is like it"—by which he was saying, "And *the second is equally important*"— "you shall love your neighbor as yourself" (22:39). Even more surprising, Paul said that the whole law was summarized in love for neighbor (Galatians 5:14) and that love for neighbor fulfills the whole law (Romans 13:10).

What's going on? Is love for God being absorbed into love for neighbor? Is theism being reduced to humanism? John offers an insight that resolves the paradox: *if you don't love your neighbor whom you have seen, you can't love God whom you have not seen* (1 John 4:20). His words recall Jesus's own words: "Just as you did it to one of the least of these who are members of my family, you did it to to me" (Matthew 25:40). Only through loving neighbors do we prepare our hearts to love God. We might even say that the way to God runs through our neighbors—especially those who are vulnerable.[7] The New Testament has been teaching us this radical truth all along, but we have been clever and perhaps even downright wicked in our persistent determination to avoid it.

FROM FAMILY TO FRIEND TO OUTSIDER TO ENEMY

If neighbors are those close to us, those with whom we share something in common, then our family members are our closest neighbors. Neighbor love begins between spouses and among parents and children, brothers and sisters, grandparents, cousins, aunts, and uncles. The Bible speaks to these relationships frequently, but much of its guidance is encoded in the cultures of the ancient world, cultures characterized by patriarchy and chauvinism. Traditional or conservative Christians have often excelled in teaching biblical skills of family love, but unfortunately, they have often preserved patriarchy and chauvinism as an essential part of the curriculum. More liberal Christians have been so determined to avoid the patriarchy and chauvinism that they have often been lax in teaching practical skills of family love at all. Today, we need to teach those practical skills clearly and effectively, but without the patriarchy or chauvinism.

These skills include common courtesies, gratitude, admitting weaknesses and failures, self-reporting emotions, expressing hurt or disappointment, confronting and forgiving, asking for help, differing graciously, surfacing and negotiating competing desires, taking the first step to resolve conflicts, upholding wise boundaries, saying yes and no, winning and losing graciously, creating win-win outcomes, speaking truth in love, speaking truth to power, asking good questions, requesting feedback, expressing affection, opening one's heart, giving gifts, and seeking wise counsel.[8] But sadly, too few parents know these skills themselves, and when parents don't know these skills, more often than not, their children won't learn them. This is how we've come to a place where millions of ill-equipped people spread damage rather than love in their homes, schools, neighborhoods, social circles (including social media!), workplaces, and societies.

To preempt this damage and to spread relational thriving instead, churches need to make these skills of family and friendship an essential part of love education, constantly teaching them through song, games, role-playing, storytelling, simulation, and through any and all other effective means.

If elementary training in neighbor love focuses on family and friends, in secondary neighbor-love studies, we learn to see the outlier, the outsider, the outcast, the stranger, the alien, and even the enemy as neighbors too. Such an education can be deeply subversive, some might even say unpatriotic. After all, political figures, military leaders, and rising demagogues consistently consolidate power by scapegoating and dehumanizing an outsider, an outcast, or an enemy. But Christian love resists their agenda by humanizing "the other" so that we see all people as brothers, sisters, neighbors, loving them *as ourselves,* standing with them in solidarity.[9] This profound shift in our attitude toward the other naturally leads to a shift in our attitude toward ourselves.

SELF, EARTH, AND GOD

Many of us suffer the shame of self-hatred or self-rejection, while others suffer from self-centered conceit or pride. Both inner maladies spread like an infection, and both can be healed when we learn to love ourselves for God's sake, as the great Cistercian monk Bernard of Clairvaux put it. He described a practice of standing with God, so to speak, and from that vantage point, regarding ourselves with divine compassion.[10] In the portion of our curriculum that might be called Love 201, Christians would learn this transformative practice.

If you love someone, you will want to understand them and accept them as they grow and change; similarly, loving yourself involves a never-ending process of self-understanding and self-acceptance through life's ups and downs. A wide range of personality tools from the Enneagram to the Myers-Briggs Type Indicator can help in this regard, as can a soul friend (or *anam cara*), as the ancient Celts called it, a friend in whose compassionate presence you can unmask and open your heart. Often it's wise to consult a professional counselor, therapist, or coach to help you in caring for yourself, especially when you are grappling with life transitions, addictions, emotional or mental illness, or trauma.

We are finally coming to understand that love for neighbor and love for self naturally lead to love for the earth, which, I propose, is the third core course of the love curriculum. For example, if you love your neighbors as yourself, you want both them and you to be able to breathe, so you need to love clean fresh air. If you love your neighbors as yourself, you want them and you to be able to drink, so you need to love pure water in all its forms. If you love your neighbors as yourself, you want them and you to be able to eat, so you need to care about the climate and about soil and about fisheries, fields, farms, and forests. If you love your neighbors as yourself, you will want all your children and your future descendants to be able to enjoy the beauty of creation too, so you will care about conservation and you will see ecology as a beautiful and holy science.

In the process of loving the earth for the sake of your neighbors and yourself, you will naturally learn to love the earth for its own sake. You will understand that just as each work of art is precious to the artist, each bird, tree, fish, plant, river, mountain, wetland, ocean, and ecosystem is precious to the Creator. You will increasingly feel the Creator's love for the earth in all its inherent, manifold beauty.[11]

People who are learning to love their neighbors, themselves, and the earth will not find it hard to learn to love God, because God will not be for them a doctrine or theory separate from or inconsistent with what they already love. Rather, in their experience of love for neighbor, self, and creation, they will have already experienced God, because, as Richard Rohr says, "God is an event of communion."[12] They will already have come, as the Quakers say, to love and reverence "that of God in every one." So in Love 401, people learn to recognize and love the familiar light they see radiant in everything they already love. They learn to inhabit God as the loving reality in which they "live and move and have their being," the all-encompassing "event of communion" in which they have experienced countless events of communion. Each experience of love itself, they will realize, has been an experience of God, for, as John said in the New Testament, "Love is from God; everyone who loves is born of God and knows God . . . for God is love" (1 John 4:7–8).

Yes, loving a distant and theoretical God who must be approached through complex belief systems can indeed be tough— even exhausting, mentally and emotionally. But loving the God who is experienced in love for neighbor, self, and creation comes as naturally as breathing. A character from Dostoevsky's *The Brothers Karamazov* captures it perfectly:

> *Love all of God's creation, both the whole of it and every grain of sand. Love every leaf, every ray of God's light. Love animals, love plants, love each thing. If you love each thing, you will perceive the mystery of God in things. Once you have perceived it, you will begin tirelessly to perceive more and more of it every day. And you will come at last to love the whole world with an entire, universal love.*[13]

Of course, I wouldn't insist that these elements of the love curriculum always be ordered in the same way. As long as we're learning to care for the earth, care for ourselves, care for each other, and care for God, in whatever order or messy disorder, I'm happy. Ecstatic, actually!

EMBEDDING LOVE IN MEANINGFUL RITUAL

When Christians put love at the top of their agenda, they can, of course, announce it—on their church website, in their mission statement, and so on.[14] But they also need to ritualize it—to weave it into the practices of their community when they gather

Sunday by Sunday, month by month, year by year.[15] How can that happen? Here are ten simple, doable ideas to stimulate your creative imagination.

Welcome: Imagine if the first words of welcome each Sunday went something like this: "Welcome, everyone! This community of faith has one great aim: to help people grow in love for neighbor, self, the earth, and God. That's why we've come together, and that's why we're glad you're here."

Prayer: What if our public prayers consistently reflected this great aim—to grow in love? What if our prayers addressed—specifically and boldly—obstacles to love like selfishness, greed, addiction, lust, pride, racism, religious bigotry, nationalism, ideology, apathy, perfectionism, unhealed trauma, and fear? What if we developed prayers that guided people to desire and seek the crucial elements of love like patience, kindness, nonviolence, gentleness, humility, and hospitality?

Confession: Imagine if love, not law, was the standard by which we learned to examine ourselves and confess our sins against God, neighbor, and the earth we share. Imagine if each week we were guided into the kind of self-examination that helped us name and turn from our unloving acts in recent days. And imagine if, along with confessing our sins, we confessed or named our hurts, the places where others have wounded us, so that we could process our pain and then respond in a way that doesn't give in to resentment or revenge.

Creeds/Confessions: What if we wrote new creeds that put love in the spotlight? Imagine if, instead of reciting a statement of beliefs, we spoke confessions of love, beginning with "We love" rather than "We believe."[16]

Communion: Imagine if we separated our understanding of the Eucharist once and for all from the language of divine appeasement, and instead celebrated the Eucharist as a family table, a love feast, a bonding to Jesus and his life and message of love, an experience of mutual self-giving with God as the "event of communion."

Sermons/Benedictions: Consider the opportunity to use twelve or twenty or more minutes each week to address the pressure points where people are struggling to love—their neighbor, the stranger or other or enemy, themselves, the earth, and God. Imagine if the fourteen qualities of 1 Corinthians 13 were more crucial to sermon development than the "five fundamentals" or "thirty-nine articles" or whatever.[17] Consider the accumulating impact if the final words of our benedictions sent us into the world as students and agents of love each and every week.

Offering: Imagine if churches taught about giving not as a duty, and not as a bargain (give and you'll get), but as an expression of love.

Songs: What if for the next three hundred years, we sang about love and justice (which has been defined by philosopher Cornel West as "what love looks like in public") as much as we've sung about sin and forgiveness over the last three hundred years? Imagine if every week God were praised and worshipped above all as the source and epitome of love.

Church Design: What if our church buildings were decorated with symbols of and quotations about love? What if the basin and towel, symbols of loving service, and the bread and cup, symbols of self-giving love, became as important as the cross in our buildings? And what if the cross itself were understood in

terms of God's nonviolent love that is "stronger than death"—
meaning stronger than the violent threat of killing or harm
that sustains the powers that be and holds people captive in the
status quo?

Holidays: Imagine if the great holidays and seasons of the Christian year were redesigned to emphasize love. Advent would be
the season of preparing our hearts to receive God's love. Epiphany
would train us to keep our eyes open for expressions of compassion in our daily lives. Lent would be an honest self-examination
of our maturity in love and a renewal of our commitment to grow
in it. Instead of giving up chocolate or coffee for Lent, we would
stop criticizing or gossiping about or interrupting others. Maundy
Thursday would refocus us on the great and new commandment;
Good Friday would present the suffering of crucifixion as the
suffering of love; Holy Saturday would allow us to lament and
grieve the lack of love in our lives and world; and Easter would
celebrate the revolutionary power of death-defying love. Pentecost
could be an "altar call" to be filled with the Spirit of love, and
"ordinary time" could be "extraordinary time" if it involved challenges to celebrate and express love in new ways—to new people,
to ourselves, to the earth, and to God—including time to tell stories about our experiences of doing so.

If we could actually deliver on a promise to provide this kind
of lifelong learning in love to children, youth, and adults of all
ages, I could easily imagine waiting lists replacing empty pews.
Such a migration to love would help our churches change their
line of business, so to speak, from the making and certification of
Christians, Baptists, Catholics, Pentecostals, or whatever, to the
lifelong formation of compassionate human beings—apprentices
of love, who live in the way of Jesus.

Do the Math

A friend of mine makes this point in a rather mathematical way.[18] We hear Jesus say "Follow me" eighty-seven times in the four Gospels. How many times does he say, *Worship me?* Zero. Name a religion after me? Zero. Recite a creed about me? Zero. Erect buildings in my honor? Zero. That's not to say these things are wrong, but succeeding at them without actually forming followers of Christ is like climbing a ladder that's leaning against the wrong building.

Similarly, the word *disciple* appears in the New Testament more than 250 times, while *Christian* appears three times, and *Christianity,* zero.

Imagine what would happen if for the next five hundred years, our churches put as much energy into the formation of generous, Christlike disciples as we have put into getting people to believe certain things or show up at certain buildings or observe certain taboos or support certain political or economic ideologies or keep certain buildings open and people gainfully employed.[19] Imagine how differently love-motivated teachers and engineers would teach and design; how differently love-directed lawyers and doctors would seek justice and promote well-being; how differently love-driven businesspeople would hire, fire, budget, and negotiate; how differently love-guided voters would vote; and how differently love-guided scholars would relate to their students and their subjects. Imagine!

Thousands of church boards will meet this month asking a predictable set of questions: How do we pay the bills? What do we do about declining numbers? Why don't young people attend anymore? How can we find good staff when we can't afford decent salaries? But sooner than many people think, tens of thousands of church boards will meet to ask this question: *What can we do to better teach our people to love?* (Perhaps you should be the one to put this on the agenda.) That's not the kind of question you answer in one meeting, but it has the potential, if it's the primary agenda item for six months, to help a congregation experience something more meaningful than survival and more powerful than revival—namely, *a great spiritual migration toward love*. I'm glad to say that for churches ready for this spiritual migration, trained coaches and consultants are available to guide the process.[20]

Your church may not be ready for this kind of migration yet. That's okay. Right now, you can form a studio of love—a home group, a learning circle, a dinner group, or a digital group—and your subgroup can become a living example of what the larger congregation can someday become. The way the subgroup honors the larger group—with humility and service rather than critique and superiority—will be your school of love's best recruitment tool. Even if you invite just one or two people to discuss this chapter with you, you could be planting the seed of a powerful spiritual movement.

"Beloved, let us love one another," we read in 1 John 4:7–8, "because love is from God; everyone who loves is born of God and knows God . . . for God is love." We must move now from the subject of love to the subject of God, because God, it turns out, has gotten into serious trouble.

CONTEMPLATION, CONVERSATION, AND ACTION: CHAPTER 3

Contemplation: In your imagination, go through the events of a normal day in your life. Imagine each event or encounter—at home, at work, and elsewhere—as an opportunity to love. Imagine yourself as a person full of and overflowing with love.

Conversation:
1. What one sentence, paragraph, image, or idea from this chapter do you most want to talk about?
2. What would a "way of life/way of love" church look like? What would it ask of its members? How would it differ from a more conventional church?
3. Choose one line from the EastLake Community Church website quotation and share what you like most about it.
4. "What will the church of the future look like?" Describe the dangers of this question.
5. Respond to this question: "Are we more serious about teaching math than we are about teaching love?"
6. The author puts "love of neighbor" first in a curriculum of love, and "love of God" last. Do you think that's a good idea or not, and why?
7. Where did you learn what you know about love? How were you taught? What gaps do you feel in your love education? How could your training in love have been improved?

Action: Each day in the coming days, pick Love 101, 201, 301, or 401 (love of neighbor, self, the earth, and God) and look for opportunities that day to specialize in that dimension of love.

PART II

THE THEOLOGICAL MIGRATION

*From a Violent God of Domination
to a Nonviolent God of Liberation*

4

THE GENOCIDE CARD IN YOUR
BACK POCKET

JOHN SHELBY SPONG IS FAMOUS FOR SAYING "CHRISTIAN-
ity must change or die."[1] There's a lot of truth to that. But
I'm actually worried about something worse than Christianity
dying. I'm worried about Christianity *killing*. And actually I'm not
just worried about potential violence that might occur in our future. I'm also angry and brokenhearted about the violence that
has already occurred because our religion has too often been not
a school of love, but a cauldron of fear, hostility, prejudice, and
worse.

Most Christians, especially Christians of European descent,
remain shockingly unaware of the violence of our history. There
is a glaring gap between what actually happened and most Christians' awareness of what happened. This gap suggests a cover-up,
a massive case of denial, or both. If Christian faith is to experience
the great spiritual migration it needs, our cover-ups and denial
must be replaced with humble awareness and a deep change of
heart, because the less aware Christians are of how dangerous
Christianity has been, the more dangerous Christianity will be.

It's been said that the truth will set you free, but first it will
probably make you mad. That's the case for this chapter. If it
doesn't make you angry, if it doesn't break your heart, then it
hasn't done its job.

A LOADED GUN AND A LICENSE TO KILL

Christianity, we might say, is driving around with a loaded gun in its glove compartment, and that loaded gun is its violent image of God. It's driving around with a license to kill, and that license is its Bible, read uncritically. Along with its loaded gun and license to kill, it's driving around with a sense of entitlement derived from a set of beliefs with a long, ugly, and largely unacknowledged history.[2]

All of this became disturbingly clear to me several months after September 11, 2001.

I was lecturing at a famous seminary in a famous city. As I walked from the subway to the school in the golden late-afternoon light, I noticed that the neighborhood around the school was populated primarily by Hindu and Muslim immigrants. With images of 9/11 still in my memory, I couldn't stop wondering if there was any neighborly interchange between the Christian seminarians inside the walls and the Muslim and Hindu mothers, fathers, kids, and grandparents I passed on the sidewalk outside. In my lecture that evening, the memory of their faces drew me off script, and I said to the seminarians and faculty present:

> *If I were a neighbor of this seminary, one of the Muslim or Hindu people who live their lives just outside your walls, there is one question I would have in my mind about you. It is not the question of what your doctrines are. It is not the question of what your religious practices and rituals are. I would only have one question.*

Then, for dramatic effect, I pulled out my wallet and from it extracted a credit card, which I raised above my head:

I would want to know if you at this seminary keep the genocide card in your theological wallet in your back pocket. I would want to know if there are any circumstances under which you might, in God's name and on the authority of the Bible that you are here to study, sanction the killing of my wife, my children, my parents, and me—as infidels, heathens, pagans, the unsaved, the unredeemed.

As you'd expect, a rather confused silence followed. I added:

In an age of religious violence like ours, people care much less about what you believe, and much more about whether you will kill for what you believe. So if you haven't figured out what you're going to do with passages like Deuteronomy 7 and 1 Samuel 15 and Psalms 137:9, you still have some important work to do.[3] If you haven't grappled with these passages and others like them, your Bible is like a loaded gun and your theology is like a license to kill. You have to find a way to disarm your faith as a potential instrument of hate and convert it into an instrument of love.[4] You have to convert Christianity from a warrior religion to a reconciling religion. Otherwise, your neighbors around this seminary will tolerate you the way they might tolerate a chemical plant that could at any moment blow up and kill them all.

There was a big crowd that night, with some students sitting on the floor. Immediately, a student named Gavin near the front quite dramatically rose to his feet. He too pulled out his wallet and he too pulled out a card and waved it for dramatic effect. "I strongly disagree," he said. "If something is in the Word of God, then we must keep it in our pocket at all times, including passages that reveal God as violent. If the Bible reveals that God is violent, and if God commands us to do violence, it must be a just and holy violence, so I will defend it with my life." Some students nodded affirmatively as he sat down. A few may have even clapped and said amen. Others grew wide-eyed, as if they had no idea what was going on, except that it wasn't what usually went on at their seminary.

Bang. There it was. You can be a good Christian, at least in the minds of some seminarians at some highly regarded schools, and boldly uphold the right to kill people of other religions in the name of Jesus, because you can justify it with a chapter and verse in the Bible.

Although I think Gavin was dangerously wrong, I'm still grateful to him for speaking up. He did everyone present an important service that night. His courage to say out loud what many people quietly think forced everyone in the room to give the relationship between Christianity, love, and violence a second thought.

About decade after my experience with Gavin, I was asked to contribute to a book called *Buffalo Shout, Salmon Cry: Conversations on Creation, Land Justice, and Life Together.*[5]

My assignment was to write a response to a chapter by Waziyatawin, a Dakota scholar and activist originally from Minnesota. The first draft of her chapter included this paragraph:

From this vantage point, Christianity has nothing—absolutely nothing—to teach Indigenous people about how to live in a good way on this land. In fact, Christians have only demonstrated that there is something profoundly wrong with the cosmology and worldview behind more than five centuries of carnage—carnage that has yet to even slow down. Christians have so much negative history and dogma to overcome within their own tradition, I do not believe the religion is even salvage-

able. The world is deep in the throes of an ecological crisis based
in Western economies of hyper-exploitation. The planet will
not survive another 500 years of Christian domination.[6]

Waziyatawin's diagnosis, "I do not believe the religion is even
salvageable," will seem an overstatement, even a sacrilege, to people
who do not know what Christianity looks like "from this vantage
point"—the perspective of people (and other living creatures) not
included in the privilege hoarded for centuries by white Christians of European descent. Unless Christianity is profoundly and
radically converted, unless it repents and changes its trajectory, I
must agree with Waziyatawin. It is not salvageable.

I must make this confession because the religion that nourishes me, saves me, and sustains me has also done great harm—to
its own adherents in many ways, yes, but immeasurably greater
harm to non-Christians and the rest of creation.

Yes, I believe there is a treasure at the heart of Christianity, a
treasure worth saving. And yes, I believe that nearly all individual
Christians are decent and well-meaning people, neither conscious
of nor consciously complicit in the wrongs done in the name of
their religion. Yes, I believe that many of the problems of Christianity are problems of all human social groups. And yes, I believe that most other religions have skeletons in their closets and
corpses in their trunks too.

But we don't do Christianity, other religions, humanity in
general, or the earth any favors by minimizing the magnitude of
dysfunction and destruction that have followed our religion wher-
ever it has gone. The only way Christianity can become salvageable is by admitting that it is unsalvageable in its present form, as
Waziyatawin said. The only way it can be saved is to admit that
it is lost. The only way it can be healed is to admit that it is blind,
deaf, lame, and sick.

If you face the dark sides of our Christian past, you will feel discomfort—even deep anger and heartbreak—but experiencing short-term discomfort is far better than living in long-term ignorance, deception, or denial.

OUR HUMBLING HISTORY

If you seek an education in the humbling dimensions of our past, you would be wise to begin with the rise of anti-Semitism, a phenomenon that began within decades of Christ and the apostles and grew like a cancer until the Holocaust exposed it for the atrocity that it was.[7] You would also include the history of Christianity's rejection of women as equal in church life and leadership, a legacy that began early and continues in many places today.[8] You would focus significant attention on Emperor Constantine and his conversion to—and of—Christianity, which married the kingdom of God to the empire of Rome, a dysfunctional marriage indeed.[9] You would ponder how, through Constantine and his supporters, a counterimperial spiritual movement centered on a man who was tortured and killed by the Roman Empire became a proimperial institution that would, in the name of its founder and the Roman emperors, torture and kill others.[10]

For American Christians like myself, this education would have to include a particular strain of Christian history that is still highly influential today, a lineage of evil that stretches from Constantine to Pope Nicholas to Columbus to contemporary American and European politics: the tradition of racial and religious privilege and supremacy—specifically white and Christian privilege and supremacy.

American schoolchildren still learn the old rhyme: "In fourteen hundred and ninety-two, Columbus sailed the ocean blue."[11] But few of us learned what came before or after that fateful year. About forty years before 1492, Pope Nicholas V issued an official document called *Romanus Pontifex,* and by sixty-five years after 1492, a succession of genocides had occurred in the New World. Here's the papal proclamation of 1455 that empowered the Christian kings of Europe to enslave, plunder, and slaughter in the name of discovery:

> *invade, search out, capture, vanquish, and subdue all Saracens and pagans whatsoever, and other enemies of Christ whereso-ever placed, and the kingdoms, dukedoms, principalities, dominions, possessions, and all movable and immovable goods whatsoever held and possessed by them and to reduce their persons to perpetual slavery, and to apply and appropriate to himself and his successors the kingdoms, dukedoms, counties, principalities, dominions, possessions, and goods, and to convert them to his and their use and profit.*[12]

The statement serves as the basis for what is commonly called the Doctrine of Discovery, the teaching that whatever Christians "discover," they can take and use as they wish. It is breathtaking in its theological horror. Muslims (then called Saracens) and all other non-Christians are reduced to "enemies of Christ." Christians, even as they plunder, enslave, and kill, count themselves friends of Christ by contrast. Christian global mission is defined as to "invade, search out, capture, vanquish, and subdue" non-Christians around the world, and to steal "all movable and immovable goods" and to "reduce their persons to perpetual slavery"—and not only them, but their descendants. And notice the stunning use of the word *convert:* "to convert them to his and their *use and profit.*"

This papal document—which has not yet been repudiated by the Catholic Church—was the basis for the Christian justification of colonialism and the building of competitive Spanish, Portuguese, British, Dutch, French, Belgian, German, and other Euro-Christian empires that spanned the world.[13]

It was the genocide card that was given to every white Christian nation.[14]

Schoolchildren don't normally learn this poem about Columbus's second voyage to Hispaniola (Haiti and the Dominican Republic today): "In fourteen hundred and ninety-five, sixteen hundred people he kidnapped alive." Columbus wrote this of his dehumanized "cargo": "It is possible, with the name of the Holy Trinity, to sell all the slaves which it is possible to sell. . . . Here there are so many of these slaves . . . although they are living things they are as good as gold." Columbus gave permission to his crew who remained in Hispaniola to enslave the native Taino people "in the amount desired." Columbus awarded a teenage Taino girl to one of his crew, Miguel Cuneo, for use as his sex slave. Cuneo bragged that when she "resisted with all her strength," he "thrashed her mercilessly and raped her." Columbus bestowed this kind of "employee benefit" on many of his men, writing to a friend about large numbers of "dealers" who specialized in supplying young girls to the so-called Christians, adding, "those from nine to ten [years old] are now in demand."[15]

SURELY MANY COURAGEOUS Christians spoke out against the savagery of their so-called civilized fellow Christians? And surely many compassionate Christians spoke out for the humanity of the so-called savages? Sadly, very, very few actually did, notable among them a Dominican friar, Bartolomé de las Casas. His 1552 account included chilling details like these:

> *With my own eyes I saw Spaniards cut off the nose, hands, and ears of Indians, male and female, without provocation, merely because it pleased them to do it. . . . Likewise, I saw how they summoned the caciques and the chief rulers to come, assuring them safety, and when they peacefully came, they were taken*

*captive and burned. . . . They laid bets as to who, with one
stroke of the sword, could split a man in two or could cut off his
head or spill out his entrails with a single stroke of the pike. . . .
They attacked the towns and spared neither the children nor
the aged nor pregnant women nor women in childbed, not only
stabbing them and dismembering them but cutting them to
pieces as if dealing with sheep in the slaughter house.* [16]

One might conclude that these were a few rogue rotten Spanish apples, acting in opposition to their faith. But notice the religious motivation for the cruelty described by Bartolomé:

*They took infants from their mothers' breasts, snatching them by
the legs and pitching them headfirst against the crags or snatched
them by the arms and threw them into the rivers, roaring with
laughter and saying as the babies fell into the water, "Boil there,
you offspring of the devil!" . . . They made some low wide
gallows on which the hanged victim's feet almost touched the
ground, stringing up their victims in lots of thirteen, in memory
of Our Redeemer and His twelve Apostles, then set burning
wood at their feet and thus burned them alive.*[17]

It was the identity of all non-Christians as "offspring of the
devil" that allowed these acts "in memory of Our Redeemer and
His twelve Apostles," not in spite of Christianity, *but because of it*.
Bartolomé, of course, knew that there were other motivations as
well:

*Their reason for killing and destroying such an infinite number
of souls is that the Christians have an ultimate aim, which is
to acquire gold, and to swell themselves with riches in a very
brief time and thus rise to a high estate disproportionate to their
merits.*[18]

Motivated thus by their beliefs in God and their lust for gold—as dangerous a cocktail today as then—the Spanish Christians ravaged Latin America, as did their Portuguese counterparts. Bartolomé concludes, "We can estimate very truly and truthfully that in the forty years that have passed, with the infernal actions of the Christians, there have been unjustly slain more than twelve million men, women, and children. In truth, I believe without trying to deceive myself that the number of the slain is more like fifteen million."[19]

WHEN THE "GOOD NEWS" ISN'T SO GOOD

But voices like Bartolomé's were a tiny minority. Queen Isabella fired Columbus from governorship because of his treatment of the Tainos in 1500, but his replacement was cut from the same racist cloth. The queen intervened again in 1503 with a decree intended to protect the native peoples from forced labor, and in 1511 a friar named Antonio de Montesinos preached that it was a sin to abuse them. But laws were passed the next year to strengthen Spanish domination (and outlaw nudity among the native people, as if nudity were a greater concern than slavery and rape!). And in 1513, the Spanish government created a kind of Miranda rights–style document that was to be read (in Spanish—incomprehensible to the indigenous peoples!) to those about to be conquered. It was the summary of the Gospel as they understood it; it was their core message, their "good news," the metanarrative that legitimized their white Christian supremacy:

> *On the part of the King, Don Fernando, and of Doña Juana I,*
> *his daughter, Queen of Castille and Léon, subduers of the bar-*
> *barous nations, we their servants notify and make known to*
> *you, as best we can, that the Lord our God, Living and Eter-*

nal, created the Heaven and the Earth, and one man and one woman, of whom you and we, all the men of the world at the time, were and are descendants, and all those who came after and before us. . . .

Of all these nations God our Lord gave charge to one man, called St. Peter, that he should be Lord and Superior of all the men in the world, that all should obey him, and that he should be the head of the whole Human Race. . . .

One of these Pontiffs, who succeeded that St. Peter as Lord of the world, in the dignity and seat which I have before mentioned, made donation of these isles and Tierra-firme to the aforesaid King and Queen and to their successors, our lords. . . .

Wherefore, as best we can, we ask and require you that you consider what we have said to you, and that you take the time that shall be necessary to understand and deliberate upon it, and that you acknowledge the Church as the Ruler and Superior of the whole world. . . .

But, if you do not do this, and maliciously make delay in it, I certify to you that, with the help of God, we shall powerfully enter into your country, and shall make war against you in all ways and manners that we can, and shall subject you to the yoke and obedience of the Church and of their Highnesses; we shall take you and your wives and your children, and shall make slaves of them, and as such shall sell and dispose of them as their Highnesses may command.[20]

Sadly, this deadly mingling of racism, empire, and Christianity was not the exception; it was the norm. Equally sadly, the compassion of Bartolomé, Antonio, and Isabella was not the norm; it was the exception. The same kind of slaughter continued in North America (known to many of its original inhabitants as Turtle Island), as Waziyatawin explains:

The people of Hispaniola had their lives unjustly and savagely taken by professed Jesus followers, and they were not, as we all know, the only ones to meet such a fate. Millions of their Indigenous sisters and brothers on Turtle Island were killed at the hands of other Europeans, as nation after imperial nation, bearing Christ on their lips and crosses on their military standards, followed suit.[21]

Horrible Christian atrocities, rooted in white Christian supremacy, spread like gangrene—in their Catholic form across the Caribbean, Central America, and South America, and in their Protestant form in what is now the United States. As the Navajo and Christian activist Mark Charles explains, when citizens of the thirteen British colonies composed the Declaration of Independence, among their complaints against King George was that he didn't allow them to apply the Doctrine of Discovery to the people of the lands to their west.[22] The Declaration described the indigenous peoples as "merciless Indian savages," clearly not counted among the "all men" whom God supposedly "created equal."

In 1830 the Indian Removal Act carried echoes of the Doctrine of Discovery, nearly four hundred years later, as indigenous peoples were rounded up at gunpoint and imprisoned in concentration camps. About fifteen thousand Cherokees and others were forced to march west in 1838 on "the Trail of Tears," during which about four thousand died from exhaustion and disease, with an equal number of traumatized deportees dying over the next year.[23] Abraham Lincoln ordered the largest mass execution in US history, taking the lives of thirty-nine indigenous people in Minnesota in 1862. Less than two years later came the Sand Creek Massacre in Colorado, in which two hundred peaceful Arapaho and Cheyenne children, women, and men were slaughtered:

In terms of sheer horror, few events matched Sand Creek.
Pregnant women were murdered and scalped, genitalia were
paraded as trophies, and scores of wanton acts of violence char-
acterize the accounts of the few Army officers who dared to re-
port them.[24]

When physical genocide ran its course, cultural genocide followed, reflected in the "compassionate" counsel of Captain Richard Henry Pratt: "A great general has said that the only good
Indian is a dead one. In a sense, I agree with the sentiment, but
only in this: that all the Indian there is in the race should be dead.
Kill the Indian in him, and save the man." Then came the Dawes
Allotment Act of 1887, which began a process that dramatically
expanded available land for white settlers and dramatically reduced the land set aside for indigenous peoples. Three years later,
the massacre at Wounded Knee left at least two hundred Lakota
men, women, and children dead and rewarded twenty US soldiers with Medals of Honor for the killing.

The United States denied voting rights to Native Americans
until 1924. States like Arizona and New Mexico found ways to
continue restricting voting rights until 1948, just as several southern states continue to do in this century to African Americans.[25]

THE DOCTRINE OF WHITE CHRISTIAN PRIVILEGE

Speaking of African Americans, the horrors of the African slave
trade are more connected to the enslavement unleashed by Columbus than most people realize.[26] The Portuguese began en-
slaving and exporting the native peoples of Labrador beginning
in 1501. Early in colonial history, the British paid some tribes
to capture members of other tribes; the British then sold these
captives as slaves. Charleston, South Carolina, was a center for

exporting indigenous American slaves before it became a center for importing African ones. Having developed a taste and skill for enslavement of the Tainos, Arawaks, and others in the New World, European colonizers quickly turned to Africa for additional "stock" for their slave market. Even Bartolomé de las Casas at one point recommended importing African slaves so that the indigenous peoples could be released, a recommendation he later regretted and repudiated.

Even though Pope Urban VIII reversed the pronouncements of his predecessors by declaring slavery unacceptable in the mid-seventeenth century, the vast majority of Protestant Christians in America considered slavery and white supremacy to be absolutely consistent with "biblical" Christianity. It would take American Protestants over a hundred years to make slavery history. Even then, they would find ways to cleverly camouflage the old Doctrine of Discovery and its white supremacist scaffolding under distinctly American terms like *Manifest Destiny* and *American exceptionalism,* terms still celebrated in many sectors of US society today. Professor Yolanda Pierce of the Princeton Theological Seminary told the bitter truth in a 2015 article in *Religion & Politics*:

> *We often fail to deconstruct how proslavery theology still influences American Christianity. But simply put: Theological arguments upheld the institution of slavery long after every other argument failed. American Christian theology was born in a cauldron of proslavery ideology, and one of the spectacular failures of the Christian church today is its inability to name, interrogate, confront, repent, and dismantle the cauldron which has shaped much of its theology. We are daily living with the remnants of a theological white supremacy, coupled with social and political power, which continues to uphold racist ideologies. . . . Can this nation afford to keep ignoring the truth that*

*black people in America live under a threat of racial violence,
never quite feeling that we are fully equal citizens in the nation
that our enslaved ancestors built?*[27]

If more Christians today summon the courage to take seriously the dark sides of our history, we will wake up to the degree to which our religion still interprets the Bible exactly as our misguided ancestors did.[28] (No, we don't draw exactly the same conclusions, but we have neither acknowledged nor rejected the method of reading the Bible that made those unacceptable interpretations acceptable.) If we face our past, we will see how many power centers within the Christian community still carry white Christian supremacy and white Christian privilege cards in their back pockets, often without even knowing they do so, and as a result can be found consistently allying themselves with oppressors rather than the oppressed. We will see behind the curtain, so to speak, exposing how many Christians still drink the old cocktails: of God and gold (including the "black gold" of fossil fuels), of Christianity and white supremacy, of Christianity and privilege, of Christianity and colonialism, of Christianity and exceptionalism, of Christianity and violence.

MY OWN AWAKENING

Two incidents in my childhood made clear to me the degree to which the Christian religion of which I am a part still drives under the influence of these unholy spirits.

When I was about eight, our family relocated from New York to Maryland, a move that placed me south of the Mason-Dixon Line for the first time in my life.[29] We found a church of our denomination, and I found myself in a Sunday school class that included kids up to twelve or thirteen years old. The teacher was a proper, well-dressed woman whose daughter, Janine, was in the class. Janine was very pretty and very much a teenager, and even though I was only eight, I couldn't help but be in awe of her. One Sunday, Janine's mother became much more serious and earnest than normal: "Boys and girls," she said, "when you get older, it is very important that you not associate with children of another race." This was the early 1960s, and because my dad watched the evening news on TV every night after supper, I knew about the civil rights movement. So Janine's mother had my attention.

"If you associate with them, you might start to date one of them," she said. "And if you date one of them, you might fall in love with one of them. And if you fall in love with one of them, you might marry one of them. And that would be a very serious sin, and clearly out of God's will." I noticed Janine rolling her eyes, and my eight-year-old political radar sensed that this lesson might be a kind of indirect mother-to-daughter preaching opportunity. But I kept listening as Janine's mother told us about something called "the curse of Ham," which I realized was not a condemnation of pork products, but a popular justification—from the Bible (Genesis 9:20–27)—of segregation and white supremacy.

Fast-forward a few years. I was on my way to becoming a young teenager myself. My grandfather was a Scotsman who had been a missionary in Angola for forty years. While on furlough, he had a minor stroke that temporarily slurred his speech and confined him to a wheelchair. Our family went to visit him in South Carolina, where he was convalescing—a drive of seven or eight hours. It was the April weekend in 1968 after Dr. Martin Luther King Jr. had been murdered and the air was humming with tension. We took my grandfather in his wheelchair to a restaurant, a rare occasion for my frugal family. There we sat, in a southern diner with a TV on the wall—another rarity in those days. Black-and-white scenes of rioting flashed on the screen, and my grandfather responded—slowly and deliberately because of the stroke—"I'm glad they got that communist devil."

I was horrified. My grandfather had lived among Africans in Africa for over half his life. How could he say this about an African American leader who had risked and now given his life for the dream of racial equality?

Not quite twelve years old, I had never heard of the Doctrine of Discovery and had no idea of its residue in British imperialism and jingoism. I didn't understand how the whole African missionary project required permission from the colonizers to enter a colonized nation, thus obligating missionaries to live by colonial rules. Nor did I yet realize that my grandfather had spent a lot of time in South Africa, where racism was disguised as anticommunism, where capitalism became camouflage for white supremacy, and where apartheid was being articulated as a matter of Christian theology—using exactly the same lines of argument that Janine's mother had used in my classroom four years before. I didn't know a lot, but I knew this: my grandfather was wrong, seriously, deeply wrong. How could my adolescent brain come to terms with the fact that my beloved grandfather simultaneously loved God and was glad that a human being—in my mind, one of the greatest human beings of my time—had been murdered?

I would like to think that I spoke up at that point. I may have; I'm not sure. But I do remember that a little lecture followed, and in my memory, it was directed at me. My grandfather, in his stroke-slurred brogue, explained that the Negro race was inferior and "completely incapable of governing themselves." They were like children, and God loved them, but because of the curse of Ham, it was God's will for white people to rule over them.

There it was again. The Bible and God used in service of racism and violence. All by my beloved grandfather. I write these words with tears.

THE DOCTRINE OF DOMINATION

As an adult, as I've become more engaged with the environmental crisis, I've come to see that just as the Doctrine of Discovery was used to justify white Christian supremacy and the exploitation of nonwhites and non-Christians, the "doctrine of dominion" (Genesis 1:28) is still being used to justify human supremacy and the exploitation of the earth and all its creatures. Aided and abetted by harmful doctrines about the future (especially "left behind" dispensationalist eschatology), industrial-era Christians have used toxic, industrial-strength beliefs to legitimize the plundering of the earth, without concern for future generations of humans, much less our fellow creatures. After all, if Jesus is coming back soon, and if God will soon destroy the earth and take righteous souls to heaven, who cares about the earth? What's a little human domination in comparison to divine damnation?

Now it's clear to me how the vicious trajectory of theologically justified genocide (mass killing of "the other") naturally leads to geocide (mass destruction of the planet). As Pope Francis has eloquently said, society's refusal to hear the "cry of the poor" is inseparable from our refusal to hear the "cry of the earth."[30] Or as my friend Sister Simone Campbell puts it, "The toxicity of what we're doing to our planet and the toxicity of racism have the same roots."

It's clear to me now that to salvage at least some sectors of Christian faith from violence against people and our planet, we must go to those roots. To be converted from all forms of supremacy and domination, we must dare to embark on a great theological migration, challenging many of our deepest assumptions about God.

CONTEMPLATION, CONVERSATION, AND ACTION: CHAPTER 4

Contemplation: This chapter should evoke strong emotions that we often suppress or dismiss. Open your heart to the presence of God, let these strong emotions surface, and ask God's Spirit to help you wisely process them.

Conversation:

1. What one sentence, paragraph, image, or idea from this chapter do you most want to talk about?
2. "Christianity, we might say, is driving around with a loaded gun in its glove compartment, and that loaded gun is its violent image of God." Respond.
3. Which part of the history overview most surprised or disturbed you, and why?
4. How aware do you think most Christians are of the historical information contained in this chapter? What are the causes and consequences of this level of awareness, and what can be done about it?
5. Respond to the Yolanda Pierce quotation included in this chapter.
6. "Now it's clear to me how the vicious trajectory of theologically justified genocide (mass killing of 'the other') naturally leads to geocide (mass destruction of the planet)." Explain how the two are related, and how a flawed view of God can underlie both.
7. Is Christianity salvageable? Try defending the position opposite to the one you would normally support, and see how things look from that perspective.

Action: Look for signs of supremacy or domination in your daily life in the coming weeks. When possible, seek a constructive way to respond. Read *Laudato Si,* and make one of the prayers at the end of the document your own.

5

GOD 5.0

GROWING NUMBERS OF US ARE ACKNOWLEDGING WITH grief that many forms of supremacy—Christian, white, male, heterosexual, and human—are deeply embedded not just in Christian history but also in Christian theology. We are coming to see that in hallowed words like *almighty, sovereignty, kingdom, dominion, supreme, elect, chosen, clean, remnant, sacrifice, lord,* and even *God,* dangerous viruses often lie hidden, malware that must be identified and purged from our software if we want our future to be different from our past. We are realizing that our ancestors didn't merely misinterpret a few Scriptures in their day; rather, they consistently practiced a dangerous form of interpretation that deserves to be discredited, rejected, and replaced by a morally wiser form of interpretation today. (We'll return to this topic in the next chapter.) And we are coming to see that this repentance and conversion do not express infidelity to Christ, but fidelity, because we are coming to see in the life and teaching of Christ, and especially in the cross and resurrection of Christ, *a radical rejection of dominating supremacy in all its forms.*

Supreme in a Supremely Different Way

The theological term for the rejection of dominating supremacy is *kenosis,* which means self-emptying. We encounter the term in a pivotal New Testament passage, Philippians 2. Rather than seizing, hoarding, and exercising power in the domineering ways of typical kings, conquistadores, and religious leaders, Jesus was consistently empowering others. He descended the ladders and pyramids of influence instead of climbing them, released power instead of grasping at it, and served instead of dominating. He ultimately overturned all conventional understandings of supremacy, lordship, sovereignty, and power by purging them of violence—to the point where he himself chose to be killed rather than kill. In this way, according to Philippians 2, Jesus manifested the true nature or image of God. And for this reason, God elevated Jesus's name above all other names, so that every knee should bow to Jesus as Lord.

Of course, for many, those words evoke the image of a conquering king forcing the vanquished to kneel at sword point and saying, "Grovel before me and acknowledge my supremacy!" But that understanding completely undermines the thrust of all that has gone before. It is far better, I am convinced, to understand the image like this: One day, all of humanity will become convinced that the ways of violence and domination, enslavement and exploitation, supremacy and privilege are ugly, wrong, suicidal, and ungodly. Then they will realize that the violent "winners" were wrong, and the nonviolent "losers"—those who walked the path of Jesus—were right. Jesus's way of self-giving was right. His humble path of gentleness was right. His form of servant leadership was the one we should have honored all along.

It's important to note that the text doesn't say they will bow and confess "Christianity is right" or "The Western Christian tradition reigns supreme." No: they will acknowledge that the powerful leaders of history—from Herod and Pilate to Constantine and Columbus, from the inquisitors and conquistadores and slave masters to those who exploit the poor and the earth today—are not the "lords" or heroes of history we thought them to be. Rather, Jesus had it right. Jesus faithfully and courageously represented the nonviolent and loving heart of God. Jesus and his way of nonviolent, self-giving love, the text suggests, will earn the trust of all humanity. We will ultimately migrate, in other words, toward the way of Jesus.

THE GOD WHOM JESUS SHOWED US

The implications of the Philippians 2 passage are staggering.[1] Simply put, God as known in Christ is not the stereotypical Supreme Being of traditional "omnitheology." That Supreme Being of Christian theology was characterized first and foremost by controlling, dominating, dictatorial power. His totalitarian regime (the masculine pronoun is appropriate here) was enhanced by the ultimate surveillance tool: *omniscience*. Its spies and informants were everywhere: *omnipresence*. And its unaccountable power was not limited by any law except the will of the Supreme Being Himself: *omnipotence*.

In sharp contrast, the God imaged by Jesus exerts no dominating supremacy. In Christ, we see an image of a God who is not armed with lightning bolts but with basin and towel, who spewed not threats but good news for all, who rode not a warhorse but a donkey, weeping in compassion for people who do not know the way of peace.[2] In Christ, God is supreme, but not in the old discredited paradigm of supremacy: God is the supreme healer, the supreme friend, the supreme lover, the supreme life-giver who self-empties in gracious love for all. The king of kings and lord of lords is the servant of all and the friend of sinners. The so-called weakness and foolishness of God are greater than the so-called power and wisdom of human regimes.

In the aftermath of Jesus and his cross, we should never again define God's sovereignty or supremacy by analogy to the kings of this world who dominate, oppress, subordinate, exploit, scapegoat and marginalize.[3] Instead, we have migrated to an entirely new universe, or, as Paul says, "a new creation" (2 Corinthians 5:17) in which old ideas of supremacy are subverted.

If this is true, to follow Jesus is to change one's understanding of God. To accept Jesus and to accept the God Jesus loved is to become an atheist in relation to the Supreme Being of violent and dominating power. We are not demoting God to a lower, weaker level; we are rising to a higher and deeper understanding of God as pure light, with no shadow of violence, conquest, exclusion, hostility, or hate at all.

We might say that two thousand years ago, Jesus inserted into the human imagination a radical new vision of God— nondominating, nonviolent, supreme in service, and self-giving. That vision was so radically new and different that we have predictably spent our first two thousand years trying to reconcile it with the old visions of God that it challenged. Maybe only now, as we acknowledge Christianity to be, in light of our history, what the novelist Walker Percy called a "failed religion," are we becoming ready to let Jesus's radical new vision replace the old vision instead of being accommodated within it. Could some sectors of Christian faith finally be ready to worship and follow the God that Jesus was trying to show them?

Such a possibility raises a question: if one dares to let one's traditional and inherited "Christian" understanding of God be converted under the influence of Jesus, can one still be considered a Christian? Or, conversely, if one *refuses* to let one's traditional understanding be converted under the influence of Jesus, can one still be considered a Christian? Be that as it may, growing numbers of us are coming to realize this simple truth: *for the world to migrate away from violence, our God must migrate away from violence.*

DANCE OF DEVELOPMENT

Of course, *God* in the previous sentence meant *our concept of God,* because, in a sense, it doesn't matter whether God is or is not violent. In fact, it doesn't even matter whether God exists, because our concept of God will form us whether or not there is any reality corresponding to that concept.[4] If we have a *concept of God* that is violent, we will be transformed into that violent image, whether or not that concept is true. Similarly, if our *concept of God* is nonviolent, we will be transformed into that nonviolent image, whether or not that concept is true. We might say that whatever our God is like, whether or not our God exists, our God is still powerful because our image of God transforms us. Like an image in a mirror, our God concept reflects back to us the image of what we aspire to become. Powerful and vengeful? Kind and merciful? Dominating and in control? Relational and respectful? Like God, like believer, we might say. Our image of God, our image of ourselves, and our processes of individual and cultural development move together as in a dance.

Speaking personally, because I believe that God is love, and love never wills harm or damage, I've had to pull the genocide card from my spiritual wallet and cut it to pieces. I've done the same with my collection of prejudice cards, favoritism cards, and other trump cards. My sense of privilege and entitlement has been fully discredited, and I've been left, as Paul said, with a huge debt, a joyful debt: the perpetual debt of love for all (Romans 13:8).

To understand how our concepts of God might convert from violence to nonviolence, you can reflect on how your understanding of God has changed in your life experience so far. You can start by acknowledging this: *you were pretty selfish as a baby.*

You didn't care whose ear you screamed in, whose lap you pooped on, whose shoulder you threw up on, whose sleep you interrupted for the ninth time in one night. *Your* hunger, *your* thirst, *your* comfort, *your* relief—all that mattered to you was *you.* "I want what I want when I want it!" was your motto, even before you had the words to say so. If you had a concept of God at this stage, we could call it *God 1.0.* God 1.0's job, generally carried out through your parents, was to come when you called, clean up your messes, satisfy your demands, kiss your scrapes and bruises, and keep you as happy as possible as much as possible. To the degree that caring adults faithfully came to your aid when you cried, you developed a primal trust in God 1.0, a God of loving faithfulness who would take care of you as you made your way through life.

As you grew from infancy into toddlerhood, you were still pretty selfish. But occasionally, you felt a generous impulse tingling in your soul. For example, one day when one of your parents was feeding you Cheerios (Cheerios being, in my opinion, the perfect toddler food), you took a few gooey Cheerios out of your mouth and offered them back in a slobbery fist. Your parent realized you were imitating a generous gesture: you were doing for another what had been done for you. Your parent received your sticky gift like a holy wafer from a priest.

A few days later, you realized that you could make your sibling laugh by making a farting sound with your mouth. You enjoyed making your sibling happy, so you repeated the sound as long as the laughter continued (which was considerably longer than your parents approved of).

A while later, after biting your best friend at preschool for three days in a row when he took your stuffed giraffe, you decided to let him play with it. Your teacher kept using the word *sharing* when you did this, and you decided that from time to time, you would share rather than bite, even though you weren't sure that your classmate could be trusted with something as precious as your giraffe.

In these episodes, you were discovering a toddler's version of the joy of generosity, and you were graduating to *God 2.0*. God 2.0's job was still to clean up your messes and satisfy your demands, but God 2.0 also had the tough job of calling you beyond selfishness to generosity. In short, God 2.0, imaged in your parents and other caring adults, wanted you to be nice and polite, to say please and thank you, and to play well with others. That's progress!

When you grew older and went to school, you entered a new world of rules and schedules. You couldn't leave your seat without permission; you had to turn in your homework on time, whether you felt like it or not. There were rules for math, rules for grammar, rules for sports. By the time you got your driver's license, there were rules of the road. As you entered young adulthood, you were graduating to *God 3.0*: the God of rules and fair play whose job it was to reward the rule keepers and punish the rule breakers. God 1.0 was still there, meeting your needs, as was God 2.0, calling you to generosity. But like growth rings on a tree, this season's new ring embraced those left by previous seasons. God 3.0, embodied in authority figures outside the home, grew predominant in a social world full of written and unwritten rules.[5]

Then, several years later, you fell in love for the first time. True, it was still a bit selfish. "I love me and you love me, which means we have a lot in common," you never said to yourself, even though that's how you felt. After a few breakups and heartbreaks—some of which you suffered, some of which were inflicted by you—you learned that love always comes with a risk of pain. And still, you took the risk. You began to anticipate how your actions would impact your significant other. You learned the art of sacrifice, the grace of granting forgiveness, the humility of asking for forgiveness. You started to think in terms of two, voluntarily linking your well-being with the well-being of another. There were no simple rules for this new territory in life, so you needed a new concept of God to guide you beyond the simplicity of rule keeping, and *God 4.0* came into view: a God of affection, fidelity, forgiveness, and family.

With God 4.0's help, you began to learn the adult commitments of service, of teamwork, of sacrifice, of professional growth, of handling money, of dealing with conflict, of citizenship, of social responsibility. At some point, you may have made special vows to a special someone—promising that no matter how you feel, for better or for worse, in health or in sickness, you would remain faithful and committed to this one person who was willing to make reciprocal vows to you.

Someday, you may have children. And guess what? You'll love them so much that you'll find their absolute selfishness adorable (most of the time). When they start sharing Cheerios with you or trying to make you laugh, you'll be even more elated to see your love for them reciprocated. You'll keep on loving them when they become teenagers and are either disgusted or embarrassed by just about everything you say or do. Inspired by the love of God 4.0, your love will remain constant through their adolescent ups and downs, until they break through into adulthood and maybe even make lifelong commitments to partners and children of their own.

In the years ahead, you may experience the joy of watching the lives of new generations unfold—whether grandchildren or nieces and nephews and their children, always bathed in your unconditional love as they make the rocky ascent from immature selfishness to mature self-giving. And someday, it will be your time to die. If all goes as it should, you will look back on your life with gratitude and you will generously surrender your space on earth to make room for someone else. You will entrust yourself to the loving presence of God, whom you will understand with so much more depth because of your changing stages and experiences in life. Your whole journey, you will see, was a journey of learning new and deeper expressions of love.

But here's the problem: we often get stuck on an early version of God. Many of us are still angry and bitter that God 1.0 hasn't solved all our problems and made life as cozy and easy as a warm blanket and a dry diaper. (The God that many alienated former believers have rejected is God 1.0.) For others, God 2.0 is all they can handle—a gracious God who wants us all to be nice and get along. Some really like a world defined by rules, so for them, God 3.0 is their favorite, and they would very much like to impose God 3.0 on everyone else too. Of course, you may then realize that you would also like to convert everyone to the loving God 4.0! You wish everyone could migrate from selfishness to other-centeredness, from self-interest to the common good, *from me to we*. You've arrived at God 4.0 and wish everyone else would too!

GOD 4.0 ISN'T ENOUGH

There's just one problem. God 4.0 is Gavin the seminarian's God, the God of the *exclusive we* whom we met in chapter 4, the one who shows favor to *us* but not *them*. God 4.0, whether it's a Christian, Muslim, Jewish, or other version, leads people to affection, fidelity, and forgiveness in family, community, and nation—but only for people from *our* religion, ethnicity, or tribe.

True, those little words *we, our,* and *us* are a big improvement over *me, myself,* and *mine.* But they can cause big problems, depending on how inclusive or exclusive they are. The same God 4.0 who inspires individuals to progress from the personal selfishness of *me* to the social maturity of *we* is the violent God whose genocide card we keep in our back pocket if *we* are threatened, or if *they* have something *we* desire. The word *we,* it turns out, can be pretty dangerous, because it can otherize and dehumanize those who aren't like *us.*

We're surrounded by examples of this exclusive we and the damage it causes. When the writers of the US Constitution wrote "We the people," their "we" excluded women, Native Americans, and African Americans. Those were not minor oversights! The same was true some years earlier when the writers of the Declaration of Independence wrote, "We hold these truths to be self-evident, that all men are created equal." Their "we" and "all men" didn't mean "everyone" or "all people." They meant privileged white men of a certain social class or religion.

This exclusive we is deeply ingrained in our species. It probably goes back well over 130,000 years, to a time when all the DNA in all living humans today was resident in a small tribe of people somewhere in Africa.[6] These hunter-gatherers needed a significant amount of territory in order to survive—enough to grow the leaves, nuts, berries, fish, and animals necessary to provide the proteins, fats, and carbohydrates their bodies needed for health and reproduction.

When a tribe's numbers increased beyond the carrying capacity of their region, it would hive off (or drive off) daughter tribes, each of which would need to find new patches of land. Eventually, with many tribes of early humans each hunting and gathering on large patches of desirable land, conflicts inevitably arose. For example, if a neighboring tribe raided *our* land to catch *our* game or raided *our* trees for *our* fruit, we would fight them and drive them away. If we didn't, our babies would starve. So along with all the other threats our ancestors faced, from droughts to floods to diseases to wild animals, other tribes of humans became a constant danger. *We* meant safety and security; *they* meant danger and anxiety. No wonder tribes marked themselves with unique sets of tattoos or paint or feathers; knowing *us* from *them* was a matter of life and death.

And no wonder our ancestors developed weapons not only to subdue prey and defend themselves from predators, but also to fight with other tribes.[7]

Driven apart by growing populations, territorial skirmishes, depleted resources, and natural disasters like flood or drought, our ancestors quickly spread across Africa—and beyond. When they reached the Middle East (where they appear to have interbred with *Homo neanderthalensis*), some took a left turn and spread across Europe. Others took a right turn and made their way across Asia, Australia, and eventually North and South America. The global spread of our species suggests just how successfully the exclusive we worked as a survival strategy.[8]

At some point, a handful of our ancestors moved beyond hunting and gathering.[9] They began to farm livestock and crops and lived in more fixed settlements. Their populations grew, and more and more people could specialize in other forms of work beyond food production. Many learned to fashion tools and works of art from wood, stone, shell, bronze, iron, and other metals. Members of a settlement would trade their goods and skills with one another, and settlements began creating regional trading networks. Regional economies developed.

Beginning about nine thousand years ago, settlements began to amalgamate into city-states, each ruled by its chief and nobility, and then into nation-states ruled by kings and their courts, and sometimes nation-states would amalgamate into empires, ruled by emperors and their elites.

In these ways, our ancestors kept enlarging their exclusive we to enhance their survival in intergroup conflict. It was a messy process, often involving war, enslavement, oppression, scapegoating, even genocide—ugly realities in our shared human history.

Our ancestors developed new kinds of governments to support and regulate life in their enlarging exclusive we. Religions evolved and adapted as well, as did God concepts. No group could thrive without helping people learn to trust (through God 1.0), to transcend selfishness (through God 2.0), to respect rules (through God 3.0), and to love one another in family and nation (through God 4.0). And no group could thrive without being ready at any moment to defend against or attack other groups—each of which was united by a different version of God 4.0. Groups with the biggest and best God 4.0 gained important survival advantages over their counterparts, and God 4.0 proved remarkably flexible, serving small tribes and global empires with equal efficiency.

Yesterday's Survival Strategy Is Today's Suicide Strategy

But here we are in this present moment, and the very exclusive-we survival strategy that brought us to this point now threatens us. We have developed weapons of mass destruction so terrifying that if they were fully deployed in the name of any God 4.0, there would be no winners. Every *we* would be decimated.

In addition, all the *we*s on earth now face problems so immense—beginning with the climate crisis, but extending to many other ecological, economic, and political challenges—that no single exclusive we can solve them alone. The very exclusive-we strategy that has served us so well for 130,000 years has now run its course. Our time-tested divine survival strategy has become suicidal. For the first time in human history, God 4.0, the exclusive-we God who is the God of *us* but not *them,* threatens our survival. Here's how the Catholic theologian James Finley puts it: "It appears that religions—and perhaps even humanity itself—will not survive if we stay within tribal consciousness, believing our religion is the only 'one true religion.' "[10]

We need *God 5.0* to emerge, a God of the *inclusive we,* the God not just of *us* but of *all of us.* Only a bigger, nondualistic God can unite us and them in an inclusive identity that is not limited to a tribe or nation, but that extends to all humanity, and not just to all humanity, but to all living things, and not just to all living things, but to all the planetary ecosystems in which we share. We need to migrate to a grown-up God, as my friend Jacqueline Lewis puts it.[11]

We need God 5.0 to lead us away from the precipice of cataclysmic war.

We need God 5.0 to save us from paralyzing polarization.

We need God 5.0 to teach us to wisely revere and care for the earth upon which we all depend.

We need God 5.0 because we now realize we have evolved together with all other forms of life on this tiny, fragile planet, which means that all creatures are our relatives, our relations.[12] We are all part of one family tree, one web of life, and we need our understanding of God to embrace that reality.

As we have seen, God 4.0 still succeeds in helping us make the personal transition from selfishness to sharing to rules to love. And God 4.0 still succeeds in strengthening the bonds of the exclusive-we community, whether we're talking about a few dozen people in a local congregation, or a billion people in a religion, a nation, or an empire. There is much that is good about "God and country" God 4.0, and the same is true of the "I'll be there for you" God 1.0, the "be nice to your sister" God 2.0, and the "play by the rules" God 3.0. Those whose lives have been enriched—even saved—by these concepts of God will have good reason to fear moving beyond them.

That's why it's important to emphasize that we're talking

about an integral change, not a wholesale rejection and replacement. Like rings on a tree, each new concept of God includes or integrates its antecedents, even as it transcends or expands beyond them. When we move to God 2.0, for example, we don't reject the primal trust we learned from God 1.0, just as we don't (or shouldn't) reject the familial generosity of God 2.0 when we embrace the social responsibilities of God 3.0. You might say we only become ready for God 5.0 after we have thoroughly learned the best lessons that Gods 1.0 through 4.0 have to offer. And just as a tree finds a way of incorporating damage from storms or disease, or just as a bone can become stronger where it healed from a previous break, our new concepts of God can acknowledge and incorporate the tragic misunderstandings and mistakes of our past and seek to become stronger through them.

We see this pattern in the Scriptures. When Moses is given the Ten Commandments, he doesn't say that Abraham's religion was wrong because he didn't have them. And when Solomon builds an elaborate temple of stone, he doesn't say Moses's religion was wrong because he had only a tent of cloth. And when the prophets Amos, Isaiah, and Micah come along, they don't advocate rejecting their religion and culture, even though they are highly critical of its spiritual hypocrisy and social injustice. They want their religion to expand, to evolve, to learn and grow. The same is true with Jesus. He came, he said, not to abolish or replace, but to fulfill what came before him.

So now Christianity, like its monotheistic sister religions, faces a critical challenge. Can Christians migrate from God 4.0 to God 5.0 without leaving their religion? Can our hearts expand to embrace a larger, grander, inclusive God who demonstrates solidarity with all rather than hostility to some? In the name of God 5.0, can we cut up the genocide and holy war cards in our back pocket once and for all, rejecting hostility and domination, and sign up for a new project of inclusive-we harmony instead?[13]

Can we seal off and transcend all the vestiges of domination, subjugation, and violence that we developed while worshipping God 4.0, and add new depths of relationality, solidarity, and self-giving?

GOD 5.0 IS ALREADY HERE

Some days I feel pessimistic about the likelihood of this migration. There are many factors—psychological, sociological, political, economic, as well as theological—that make Christian tribes afraid of moving beyond the exclusive we of God 4.0. In fact, at this very moment many sectors of Christian faith (and other religions) seem to be doubling down and constricting in fear rather than opening up in a gesture of embrace.

When I feel cynical about the possibility of Christianity (and other religions) moving beyond our love affair with violence, I'm glad we don't have to wait for our religious leaders in an office or a cathedral (or a mosque or a temple) somewhere to take the lead. I'm glad we don't have to wait for a majority vote of some group somewhere to give us permission to begin. You and I, along with the people we influence, can simply migrate to God 5.0 ourselves—with the help of our religious leaders when possible, and without it when necessary. If more and more of us experience this migration, hundreds and thousands of us could soon be millions and eventually billions. Then, if our religious leaders and institutions don't lead, they can at least follow.[14]

We are surrounded with reasons for hope. Again and again over recent decades and in place after place around the world, people are beginning to move in a great theological migration.

Think back fifty years in the United States, when leaders like Dr. King, Dorothy Height, Bayard Rustin, and Fannie Lou Hamer dared to challenge the dominant view of a segregation-

ist God who upheld white privilege. They faced not only the opposition of white religious and political institutions but also the
misgivings of many African Americans who feared they were
pushing too hard and too fast. But now, virtually all Christians
agree, at least in theory, that Dr. King's dream was God's dream,
and that God was imaged more truly by the marchers being
beaten on the Edmund Pettus Bridge in Selma than by those
swinging the clubs in the name of tradition, law, and order. In
word and deed, with their words and with their feet, courageous
demonstrators literally embodied for us the nonviolent dream of
God 5.0's beloved community.

Similarly, in Africa through the late twentieth century, brilliant Christian theologians and courageous Christian leaders like
Kwame Bediako, Emmanuel Katongole, Desmond Tutu, and
Mabiala Kenzo, joined by intrepid white missionaries like Vincent Donovan and David Bosch, have dared speak truths that
were rarely spoken: that the version of God brought by the white
colonial missionaries wasn't the only possible Christian version;
that black Africans themselves could be bona fide Christian theologians too; that the Gospel was more truly understood from the
perspective of the colonized than from that of the colonizers; and
that African traditions could illuminate the Gospel no less than
European traditions. They boldly proclaimed God 5.0 as the God
of *ubuntu,* the God of mutuality and solidarity.

Meanwhile in Asia, a land where religious plurality had long
been the norm, Christian theologians like Raimon Panikkar,
Anthony de Mello, Bede Griffiths, and E. Stanley Jones spoke of
God in conversation with Hinduism, Buddhism, and other East-
ern religions, without the us-versus-them hostility so typical of
Western Christians. They allowed themselves the same freedom
that Western Christians had enjoyed centuries earlier: they let the
Christian Gospel interact with the Upanishads or the Four Noble
Truths as their counterparts had done with Plato in the age of

Augustine or with Aristotle in the age of Aquinas. As a result, they dared to imagine God in a nondual relationship to the universe, and in so doing, courageous Asian-influenced theologians boldly proclaimed God 5.0.

In Latin America, twentieth-century liberation theologians like Elsa Tamez, Oscar Romero, Gustavo Gutiérrez, Maria Pilar Aquino, Leonardo Boff, Jon Sobrino, and René Padilla dared to challenge the dominant view of a law-and-order God who upheld rich dictators and told the poor to stay compliantly in their place. These daring theologians proclaimed a dynamic God 5.0 who loved the landless, the farmworkers, the slum dwellers, the illiterate, and the indigenous people living in the jungles, a God 5.0 who heard both the cries of the earth and the cries of the poor who suffer under an unjust status quo.

In Europe and the English-Speaking World

In Europe, a generation of midcentury theologians like Jürgen Moltmann, Dietrich Bonhoeffer, and Wolfhart Pannenberg saw at close range how the God 4.0 of European nationalism did indeed carry a genocide card in his back pocket. Amid the lingering smoke of twentieth-century bombs and ovens, they began to envision a God 5.0 who suffers with all creation, who groans with all creation for a better future, who is profoundly with all humanity in our pain and hope, and who is found in the ghetto and the concentration camp. They have been joined by twenty-first-century Christian thinkers schooled in continental postmodern philosophy, from John Caputo to Peter Rollins, who seek to deconstruct from within the metanarratives of genocide-card-carrying Christian colonizers, to see if, perhaps, a new trace of God 5.0 might be discerned.

Others have been rediscovering in the Anabaptist tradition a vision of a nonviolent God of peace rather than a violent God of war. Groups like Sojourners in the United States and festivals like Greenbelt in the United Kingdom have raised colorful banners of faith and justice, as have bold advocates for justice like Alexia Salvatierra, Dave Andrews, and Shane Claiborne. Theologians and educators like James Alison, Michael Hardin, and Suzanne Ross have been unlocking in the work of René Girard new anthropological insights as to why the concept of God has had such a bloody history. In mass media, powerful figures like Oprah Winfrey, Bill Moyers, and Krista Tippett have given creative Christian thinkers like Father Richard Rohr, Katharine Hayhoe, Barbara Brown Taylor, and Rob Bell a platform. Online, a wide range of voices, from authors and bloggers Glennon Melton and Rachel Held Evans to theologians Michael Hardin, Peter Enns, Peter Heltzel, Sharon Putt, Brad Jersak, and Brian Zahnd, have discovered they were singing in virtual harmony—and more and more people around the world have begun singing along.

A WORLDWIDE CONVERSATION

And while all this has been going on, from Taizé in France to Iona in Scotland to retreat centers around the world, thousands of Christians across denominations have been rediscovering the contemplative and monastic traditions. These spiritual seekers have, with the help of contemplatives and mystics, embraced a vision of God that is bigger and deeper than God 4.0: a God of unfathomable compassion who can be encountered through spiritual practices and silent solitude, not just through words and arguments and longer words and hotter arguments.

As if that weren't enough, the vibrant voices of feminist theologians around the world—Sallie McFague, Marjorie Suchocki, Elisabeth Schüssler Fiorenza, Diana Butler Bass, Ilia Delio, and many others—have been making invaluable contributions, proclaiming a God beyond patriarchy, a God beyond domination, a God beyond modernity and its technologically enhanced violence, a God 5.0. They have been joined by queer theologians who discovered that even though God 4.0 had no room for them, God 5.0 welcomed them to the table—not just to receive, but to serve and lead with their unique and precious gifts.

Over these same decades, indigenous theologians and Christian thinkers around the world like George Tinker, Randy Woodley, Ray Aldred, Terry LeBlanc, Andrea Smith, and Richard Twiss have drawn from the deep wells of their tradition and experience. Having seen the genocide card played against their people, how can they *not* proclaim that the God of the conquistadores and cowboys must not get the last word? How can they *not* proclaim that it is time for God 5.0 to emerge?

Of course, these diverse people and groups don't agree on everything, and none of them would use a clumsy term like *5.0*. (I don't normally use it either. It's just an unwieldy but useful tool that I promise to abandon when this chapter is finished, and I hope you'll do the same.) I've only employed it here to help us grasp this simple truth: our understandings of God must continue to change and grow—not because Christianity will die if we don't, but because of its proven capacity to kill.

At this very moment, inspired by all this foment and theological creativity, a grassroots movement of Christians is springing up around the world. Christians everywhere are reading new books, following new blogs, attending new conferences and festivals and retreats where new ways of thinking are possible. Courageous leaders of previous generations have opened many doors, and today's emerging trailblazers are walking through them. They aren't waiting for anyone's permission. They have all the permission they need. A great theological migration has begun.

CONTEMPLATION, CONVERSATION, AND ACTION: CHAPTER 5

Contemplation: Let this chapter settle in your mind, and in a quiet place, sitting or walking, let your heart form one simple sentence uttered to God in response.

Conversation:
1. What one sentence, paragraph, image, or idea from this chapter do you most want to talk about?
2. "We are coming to see in the life and teaching of Christ, and especially in the cross and resurrection of Christ, *a radical rejection of dominating supremacy in all its forms.*" Respond.
3. Read Philippians 2:1–11, and respond to the reflection on this text from the chapter.
4. The author speaks of becoming "an atheist" in relation to one view of God in order to migrate to another understanding of God. Explain in your own words.
5. In one of his most easily misunderstood statements, the author says, "It doesn't even matter whether God exists." What does he mean, in context? Do you agree or disagree?
6. Discuss the strengths of God 1.0, 2.0, 3.0, and 4.0. And then discuss their weaknesses.
7. What is the difference between "an integral change" that transcends and includes as opposed to "wholesale rejection and replacement"?

Action: This chapter begins and ends with signs of hope that our view of God is slowly but surely maturing. Keep track of signs of this hope around you in the days to come.

6

THE BIBLE IN LABOR

I WAS IN NEW ZEALAND RECENTLY, SPEAKING ABOUT THE great theological migration we considered in the previous chapter. In one lecture, I focused on the Bible's role in upholding violent and supremacist understandings of God.

After my talk, a woman named Fiona came up to me and told me a story. Her family had moved to a new city a few years earlier and had trouble finding a church. For a while, they did "home church," which gave the whole family a chance to develop a shared weekly worship experience together. One Sunday, her daughter Lucy, then about nine years old, offered to prepare a sermon. Fiona thought I would be interested in the sermon, and offered to send it to me if Lucy was agreeable. A week later, the sermon arrived in my in-box. Lucy was ten now, Fiona said, and would probably word a few things differently, but she still felt good about the basic message of her sermon and was happy for me to read it and share it with others.

The sermon was poignantly short and perfectly designed to achieve her rhetorical intent, as expressed in the last sentence. Here's what she said:

> When I think about God I think of a person who would never murder or kill anyone. But when you think about it you wonder because wasn't it God who swept the angel of death over

Egypt? It makes you think doesn't it? Is God against it or is he
not? I mean what had the boys done to die? It was the Pharaoh
wasn't it? Now do you realise how little we know about God?
I hope this made you think, thanks for listening.[1]

It took me a long time—at least thirty years longer than Lucy,
in fact—to confront the paradox she already sees: that the Bible
presents God as violent in many places, while in many other
places it presents God as someone "who would never murder or
kill anyone."[2] I may have had misgivings like Lucy's when I was
younger, but I didn't dare voice them. I saw it as my job to be satisfied with any and every version of God presented to me in the
Bible. If the Bible said it, it was my job to accept it and believe it,
and that settled it.

My inherited understanding of the Bible motivated me to
learn and grow, to mature and work hard, seeking to love, serve,
and please the God of the exclusive we. Well into my twenties,
this biblical orientation helped me become a much better husband, father, friend, church member, and citizen than I otherwise
would have been.[3]

But in my thirties, I began to feel a clammy sense of spiritual
claustrophobia. The air was growing stale; the windows seemed
shuttered, the doors locked tight. For starters, I didn't feel right
about how my inherited approach to the Bible was influencing my
behavior toward my neighbors. When I met a gay person, when
I interacted with an atheist, an agnostic, or a person of another
religion, even when I met a fellow Christian who understood the
Bible differently, my Bible-quoting inner fundamentalist seemed
to whisper in my ear, "Don't trust them. Don't open your heart to
them. They are not safe. They are not one of *us*. Don't fully love
them. If they're open, you should try to convert them, but otherwise keep your distance. Come apart from among them and be
separate!" I started to feel that my inherited way of reading the

Bible was making me a less open, less loving, less generous person than I otherwise would have been.

For a long time, I felt torn. As much as I wanted to, I couldn't face the kind of questions nine-year-old Lucy asked. In my early years as a pastor, like Gavin the seminarian, I felt constrained by the Bible to hold on to and even defend a vision of God that was gracious toward *us* and hostile toward *them,* even though I was beginning to see how dangerous that view had been and could be again.

Why couldn't I change? Because all my life, I had been taught that a patriarchal God issued the Bible as a kind of constitution or social contract between himself and his exclusive tribe, and the consequences for questioning that constitution were dire. To question the Bible was to risk being forever banished from *us* and condemned to suffer forever among *them* in an unair-conditioned prison.

Like many conservative Christians, I had been taught that there were only two ways of reading the Bible—our way and the wrong way. We alone held to a "high view of Scriptural authority." We alone "took Scripture seriously," which meant we "read it literally" and believed in its inerrancy. Here's the kind of thing I frequently heard among my tribe of conservative Christians: *If the Bible says the whale swallowed Jonah, I believe it. If the Bible says Jonah swallowed the whale, I'll believe that too. What the Bible says, God says, and any child can understand it.*

The only alternative to our *literal* approach, we were told, was a *liberal* approach. Liberals, according to our teachers, put the authority of human reason above the authority of the Bible, which meant (in our view), they put themselves above God. They "demythologized" the Bible, and like a person peeling an onion, when they peeled away what they called myths, there would be nothing left but tears. If there was one thing I didn't want to be, it was *liberal*! So I felt trapped between an unacceptable conservatism and an equally unacceptable liberalism.

Beyond "Literal" and "Liberal"

Gradually, through a lot of reading, a lot of pastoral experience, and a lot of pain (including my theological meltdown in front of the palo verde tree), I realized that this stark binary between conservative and liberal was neither accurate nor fair. I began to see a wide range of possible approaches to the Bible, which can be plotted on a simple matrix.

First, instead of contrasting two distinct buckets, one conservative and one liberal, I thought in terms of a spectrum that stretched between two ways of reading the Bible, *literal* and *literary*.[4]

◄───►

LITERAL   **LITERARY**

A literal reading begins with the assumption that the Bible is intended to be a source of factual information, the kind of information we would expect from a science, math, or history textbook. In contrast, in a literary reading, the Bible is a collection of literary artifacts intended to convey meaning, whether through poetry or story, law or proverb, fiction or nonfiction. If a literal approach looks for *accuracy* and *factuality,* then a literary approach looks for *artistry* and *meaning.* If a literal approach seeks *information* as raw material for a belief system, a literary approach seeks *formation* of the imagination, the soul, the character. If a literal approach seeks *metaphysical truth*—objective facts about the spiritual world—then a literary approach seeks *metaphorical truth,* an understanding that comes through imagination and intuition, reaching through what is seen and understood toward what is unseen and beyond human understanding. If a literal approach seeks *universal and unchanging absolutes,* then a literary approach seeks *timely insight* and is sensitive to *changing cultural and historical contexts.*

Those simple moves—from two discrete buckets to a spectrum, and from conservative/liberal to literal/literary—helped me understand how people from my conservative background were most comfortable at the left end of the line, but could occasionally move to the right, such as, for example, when we read one of Jesus's parables.

Then I added a vertical axis stretching from *innocent* to *critical* to *postcritical* (or *integral*).[5]

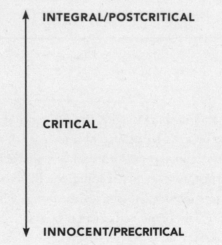

INTEGRAL/POSTCRITICAL

CRITICAL

INNOCENT/PRECRITICAL

At the *innocent* end of the vertical axis, readers of the Bible ask few or no questions about its sources, development, internal tensions, biases, historical or scientific accuracy, or literary genre. They don't concern themselves much with the history of how a text has been interpreted over time and in different cultural contexts, nor are they sensitive to the vested interests of writers and interpreters. They spend little if any energy exploring ways a passage from the Bible may be similar to or different from texts in other religious communities. They may consider questions about these matters irreverent or inappropriate, or they may simply have never been given the opportunity even to entertain such questions. For them, the Bible is God's Word, God's timeless Instruction Manual, God's Law or Constitution, and that's all they need or want—or are allowed—to know.

As readers move toward the center area of the vertical axis, they are given more and more permission to think critically about the Bible. They not only gain freedom to ask questions about the Bible's sources, development, internal tensions, and so on; they see it as their duty to do so. No question is outlawed and no answer is predetermined. For critical readers, to "take the text seriously" means applying their most rigorous critical analysis to it. If critical thinking leads them to identify inaccuracies or misinformation in the text, so be it. If critical thinking requires suspicion about how the text plays a role in power dynamics, that's an asset, not a liability. If critical thinking leads readers to see how texts evolve over time, or how texts wrestle in dynamic tension with one another, or how texts change the conditions they were meant to address—thus creating new conditions that will require new texts to speak—that's what *taking the texts seriously* requires. Although critical reading was scary for people from my tradition, it was the pinnacle of biblical scholarship for others.

Beyond that critical zone lies territory that is much less familiar to the average Christian. We might call it a postcritical zone or an integral zone—a zone of *second naïveté*.[6] In this zone, having applied all their critical skills to "deconstruct" the Bible, readers now try to put the pieces back together, to get a fresh vision of a text in its wholeness, and of many texts in concert. If critical analysis meant we took things apart, this second naïveté or second innocence means we seek to see things whole again.

We are like art connoisseurs who have critically examined a painting up close, analyzing each brushstroke with a magnifying glass, understanding each convention followed and broken by the artist. We have located the painting in its genre and in the larger history of art. We have identified similarities and differences between it and other paintings by the same artist, and by other painters of its era. We may have even studied the chemical composition of the paints chosen by the artist. But now, we step back to take in the painting as a whole again, letting the work of art once again work its magic upon us. We don't just study and analyze the text from an objective critical distance; having sought to understand it, we now render ourselves vulnerable to it again, letting it speak to us, touch us, move upon us.

This end of the vertical axis is, in this sense, *post*critical. We might also call it *integral* in that it integrates the personal vulnerability of an innocent reader who "stands under" the text with the more objective curiosity of a critical reader who stands over it, subjecting it to scrutiny. We might say that postcritical or integral readers stand imaginatively inside the text, trying to see the world through its window. Or we could say that integral readers let the text enter them, getting under their skin, enriching their vision. Either way, readers move through uncritical submission and through critical distance to a new and intimate space of postcritical engagement.

Obviously, people can locate themselves at any point along the vertical axis, and over time they can move, becoming more or less innocent, and more or less involved in critical and postcritical thinking about the Bible.

If we put the horizontal and vertical axes together, we create a matrix that clusters these approaches in six zones, and the dotted lines remind us that these are porous zones, not discrete boxes.

INTEGRAL	Integral/Literal: The Bible is valued as a multilayered and complex whole. Objective/factual information and academic interpretative approaches (Marxist, Jungian, etc.) are preferred.	Integral/Literary: The Bible is valued as a multilayered and complex whole and as a potential source of wisdom and guidance for individuals and groups today.
CRITICAL	Critical/Literal: The Bible is subject to scrutiny and challenge. Factually false meanings are exposed. Historic and scientific analyses are preferred.	Critical/Literary: The Bible is subject to scrutiny and challenge. Multiple dimensions of meaning are permitted and multiple interpretive approaches are allowed.
INNOCENT	Innocent/Literal: The Bible is accepted without question as authoritative; objective and factual meanings are favored.	Innocent/Literary: The Bible is accepted without question as authoritative; subjective and personal meanings are favored.
	LITERAL	LITERARY

Conservatives or fundamentalists like me were raised to read the Bible with a fervent *innocence*. Most of us were innocent literalists who focused on a text's objective literal meaning ("What does the text say?"). Those of us with a more pietistic and charismatic bent were innocent/literary readers, who habitually searched the Scriptures for subjective, personal meaning ("What does the text mean to me?").[7] We liked to extract inspiring verses and promises, often memorizing them and putting them on cards and plaques. We cared about the original context or meaning of a passage, but only as a means to the end: letting God speak to us personally, with inspiration, warning, or encouragement. Many of us learned to move adeptly back and forth between the two lower zones, using the innocent/literal approach for doctrine and argument, and the innocent/literary approach for devotion and inspiration.

Our archenemies, the "liberals," read the Bible in the critical/literal zone. They dared to say that the Bible's information was scientifically, historically, or metaphysically inaccurate. They imagined it developed over time rather than being revealed by divine fiat, or that it was simply a primitive collection of fables, myths, and other untruths. The critical/literary readers weren't much better. They made the claim—irrational to us—that a text could be literally false in terms of historical or scientific fact but true in terms of literary meaning. Ventures into this critical zone were seen in my tribe not as courageous steps up into enlightenment but as dangerous steps down a slippery slope that would end in chaos and despair.

Texts in Travail

Frankly, in my conservative Evangelical days, I almost never encountered anyone who read in the upper postcritical or integral zones, especially in the upper-right integral/literary zone. I think the same was true for many of my liberal Christian friends, who tended to look down on literalists without imagining that anyone could have climbed to a higher vantage point where even more could be seen. One author, however, seemed to lead in a postconservative and postliberal direction: C. S. Lewis. I think Lewis became so popular for many Evangelicals because he was conservative by nature and shared our antipathy toward the liberal critical literalists, yet he opened the way for us to bring imagination and literary sensibilities to the text, letting the Bible speak to us in a postcritical way. You might say he drew us farther up and to the right, allowing innocent literalists like myself to rush quickly over the critical phase that we felt was so dangerous and distasteful.[8]

With C. S. Lewis serving as a kind of gateway into the upper right area of the matrix, we discovered more and more scholars who read the Bible with their critical, postcritical, and literary skills and sensibilities intact—from N. T. Wright to Walter Brueggemann, from Jo-Ann Badley to Marcus Borg, from Walter Wink to John Dominic Crossan, from Paul Tournier to Ched Myers to James Alison, from Tom Boomershine to Derek Flood to Barbara Brown Taylor. Their conclusions often differed, but they shared a common aim: not to discredit, ridicule, or expose the Bible as false, but rather to find broader and deeper meaning and truth within it. They saw tensions among biblical texts not as contradictions, but as contractions. Like a woman in labor, biblical texts were for them "in travail," giving birth to new ways of seeing God, ourselves, and the world around us.[9]

For example, we read in some texts that the Israelite monarchy was a great gift of God, but in other texts it is seen as a rejection of God as king. We could attempt to subordinate the antimonarchy texts to the promonarchy texts, or vice versa, upholding the idea that the Bible speaks simply and with one voice (an innocent/literal approach). Or we could see the tension as a mere contradiction, discrediting the whole Bible (a critical/literal approach). But an integral approach allows us to see that different voices in the biblical library held opposing viewpoints, and the tension between those viewpoints forces us to see both the wisdom and the weaknesses of both sides.

Seen in this light, the dynamic tensions or contractions that arise among the texts give birth to a richer, deeper, and more nuanced insight; namely, that centralized government can indeed be a gift that solves many problems, but it can also become dictatorial and create new problems. Having given birth to this more mature viewpoint, the tensions between biblical texts don't represent a failure in the texts, but an invaluable heuristic device. Like unanswered problems in a math text, they don't simply tell us what to memorize, doling out answers we must accept without thinking. Instead, they challenge us to think individually and grapple with unanswered questions in community. If learning and wisdom are indeed the consequence of thinking rather than rote memorization, there could be no better way for the biblical library to be designed.

Working in this new space, this new generation of postcritical/ literary scholars didn't try to find "proof" of factual accuracy on the one hand or to reduce the biblical texts to the level of primitive superstitions on the other. Nor did they locate divine revelation in this or that isolated statement or story. Rather, they saw revelation arising like sparks in the interplay of passage and passage, story and story, statement and counterstatement, over time. For them, Scripture wasn't univocal; instead, God's manifold wisdom emerged in the multiplicity of biblical voices.[10] It was a conversation rather than a legal constitution, an art gallery rather than a single painting. In the presence of these scholars and teachers who read the Bible with literary sensibilities and with critical and postcritical or integral understanding, I felt a new freedom. I felt that I was given permission to migrate from the limited universe of the conventional, exclusive, and often violent Supreme Being to the ever-expanding universe of a more awesome and wonderful God, all while keeping my Bible firmly in hand.

In that new space, I could allow the Bible to show me a succession of understandings of God. I could see the tension between these understandings as contractions, giving birth to not just a new understanding of God, but more: to a new *experience* of God as the Holy Spirit of justice, joy, and peace, present in Christ, in my own life, in human justice and kindness, and in all creation. In short, I could leave the genocidal God of some biblical passages behind and honor the generous God revealed in Jesus.

So yes, Lucy was right: the exclusive-we Supreme Being God of conventional religion can be found in the Bible, controlling, excluding, harming, killing, and animating various forms of oppressive human supremacy—religious, racial, political, gender based. But repeatedly, insistently, from Genesis to Revelation, the exclusive-we God is challenged, and a grander vision of an infinitely compassionate, generous, and gracious God rises into view, as Lucy said, a God "who would never murder or kill anyone." The biblical library brings us through a long night of wrestling to a new dawn, revealing a luminous, life-giving, healing, and liberating presence, the generous, gracious, and holy Spirit who invites and beckons the arc of the universe—and our lives—toward ever-greater goodness, wholeness, beauty, harmony, and aliveness.[11]

That's a small taste of how a more expansive approach to the Bible nourishes a more expansive view of God. It's liberating. Beautiful. All-encompassing. Wonderful. *Good.*

WILL JESUS STILL MATTER?

Many Christians feel terrified about rethinking their approach to the Bible or their understanding of God because they fear that if they do, Jesus will no longer matter. In their inherited system of belief, Jesus matters supremely because he is the solution to a supremely serious problem. God, in the traditional view, possesses a reservoir of infinite wrath that must be vented on all who are not perfect.[12] By accepting the penalty of our sinful status and behavior, Jesus becomes our substitute and allows God's wrath to be satisfied and spent on him rather than us. An angry God is thus appeased—at least for those who hold the right beliefs so they can be considered Christians. It's a very tight formula that has provided an invaluable moral framework for millions of Christians over the last thousand years or so, and although this understanding produces a host of negative unintended consequences (as we saw in the previous chapter), at least within it there's no question whether or why Jesus matters.

No wonder traditionalists would issue a dire warning: *Lose your innocent/literal approach to the Bible, and you lose the angry God it proclaims. Lose the angry God, and you lose the need for Jesus as the shock absorber of God's infinite wrath.*

But the truth is, when we read the Bible from an integral/literary point of view, Jesus becomes even more beautiful, important, and essential. Rather than satisfying a wrathful God, we could say, Jesus deconstructs the conventional concept of a Supreme Being who is capable of murder, genocide, or geocide. Through his life and teachings, in his compassionate interactions with individuals and groups, in his profound nonviolence even to the point of enduring a violent death, Jesus reveals a generous God, a God in profound solidarity with all creation, a God whose power is manifest in gentleness, kindness, and love. Through his promise that he would rise and be present in and with us, he invites us to experience God as the holy and creative Spirit of justice, joy, and peace, moving through all creation, at work in all human history, present in our personal experience. This vision of God could never send us into the world armed with swords and spears (or guns and bombs), ready to dominate through a violent supremacy. Rather, this vision inspires and empowers us to become nonviolent ambassadors of a new way of life, servants of all, ministers of reconciliation, agents of a liberating mission (as we will see more fully in subsequent chapters).

Christians who are afraid that Jesus only matters when the Bible is read from the lower left zone have no reason to fear. When we read the Bible from an integral/literary angle, Jesus disarms both the Bible and our understanding of God.[13] That makes Jesus pretty important!

We can't receive the liberating vision of God and life offered by Jesus if we lock ourselves in the lower left zone of the matrix we've considered in this chapter. We need more space to learn, to grow, to see afresh. We have nothing to fear. We can migrate. If we do, the Bible can become an expansive library of texts in travail that give birth to a new vision of God, a new way of life and mission, and a new chapter in the story of Christian faith.

To quote nine-year-old Lucy, "I hope this made you think, thanks for listening."

CONTEMPLATION, CONVERSATION, AND ACTION: CHAPTER 6

Contemplation: Slowly reread Lucy's sermon from this chapter two or three times. Then imagine what you would say to her in response.

Conversation:

1. What one sentence, paragraph, image, or idea from this chapter do you most want to talk about?
2. Respond to this statement: "I started to think that my understanding of God was making me a less open, less loving, less generous person than I otherwise would have been."
3. Describe the difference between a literal and literary way of reading the Bible.
4. Describe innocent, critical, and integral or postcritical ways of reading the Bible. The author uses the analogy of viewing a painting. Try using a different analogy, perhaps watching a film, enjoying a meal, listening to a speech, driving a car.
5. Tell the story of your experience with the Bible, using the matrix as a tool if it is helpful. (Or explain why the matrix isn't helpful if that's the case.)
6. Respond to this statement: "For Jesus to remain important, we must preserve an innocent/literal way of reading the Bible."
7. Is there a story or passage of the Bible that especially inspires—or troubles—you? Explain why, and practice looking at that story or passage from different zones of the matrix presented in this chapter.

Action: This week, choose a passage from the Bible and reflect upon it from an integral/literary point of view.

PART III

THE MISSIONAL MIGRATION

{ *From Organized Religion*
to Organizing Religion }

7

THAT BEAUTIFUL ROMANCE

BACK IN 1974, AN ANTHROPOLOGIST WROTE THAT "A change in the conception of God is a cultural event of some magnitude."[1] In other words, because cultures and civilizations are deeply influenced by their conceptions of God, theological migrations will naturally lead to cultural transformations. That insight raises a natural question: *how?* How can the spiritual and theological migrations we have considered over the previous six chapters positively transform the character of our culture?

My thinking in this regard got unstuck a few years ago when I got stuck in an unusual place with an unexpected companion.

I was leaving one of my favorite places in the world: Burundi, East Africa. Like its twin sister and neighbor, Rwanda, the country has a tragic history of genocide, but as is so often the case, where ugliness and sin abound, grace and beauty abound all the more. I had been supporting a weeklong conference of emerging African leaders, and my hosts had just dropped me off at the airport, about an hour's drive outside of Bujumbura, the capital city. After another hour of waiting in a long, long line, I finally reached the check-in desk. "I'm sorry, sir," the ticket agent said. "That airline no longer flies on weekends. They stopped weekend service three or four months ago. They should have notified you." It was Friday afternoon, and suddenly I was all packed up with nowhere to go.

"Who can I talk to about getting a flight?" I asked.

"Since there are no more flights on your airline until Monday, there is no ticket agent here until then. But they do have an office in town, and it might still be open."

I was completely flummoxed. "How could this happen?" I asked. She replied with a gentle smile and meaningful under-statement: "Sir, this is Africa."

THIS TOO IS AFRICA

My African friends who dropped me off were long gone and I had no cell phone and knew nobody's number even if I'd had one. I asked the ticket agent if there were taxis available. "I'm sorry, sir." When she saw my consternation, she said something that would be almost unthinkable anywhere except in Africa: "Sir, I have to work for another hour. If you don't mind waiting, I have a car and I'll be glad to drop you off at your airline's office in the city." This too was Africa: *unexpected kindness.*

I waited an hour for her, and then I waited for another hour on the sidewalk in front of the airline office in the capital city. (The office staff took a long late lunch.) With their help, I was able to schedule a flight home with another airline on Sunday. Suddenly I had some free time on my hands—although Bujum-bura probably isn't on most people's list of places for a relaxing getaway. Someone in the airline office suggested a nearby hotel, and I lugged my suitcase there and rented an overpriced room. It smelled musty. It had a balcony, but the balcony doors wouldn't lock, which seemed to me a perfect setup for theft. The air-conditioning didn't work and there was no fan. I lay sweating on the bed in the stifling heat, feeling sorry for myself. "It's going to be quite a weekend," I groaned. When I could stand the sauna no longer, I decided to go downstairs for a cold drink.

The little hotel bar opened out onto the street. There were small tables and rickety chairs scattered around, most filled with local folks unwinding at the end of a workweek, smoking cigarettes and drinking beer. Inches from the sidewalk tables, bicycles flew by and taxi-vans with flatulent mufflers spewed diesel in the tropical humidity. A few little boys wandered between the tables begging for spare change and sneaking food off plates. Street hawkers made eye contact with everyone they could, selling wallets, ties, used T-shirts, fresh avocados. "This is Africa," I thought. I ordered a beer and looked for an empty table, preferably under a ceiling fan.

You can imagine my surprise when I looked across the bar and saw, sitting in a corner, one of the very few Americans who had been at the conference, a man named Greg. I had hardly spoken with Greg because I generally try to spend my time with local people when I go to events overseas. Now it was different. I went over and said hi, explaining my sad story. Greg was also waiting for a flight in a day or two. He invited me to sit down.

As we got better acquainted, I learned that Greg Leffel, a Kentuckian, had recently completed a PhD on social movement theory and its relation to ecclesiology, or church life. Because the subject of this book was percolating in my mind, I had been researching a number of movements in Christian history, including the monastic movement, the Franciscan movement, the Protestant movement, the Methodist movement, the Great Awakenings, the Social Gospel movement, and the American Evangelical movement. It was as if God had arranged a private postconference tutoring session just for me, and Greg's influence continued even after my return home through his published dissertation.[2]

"Christian leaders could learn a lot from social movement theory," Greg explained. "Tell me about it," I said. Over dinner, he did.

A PRIMER IN SOCIAL MOVEMENT THEORY

Greg began by defining three basic terms. First, we live in *communities*—groups of individuals and families who are bound together through their dependence upon the same environment.[3] Then, Greg explained, *institutions* evolve within our communities to serve the individuals and families who constitute them. Each institution seeks to enhance some dimension of community life. For example, schools ideally enhance learning, companies enhance trade, governments enhance peace and freedom, hospitals enhance health, courts enhance fairness, banks enhance wealth, and churches enhance personal, social, and spiritual well-being. Of course, the critical word in the previous sentence is *ideally,* because we can easily come up with examples where institutions actually harm or limit the dimension of community life they are supposed to enhance.

When institutions fail us, Greg explained, members of a community arise, organize, and confront those institutions by forming a *movement*.[4] Movements, we could say, exist to propose positive change to institutions. Movements organize people to articulate what's wrong with current institutions and propose what should be done to make things right.[5]

Institutions can go wrong in many ways. For example, a hospital that was established to help sick people can be diverted to the purpose of providing a high salary to its top doctors and administrators, or providing maximum profit to its investors. A government can be established to protect and serve its citizens, but its actual purpose can degenerate into providing a mechanism for its politicians and their cronies to amass wealth and power. A school can be established to educate students with cutting-edge and mind-liberating knowledge, but its actual purpose can degenerate into dispensing diplomas with minimal effort on the part of students and faculty, or forming compliant drones for corporate or political exploitation. A court system can be established to protect citizens from crime, but it can degenerate into an instrument of racism through mass incarceration. The words used to describe failures like these are familiar to us all: *institutionalism, bureaucracy, organizational ego, stagnancy, rigidity, systemic injustice, corruption.*

To serve and strengthen the Christian community, institutions abound: congregations, denominations, mission agencies, book publishers, music publishers, radio and TV networks, seminaries and other schools, parachurch organizations like youth and college ministries, retreat centers, and summer camps. When these institutions work well, Christians thrive from one generation to the next and bring benefit and blessing to the world. When they break down or malfunction, Christians suffer and their positive influence is reduced, until a movement arises to bring needed change.

Whenever movements gain momentum, Greg said, they soon run into opposition from elites, people who benefit disproportionately from positions of power in current institutions. Since institutional change will likely cost them control, comfort, money, privilege, or prestige, they do all they can to preserve the status quo. That's why movement leaders must build "collective intention" among people for whom the status quo is unsatisfying, so together they can "disrupt the actions of socio-political elites and their control over social, political and cultural institutions."[6]

This growing collective *intention,* he explained, creates social *contention,* which often leads institutional elites to respond aggressively, labeling movement leaders as divisive agitators, ignorant troublemakers, disloyal heretics, and so on. In the presence of rising opposition, nonviolent movement leaders must not discredit themselves by mirroring the hostility of their critics. They must stay positive, attracting and aligning individuals and existing organizations into effective alliances.

FOUR POSSIBLE OUTCOMES

As we finished our meal, Greg explained that movements really have only four options. First, if conditions change and render the movement irrelevant, if its leaders alienate or lose the interest of the followers, or if elites manage to intimidate leaders and followers into silence and inaction, a movement might simply fail. Second, a movement might succeed in convincing relevant institutions to accept its proposals; in this way, it might fulfill its mission and go out of existence. Third, a movement might succeed and then retool around a new set of proposals and thus be renewed or reborn. Fourth, if the institution in question decisively refuses movement proposals, the movement may form a new competing institution.

I interrupted to observe that this fourth option has occurred again and again in Protestant church history. Reform movements in Protestant denominations frequently break away and form their own new denominations, which means that movement leaders quickly morph into institutional leaders.

Of course, the opposite can happen too, Greg explained. Institutional leaders can encounter so much conflict, paralysis, or corruption inside their institution that they want to change it rather than defend it from change. Or they may see outside forces, trends, and events converging that convince them that the status quo is a sinking ship. As a result, they "defect" and stop acting as elites. They start working either from within or from outside their institutions on behalf of a movement. In this way, institutional leaders can become movement leaders, and when they do, they have insider knowledge that noninstitutional leaders lack.

Greg's analysis reminded me of something I had learned years earlier from Jim Wallis, the founder of Sojourners. Jim would often say that movements can simmer on the margins for years, knocking on doors that are never opened. But sometimes an institutional leader opens one of those doors. When a door opens so movement leaders and institutional leaders can begin working together, breakthroughs occur. I've often heard Jim mention the relationship between movement leader Dr. Martin Luther King Jr. and President Lyndon Johnson in the 1960s as an example of this moment of convergence.

Greg and I paid our bill and continued our conversation in the hotel lobby. We discussed the deep differences between movements and institutions. For example, movements typically strive for radical or revolutionary change—they try to leap forward. In contrast, institutions seek either to maintain the status quo or to achieve change gradually and incrementally, taking small steps forward. Movements engender loyalty to their cause or dream and value passion and agility; institutions build loyalty to their legacy and value moderation and stability. When movements succeed, their leaders declare "Mission accomplished!" and everyone goes home, but when institutions succeed, everyone keeps their job.[7] We also considered how closely movements and institutions are related, and how, in fact, they help define each other: institutions are enduring organizations that preserve the gains made by past social movements, and movements are ad hoc organizations that propose new gains to current institutions.[8]

By this time, it was growing late. Greg agreed to meet again the next morning and promised to share with me the heart of his doctoral research.

OPEN SEASON FOR CHANGE

It was a noisy, sweaty, uncomfortable night in my shabby little hotel room, but that wasn't the only reason I couldn't sleep. My imagination was bubbling with possibilities for how a vibrant

spiritual movement could help Christian individuals and institutions experience the deep and healing spiritual migration we
needed.

When morning finally came, I didn't mind that there was no
hot water for a shower; the cool water was refreshing. I grabbed
a notebook and pen, and I went down to breakfast and ordered
some Burundian coffee. Greg arrived, and soon we were deep
in discussion about the six characteristics of vibrant social movements he had identified in his research.

First, Greg explained, movement leaders identify the *opportunity structure,* the context and incentives that make a social movement both necessary and possible. To map that context, leaders
ask questions like these:

> *What problems are not being solved by current institutions?*
> *What negative effects are current institutions creating? What
>   opportunities are they missing?*
> *Which elites have a vested interest in resisting needed change?*
> *What fissures or conflicts fragment existing elites so their
>   combined strength is weakened?*
> *What values can be articulated that rally people against the
>   interests of elites?*
> *Which allies and advocates can be rallied together across various
>   sectors of public life—from the academy, civil society,
>   the arts, the church, government, business, or science, for
>   example?*
> *What communication tools are available to help the movement
>   spread its message?*

Greg and I discussed one key component of the opportunity
structure of the twenty-first century: what some have called the
"exhaustion" of the corporate, militaristic, consumeristic, extractive, democratic capitalism that dominates the global economy,

in both its conservative and its liberal forms.[9] This system is addicted to unsustainable fossil fuels, dependent on cheap and unorganized labor, closely aligned with military forces, shielded by bureaucracy, and thoroughly advantaged by left-right political polarization (both sides of which it owns and controls). There are reasons to believe that at the very peak of its power, this system is growing increasingly vulnerable year by year, making the twenty-first century ripe for dynamic social movements.[10]

Then we considered how traditional religious structures in the West are similarly fragile—with their conflicted, constricted, aging, divided, and declining denominations, their struggling mission agencies, and their desperate and scandal-ridden religious media empires, not to mention the rise of extremist, fractious, and reactionary fundamentalist movements on the one hand and tepid nominalism on the other. It's hard to imagine conditions more ripe for a vital spiritual movement to arise.

We also discussed a relatively new factor in today's opportunity structure: globalism, which is the experience of the world as one place and humanity as a single species. We discussed how globalism (for better or worse) transforms personal and ethnic identities, creating hyphenated and cosmopolitan identities—in which people consider themselves first and foremost citizens of the earth and members of the earth's ecosystem more than as citizens of a nation or members of a religion. This identity disruption creates fissures and fractures among existing elites who are still managing parochial national, cultural, ethnic, or religious systems.[11]

We then discussed the game-changing impact of the Internet, with its potential to help self-organizing networks develop, expand, educate, and deepen their movement potential. Greg and I could feel how the conditions, taken together, were becoming ideal for aspiring social and spiritual movements to be born and to grow, if social and spiritual entrepreneurs were ready to seize the moment wisely and well.

Message and Medium

Greg then introduced the concept of *rhetorical framing and conceptual architecture*. Movement leaders, he said, must make a conceptual and verbal case for their movement by answering questions like these:

> *What's wrong with the status quo? What needs to be changed?*
> *How do we name our grievances? How do we articulate our*
>   *positive vision for the way forward?*
> *What are our specific proposals or demands for change?*
> *How do we motivate and sustain dissatisfaction with the status*
>   *quo, and how do we inspire affection for our shared vision?*
> *How do we justify our aims along traditional lines of moral*
>   *argument (as articulated, for example, by social psychologist*
>   *Jonathan Haidt): justice, compassion, tradition, loyalty, and*
>   *purity?*[12]
> *How is the movement liberating? How does the movement*
>   *challenge the status quo while conserving needed values,*
>   *truths, and practices?*

In answering these questions, movement leaders define their proposals and demands, clarify their ways of calling people to affiliation and action, and crystallize their central symbols and slogans.

Next, when the moment is right and the message is clear, movements must gain attention through a *protest or messaging strategy*—employing demonstrations, teach-ins, sit-ins, declarations, publications, and other methods to spread their message through many media. Movement leaders must attract growing numbers of active participants, and from among them develop additional leaders whom they can deploy as organizers to attract and deploy even more participants. Inevitably, as they win allies, they also gain opponents and critics. They must learn to "dance" with their opponents and critics wisely, using every criticism as an opportunity to clarify and amplify their message, always aware of how their public image is improving—or deteriorating.

At this point, Greg and I shared stories of movements we had been part of, beginning with the Jesus Movement of the late 1960s and early 1970s. We reflected on the Jesus Movement's strategies and tactics—from free papers and tracts, to concerts and festivals, to signs and slogans (like the "one way" sign or the proliferation of bumper stickers, some clever and some not so much). We spoke of the movement's proposals and demands and whether or not it achieved them.[13]

We also spoke about the challenges of movement leadership. As conditions change, movement leaders must continually evaluate, revise, and augment their strategies, tactics, and campaigns. They must demonstrate and celebrate past results, name future goals, and maintain momentum. They must balance the autonomy of key players with the need for harmony and collaboration among them. At critical junctures, they must make breaks with counterproductive allies, precipitate constructive crises, manage stigmatization and pushback by elites, define acceptable levels of disruption, and avoid overreaction to attacks and provocations.

We discussed how movement leaders must walk a tightrope, balancing the *convergent* and *insurgent* dimensions of movement building. On the one hand, leaders must build broad, vigorous alliances—convening people around a broadly shared vision. On the other hand, they must be bold and confrontational enough to disturb the peace of privileged elites and those who actually prefer the status quo, inevitably alienating some potential participants.

As we finished breakfast, Greg told me he had more to share. We agreed to pick up our conversation later that morning on a trip to the Bujumbura zoo.

Structure and Culture

Frankly, I don't have great memories of the zoo. I remember standing under a tree and wondering how it was raining on such a sunny day, only to realize that the tree was full of fruit bats, and what was falling on us through the tree branches was not rainfall. And I remember the gruesome sight of the zookeeper feeding the crocodiles with live . . . well, I won't go into it here. The best thing about the zoo that day was that it provided the setting for our fascinating conversation to continue.

As we walked under the trees (and tried to avoid being misted by fruit bats), Greg explained how movement leaders must create and monitor *mobilizing structures*—formal and informal lines of organization, communication, relationship building, coalition building, and resource development. They must balance the need for centralized and decentralized decision making, along with the oft-conflicting needs for privacy and transparency. They must create a way for viable and distinct submovements to practice collaboration without assimilation or competition. They must find ways to "fly in formation" without undermining the distinct identities of submovements. Since burnout is endemic in movement cultures, leaders must also assure their own health and well-being, building needed rest, renewal, and personal development into their structural design. We identified a long list of specific questions movement leaders must ask again and again:

> *How will we make decisions?*
> *How will decisions be communicated?*
> *Who has authority, of what kind, and why?*
> *How will we maintain the values of transparency, privacy, and*
> *confidentiality?*

How will new and current leaders be developed?

How will friendships be encouraged and supported among participants?

How will needless conflicts be avoided and necessary ones be managed?

How will counterproductive behavior be dealt with?

How will coalitions be developed and expanded?

How will money, technology, and other resources be acquired, managed, and disposed of?

How will our message be spread, new participants attracted, activists recruited, inducted, and, when necessary, removed?

How will key institutions become hosts, supporters, and enhancers of this movement?

How will commitment be maintained, increased, and renewed at all levels of the movement?[14]

Greg seemed especially animated when we discussed *movement culture.* If a movement proposes nonviolence, it must be nonviolent. If it proposes environmental responsibility, it must model it. If it advocates justice and generosity, it must embody these virtues. In other words, a movement must be an "experimental field" where people can actually observe and experience the new way of life it advocates. That's why, he explained, a movement is more than a structure mobilizing people around a message to seize opportunities for change. It is also a culture or set of cultures that sustains a community of people as they experience belonging and meaning together.

We again recounted our experience in the Jesus Movement and the elements of its unique culture: its music and slogans, its values and virtues, its distinctive style of clothing and graphics, its moral ethos and vibe or feel. We talked about how some streams of the Jesus Movement were serious, some playful; some grim, some hopeful; some regimented, some spontaneous; some secretive, some public; some austere, some extravagant; some enthusiastic, some apocalyptic. In that light, it was clear how important it is for leaders to consciously craft and cultivate their movement culture. Otherwise, movements can unintentionally become incoherent and confusing to potential members, or exclusive in terms of race, education, or economic level. And if the movement culture isn't healthy and enjoyable, it will wound and damage people, which will eventually lead to its own demise.[15]

That brought us to the final characteristic of movements that Greg had studied. A movement not only makes a difference in the world, he explained; it also makes a difference in the lives of participants, enriching the *participant biography* of all who are involved. People experience costs and rewards, help and harm, scars and strengths through their involvement. If the costs outweigh the rewards too much for too long, the movement will collapse. But if the costs are minimal, rewards will probably be minimal as well. That's why wise movement leaders can't take these matters for granted. They regularly monitor how the movement is contributing to the personal formation of participants in terms of character, attitudes, knowledge, recovery from trauma, relationships, and renewal. They make sure that healthy pride doesn't slip into arrogance, or that humility doesn't descend into discouragement.

Greg and I continued our conversation over dinner on Saturday and over breakfast on Sunday. When the time came for me to return to the airport to begin my journey home, my mind was buzzing with new ideas and my heart was stirred with new possibilities. What kind of spiritual movement could challenge willing sectors of Christian faith to migrate from their systems of belief to a shared way of life centered in love? I wondered. What kind of theological movement could help us migrate from conventional violent understandings of God to the nonviolent vision of God embodied in Jesus? And how could these changes in spirituality and theology be expressed as a transformative movement in the culture at large?

THE GOSPELS AS MOVEMENT HISTORY

On my long flight home, I took out my Bible to see where it resonated with what I had learned from Greg about movement theory. As I surveyed the Hebrew Scriptures, I could see how Moses faced dual movement challenges: first, confronting the leader of a dictatorial institution, and then mobilizing an oppressed people for a very literal migration. As the newly liberated Hebrew children settled in the Promised Land, they faced the difficult challenge of developing religious and political institutions of their own, passing through the chaotic period of the judges and eventually centralizing institutional power in a monarchy. A charismatic young leader named David rose to movement leadership just as the monarchy was being established, and predictably, King Saul saw young David as a threat. Eventually, David replaced Saul and took the throne of institutional leadership. Before long, David fell prey to the temptations of institutional power, and soon he was confronted by the prophet Nathan. Many of the prophets seemed to function as movement leaders, complete with staging dramatic demonstrations that involved creative messaging, nudity, excrement, and scandalous behavior.[16] When I read about the "school of the prophets," I couldn't help but think of the Freedom Schools of the American civil rights movement in 1964.[17]

When I moved to the Gospels, on page after page, Jesus and his disciples practiced movement dynamics in Galilee, Judea, and Samaria. Jesus seized the *opportunity* for change created by unrest in Galilee, by tensions between Pharisees and Sadducees, by divisions between Zealots and Herodians, by the injustices of the Roman occupation, and by corruption among the religious elite. He *framed his message* through a powerful central image (kingdom of God), a unique art form (parables), and through powerful slogans ("Repent for the kingdom of God is at hand," "Render unto Caesar . . . ," "Love your enemies," "Deny yourself, take up your cross, and follow me," for example). He developed a *protest and messaging strategy* that included public teach-ins (the Sermon on the Mount), demonstrations (healings, exorcisms, feeding of the five thousand), guerrilla theater (his triumphal entry into Jerusalem), and advanced action-reflection leadership training (deployments and retreats with disciples).

His *mobilizing structures* included the three, the twelve, the seventy, and special two-by-two initiatives. In addition, he taught his disciples to build allies among "people of peace," and to be willing to let people walk away if they were not ready for the demands of movement involvement. He developed rituals of initiation (baptism) and renewal (Eucharist), calling people to initial commitment and strengthening them for the long haul. His *movement culture* was unique and distinctive, characterized by feasts, parties, joyful processions, and outdoor festivals at which usually stigmatized and outcast people were warmly welcomed. He gave women an unprecedented level of responsibility in his movement, and among his inner circle he included people of diverse gifts and temperament, from a poet like John to an activist like Simon the Zealot to a steady pillar like Peter (at his best). His movement culture also emphasized the value of contemplative solitude and withdrawal to nourish the inner life and sustain the struggle over the long haul. The New Testament contains many examples of *participant biographies* of those caught up in the movement. Their lives in the movement were characterized by great joy, great sorrow, and great love.

The Movement Continues

I could see these same dynamics at work in Paul and his colleagues around the Mediterranean, as the "kingdom of God" movement expanded to the far corners of the earth. And I could see similar patterns reemerging throughout Christian history—in the desert fathers and mothers, in Saint Patrick and the Celts, in Saint Francis and Saint Clare, in the Wesleys and the early Pentecostals, in Dr. King and Desmond Tutu, in Dorothy Day and Oscar Romero. Since its earliest and most dynamic centuries, Christianity has been most vital when it has been energized by movements of self-organizing—or perhaps we should say "Spirit-organizing"—cells. These cells have taken root and grown like seeds in communities and institutions. There they have grown, multiplied, and borne fruit—fruit in just and vibrant institutions, fruit in thriving, peaceful, joyful communities.

In the Catholic Church, some movements (like the one led by Martin Luther in the sixteenth century, and the one led by liberation theologians in the twentieth century) were initially rejected or silenced as heretical, but others (like the ones led by Saint Benedict, Saint Clare, and Saint Francis) were accepted and encouraged. Some would argue that the accepted movements were simply co-opted and domesticated, so that acceptance was as effective a way to neutralize a movement as persecution or excommunication. But long term, the legacy of these movement leaders keeps resurfacing. Who would have guessed that the joyful, courageous spirit of Saint Francis would be seen in a twenty-first-century Jesuit pope?

Among more fractious Protestants, movements often led to schism and the formation of new denominations, whose leaders typically institutionalized their original proposals and then resisted or rejected proposals from future movements, leading to further schism. In recent centuries, several movements have had remarkable success in embedding proposals in some church institutions, including the Social Gospel movement, the movement for equality of women, the Pentecostal and charismatic movements, the Jesus Movement in which Greg and I participated, and the LGBT equality movement.

PRACTICE OF THE BETTER

One of the most powerful religious movements in recent history isn't often recognized as a movement—especially by those who think that all movements are progressive. In recent decades, the so-called *religious right* has brilliantly seized opportunities, framed a message, promoted that message, mobilized people to action around it, created a beloved culture for participants, and given participants intense and meaningful experiences that they will always treasure. This conservative movement has been so successful that it has redefined Christianity for many inside and outside the church.

Moderate and progressive Christians love to complain about the success of the religious right and criticize its leaders.[18] But as Father Richard Rohr likes to say, "The best criticism of the bad is the practice of the better."[19] In other words, the time for complaining and criticizing is over. It's time to get moving.

Nearly all bishops and other denominational leaders I meet in my travels are ready to answer when the forward-leaning spiritual movement we need knocks on their doors. They know that this movement must transcend denominational silos, working both within and across each denomination. They know that Episcopalians alone can't solve Episcopal problems; Methodists alone can't solve Methodist problems, and so on. That's because the problems we need to solve are bigger than Lutheranism, Orthodoxy, Presbyterianism, or Catholicism. We have *Christian* problems, and so our future must be more connected and collaborative than our past.

When we better come together as Christians, we can better join with parallel movements from other faith traditions, because ultimately, the problems we face are not just *Christian* problems, they are *human* problems.

Since Christianity is a global and diverse religion with no single institutional center from which innovation can be disseminated, the spiritual movement we need must be global and multicultural as well as transdenominational. It must involve partnership between global north and global south, between rich and poor, and across racial divides. It must bring the descendants of the colonizers and enslavers together with the descendants of the colonized and enslaved. It must forge an unprecedented partnership between clergy and laity. It must empower people everywhere to self-organize around shared movement opportunity, message, strategy, structure, culture, and personal experience. And then the global spiritual movement we need must help those local self-organizing movements to link up and synergize.

In fact, that's exactly why Greg and I found ourselves in Burundi that weekend when my flight was canceled. We had learned that a grassroots movement of young Christians was emerging in East Africa, and both of us were drawn there to offer encouragement and support. These young African Christians weren't satisfied simply to show up in their (mostly Pentecostal) churches week after week, singing and dancing and listening to sermons about how God can solve their problems and help them prosper. That was good, but they felt the Spirit calling them to go further.

They were coming to care about the poor, the marginalized, the outcasts. They realized that the Gospel of Jesus Christ addresses social, political, and economic issues of the day, and so must they—including the issues of tribalism, systemic economic injustice, religious pluralism, ethical business, equality for women, mental illness, health care, education, climate change, and environmental stewardship. They realized that as Africa became more educated, its churches would need better training for church leaders—including more thoughtful ways of reading and interpreting the Bible. They also realized that much of the influence coming from the West, and especially the United States, was aligned with the religious right, and they knew that they needed an authentically indigenous movement to address the actual needs of their communities.[20]

In the months after my return home from Africa, I kept feeling that the church in the West is stuck in a dangerous stalemate. On the one side we have good-hearted people who are loyal to their religious institutions, zealous for their traditions, and so fearful of compromise that they are willing to excommunicate anyone who calls for change. On the other side we have their morally passionate counterparts: sick of traditions that no longer speak to them, disgusted by the money and energy necessary to keep institutional ships afloat, and increasingly defining themselves as noninstitutional or even anti-institutional. "If either side wins," I said to myself, "we all lose," because both vital institutions and vibrant movements are necessary to human thriving.

In fact, rekindling that beautiful romance between institutions and movements may soon become a matter of human survival.

CONTEMPLATION, CONVERSATION, AND ACTION:
CHAPTER 7

Contemplation: Meditate on Jesus's words "Follow me" as an invitation to join a spiritual movement.

Conversation:

1. What one sentence, paragraph, image, or idea from this chapter do you most want to talk about?
2. Describe how institutions, movements, and communities are related.
3. "Christian leaders could learn a lot from social movement theory." Respond to this statement.
4. The author looks at Jesus and Paul as movement leaders. How do you respond?
5. Have you ever felt that you were part of a movement? How have these experiences affected your "participant biography"?
6. Which of the six movement components—opportunity structure, rhetorical framing and conceptual architecture, protest and messaging strategies, mobilizing structures, movement culture, and participant biography—was most interesting to you, and why?
7. What emotions do you feel after reading this chapter?

Action: Be alert this week for signs of movements that are challenging institutions to improve their service to communities.

8

SALVATION FROM THE SUICIDE MACHINE

THE PRIMARY CONCERN FOR MANY OF US CHRISTIANS IS our churches. We see how they're wrinkling and shrinking, how they're aging and experiencing numerical decline. We know how important church has been in our lives and we want to save our churches from going the way of the phone booth, cassette tape, or landline. But whenever I find myself in conversations about "saving the church," I can't help but recall Jesus's words: *if you want to save your life, you will lose it, but if you lose your life for my sake, you will find it.*[1] Jesus's words make me wonder: could our desire to save our precious religious institutions and traditions actually hasten their demise? Could it be that the Spirit of God is calling the church to stop trying to save itself, and instead to join God in saving the world? Could pouring out itself for the good of the world be the only way for the church to save its own soul?

SPEAKING OF SALVATION

Our world, it turns out, needs saving. In an earlier book, I described our civilization as a kind of "suicide machine."

We act as though the resources we consume are infinite and the wastes we deposit are invisible. Just as our bodies consume food

*and produce excrement, in this economy we consume trees and
produce smoke, consume clean air and produce smog, consume
clean water and produce sewage and toxic waste, consume rock
and produce radiation, consume oil and coal and produce gases
that turn our planet into an overheating oven in which storms
boil and oceans rise and deserts spread and forests wither. Our
prosperity system thus becomes an excrement factory.*[2]

To many of us, the suicidal nature of our civilization remains invisible. We don't see it because we don't measure it. Our economists typically measure only consumption via GDP or GNP (gross domestic/national product). Those measurements tell us a lot about how things are going for the elite "one percent," but they tell us next to nothing about life lower down on the economic pyramid: how family farms are disappearing, migrant farmworkers are suffering, slums are proliferating, ecosystems are degrading, middle class families are breaking under economic strain, or ice caps are melting. You might say we are blinded by our measurements.

As a result, when the economy experiences a recession or a crash, next to nobody questions whether the system itself is sound and sustainable. The only question is how to get it growing again at its pace of extraction, consumption, and destruction. About this consumptive way of life, the economist Herman Daly has said, "There is something fundamentally wrong with treating the earth as if it were a business in liquidation."[3]

Sadly, many religious communities, especially within Christianity, have by and large been chaplaincies to this destructive, suicidal economy. With a few rare exceptions, we have baptized it as "Christian," and we have been rewarded handsomely for doing so. (We have also avoided the punishments that would have come from confronting our civilization with the truth that it is unjust, unloving, and unsustainable.) Our compliant priests have profited, while our prophetic voices have been silenced, ignored, or bought off.[4] Nearly all our institutions—political, economic, educational, social, and, yes, religious—have become part of this suicidal system.[5]

EXTERNAL AND INTERNAL FUELS

Our consumptive, suicidal system currently depends upon two kinds of fuel, each of which is toxic in its own way. Internally or personally, it requires an endless supply of greed or unfulfilled desire, because the system doesn't work if consumers ever reach a point where they say, "Okay. I'm satisfied. I have enough." As the work of the anthropologist René Girard has made clear, because human beings are imitative, when one person wants something, another person wants it too, creating an epidemic of contagious desire: I catch your desires, and you catch mine. The cascade of unfulfilled desires spreads like Ebola, creating a fevered competition to acquire more and more stuff. The desired stuff may be a new car or a house in a better neighborhood, a more youthful figure or improved sexual performance. But on a deeper level, it may be something more simple and less tangible, like prestige, and when prestige is gained by owning more than the next guy, we create what the economist Mark Anspach calls "perpetual scarcity":

> In placing the struggle for prestige at the heart of consumer mo-
> tivation . . . it now becomes possible to explain the phenomenon
> of perpetual scarcity as the result of a deliberate and relentless
> effort to acquire new badges of distinction. This is the price that
> everyone must pay in order to maintain, if not also improve, his
> position on the social ladder.[6]

If our suicidal system is fueled by an endless supply of "desire to acquire" *internally,* it requires an endless supply of cheap fossil fuels *externally.* But we do not have an endless supply of cheap fossil fuels.[7] And the supply we do have threatens our survival, because every time we burn coal, oil, or natural gas, we pump pollutants into the air, including carbon, which accumulates in the atmosphere and traps the sun's heat like an invisible blanket, thus destabilizing the earth's climate. That destabilization is becoming harder for even the hard-core skeptics (and fossil-fuel companies themselves) to deny.

We keep reaching and surpassing dangerous milestones in this regard: 350 parts per million of carbon in the atmosphere, the hottest year on record, the lowest coverage of Arctic ice, the most severe hurricane, the fastest reduction in glacier size, the most intense El Niño weather pattern, and so on. Thankfully, we reached a rare positive milestone in late 2015, when world leaders met in Paris and agreed on a plan to reduce carbon emissions. Pope Francis prepared the way for this positive step earlier in the year by using his position of global influence to call the world to repentance and to constructive action in regard to climate, calling all citizens of the earth to hear "the cry of the earth and the cry of the poor."[8]

The two cries go together, because the poor will suffer most from the devastation of rising temperatures, intensifying storms and droughts, melting glaciers, and rising sea levels. Even the rich will eventually see their money party coming to an end as turmoil spreads within and among nations, until civilization as we know it becomes increasingly insecure and the whole system goes staggering, catastrophe by catastrophe, toward collapse. Whether it ends with a big bang of war or a pathetic whimper of slow decline, the extractive and consumptive way of life that we have created will not stand. We are headed for self-destruction, and our destructive way of life needs more than minor tweaking, more than modest incremental change. It is time for a great spiritual migration to a new way of life, supported by a new kind of Christian faith.

MIGRATION AS SALVATION

Only a powerful spiritual movement can challenge our institutions and communities to defect from competitive consumerism and take part in collaborative regeneration. Only a powerful spiritual movement can challenge Christians to extract ourselves from being the docile chaplaincy of an extractive economy. Only a powerful spiritual movement can help us migrate away from our trivial pursuits and ridiculous arguments (organs and pianos or guitars and drums? suits and ties or blue jeans and sneakers?) so that we can instead join God in God's holy work, God's primary mission: *saving the earth and its inhabitants from human evil and folly.*

Sadly, Christianity as a system of belief remains largely oblivious to the role it has played in supporting our suicidal system. If economists have been blinded by their measurements, we Christians have been blinded by our beliefs.

As my friend and colleague Diana Butler Bass puts it, we have been an elevator religion, focused on getting people up, up, and away from this troubled earth to heaven, where God and the angels sit in cloudy bliss, having left behind the problems of earth.[9] By keeping us looking up and away, elevator Christianity has kept us from noticing or taking seriously what is happening around us—growing economic inequality, deteriorating environmental quality, expanding militarization and weaponization. If we do notice, elevator Christianity teaches us to chalk up our troubles to the God of Supremacy's preordained "last days" scenarios. After all, our belief system tells us, God loves immaterial souls, not matter, and if all this material stuff is destroyed, well ... good riddance. In short, belief-system Christianity keeps us arguing about our beliefs and singing songs about evacuating to heaven while the earth burns. Greedy and exploitive politicians and their corporate allies could not ask for a better partner in crime.

Similarly, as we've seen already, conventional Christianity as the worship of a violent, exclusive God of Supremacy is oblivious to the ways it has created a civilization in the image of its God: violent, hostile to the other, and living by the supremacist's sword—whether white (over nonwhite), Christian (over non-Christian), Western (over non-Western), hetero-masculine (over female and LGBT), or human (over nonhuman).[10] If our God is happy to make *us* rich and *them* poor, we have been happy to cooperate. If our God is happy to make *us* slave masters and *them* slaves, or *us* privileged and *them* marginalized, we have been happy to cooperate, without asking too many questions. Obliviousness has reigned, but now we must face the inconvenient truth that can set us free: the version of Christianity which we have supported is perfectly designed to produce a civilization that is unsustainable, conflicted, out of balance, and vulnerable to catastrophic collapse.

Because we have been so oblivious for so long, because we have been so obsessed with our systems of belief and our conventional vision of God for so long, we may have sped past all the warning signs and passed a point of no return. If that's the case, then we need to acknowledge our complicity, and should civilization collapse, the Christian community needs to prepare to pick up the pieces, as we have done quite effectively in the past.

But it may not be too late. And that's why we so desperately need this third migration: from *a religion organized for self-preservation and privilege to a religion organizing for the common good of all.*

Seeing from the Bottom Up

Increasing numbers of Christians around the world and across denominations are coming to understand the urgency of our situation. A few years ago, several dozen of us who had read each other's books or been in touch online wanted to spend some time together, face-to-face in one place. We decided to gather in Bangkok, Thailand, to talk together about a way forward.[11]

We didn't simply want to meet in a nice resort or retreat center, shielded from the realities we were seeking to understand and address. So we traveled by bus north to a small rural village where we spent a few days living with local people, working with them in the fields, planting rice, picking peppers and maize. At the end of the day, our muscles aching, we learned we had earned maybe $2 for that day's work. Our hosts did this for ten hours a day, 365 days a year, working harder than any of us ever worked in our lives, and they were stuck in poverty, barely subsisting.

Then we traveled to Pattaya, known as the global capital of the sex trafficking industry. There we learned that a teenage girl could make as much money for her family in one night as a sex worker as she could have made in many months as a farmworker. These realities of our extractive, exploitive, industrial economy helped us to see our "opportunity structure" from the bottom of the pyramid looking up, so to speak, and profoundly informed the conversations that followed.

We knew that courageous Christians around the world were dedicating their lives to the global and local challenges we were witnessing. But we also knew that the Christian church in general was too often part of the problem and too seldom part of the solution. We dared to believe that willing sectors of the Christian community could be mobilized to make a difference. We tried to summarize our conversations and shared conclusions in the Mesa

Document.[12] A few years later, a group of us in the United States adapted that document to our own situation as a Charter for a Just and Generous Christianity.[13] Speaking personally, every day since our gathering I have continued to struggle to find ways I can help support and build the global spiritual movement we so desperately need. This book, in fact, is an expression of that ongoing struggle.

But how does a conversation become a movement? In the fullness of time, people in conversation may come to agreement upon two things: what's wrong, and what needs to be done about it. And if they then translate their agreement into specific *proposals, demands,* and *refusals to comply,* their conversation gives birth to a movement. Here are three preliminary examples of the kinds of movement proposals, demands, and refusals to comply that are taking shape for many of us.

1. We call upon just and generous Christian communities who have embarked on this great spiritual migration to identify themselves. Where no such communities exist, we call upon Christians to start creative new ones. Because this spiritual migration can only be sustained in community, we need sustainable congregations to embody the kind of radical, regenerative Christian faith the world needs now. And we need these communities to go public so others know this new option is available. But how can these congregations go public without being divisive? We don't want them to leave their existing denominations or traditions—Catholic, Baptist, Presbyterian, Methodist, Mennonite, nondenominational, and so on. The last thing we need is another schism or another sectarian institution claiming to finally have it right. Instead we need a movement that takes root and organizes enthusiastic participants across institutions and communities.

Building such a movement is complicated because many congregations (especially in the United States) are already polarized and paralyzed by partisan affiliation in the so-called culture wars—liberal versus conservative, which in America tends to mean Democratic-leaning versus Republican-leaning. We can no longer comply with this polarizing paralysis for at least three reasons. First, we believe that this binary culture-war mind-set is part of the problem. We need to stop pulling apart and start pulling together, converging and collaborating to build a more just, generous, peaceful, regenerative, and joyful world. That agenda, we believe, can convene open-hearted and open-minded people from both conservative and liberal backgrounds.[14]

Second, we believe that in many cases, both liberals and conservatives are simply two wings of the wrong bird—the extractive industrial economy that threatens us. Each provides solutions within the box of that suicidal system, and neither seems capable of thinking outside the box. Both wings need to be challenged to rethink the system as a whole, and to bring their distinctive emphases together, collaboratively.

Third, conventional bipolar identities quickly degenerate into stereotypes that are neither accurate nor helpful—the angry and compassionless conservative, the arrogant and passionless liberal, or whatever. We know that real people and real congregations are far more interesting and multidimensional than these flat stereotypes.

The recent rise of hope around Pope Francis tells us that when people climb out of their two familiar ruts on the left and the right, Christian faith can actually become interesting again. So the question returns: how can we let the world know that there is "a new kind of Christianity" on the block, that Christians and congregations are migrating to a more just, generous, and joyful faith? How can we get the word out that many of us are abandoning the status quo and seeking instead to be builders of a brighter future, and that there is plenty of room at the table for new participants? To the degree that many conventional religious "brands" have been discredited, how can we announce the emergence of a needed alternative?

We are working on a way for these churches to stand together (through one or more charters),[15] be findable online (through various websites),[16] raise their voices together (through news, advocacy, and action),[17] and support and encourage one another (through self-organizing online connections and in-person gatherings).[18] In so doing, we hope to help congregations augment rather than replace their denominational identities, transcending rather than perpetuating the stale left/right, liberal/conservative polarization we are all too familiar with.

This emerging Christianity-in-migration, we believe, represents a convergence of several streams. In the United States, progressive Evangelicals, missional mainliners, and many in the historic peace churches are discovering one another. They are building relationships with Roman Catholic and Eastern Orthodox Christians rooted in the social justice and contemplative traditions, together with churches of color who draw inspiration from faith leaders like Martin Luther King Jr., Dorothy Height, Fannie Lou Hamer, Desmond Tutu, René Padilla, and Oscar Romero. Bringing these streams together isn't easy; we have centuries of living in silos and seeing one another with suspicion. But now, as we face the realities of an unsustainable civilization, we can rediscover one another as collaborators and companions, not competitors.

Many congregations won't be able to participate in this migration en masse because their membership includes people who are Christian believers but who resist the idea of a great spiritual migration. So we are encouraging groups within these churches— home groups, classes, reading groups, youth groups, and so on—to come together and identify themselves as "just and generous communities." As *ecclesiolae in ecclesia,* little churches within

a bigger church, these groups can move forward without needing
the larger group's permission or approval, and perhaps, like yeast
in dough, their influence will spread.

Meanwhile, in many places, no such congregations or groups
yet exist. In those places, we must encourage and support people
in forming new faith communities, simple and flexible in structure, in hopes that their presence will draw more people into this
great spiritual migration.[19] Where denominations impose too
much red tape or otherwise limit needed creativity, innovative
leaders can quietly experiment with new faith community development "on the side." In some cases, they will need to graciously
refuse to comply and, if necessary, invest their energies elsewhere,
where there is more freedom to innovate.

Once congregations and cohorts in this great spiritual migration have "come out" and "gone public," we have to think seriously about the future, which brings us to a second movement
proposal.

**2. We call upon Christian leaders and parents to begin afresh
with children, youth, and college-aged adults.** It has been said
that Christianity is always one generation away from extinction—
meaning that if one generation doesn't pass on the faith to the
next, it is gone. We could also say that Christianity is also one
generation away from conversion and rebirth—if only we would
seize the moment. The historian William G. McLoughlin put it
like this:

> *The reason an awakening takes a generation or more to work
> itself out is that it must grow with the young; it must escape the
> enculturation of old ways. It is not worthwhile to ask who the
> prophet of this awakening is or to search for new ideological
> blueprints in the works of the learned. Revitalization is grow-
> ing up around us in our children, who are both more innocent*

and more knowing than their parents and grandparents. It is their world that has yet to be reborn.[20]

Similarly, the physicist Max Planck said regarding new scientific understandings, "An important scientific innovation rarely makes its way by gradually winning over and converting its opponents: it rarely happens that Saul becomes Paul. What does happen is that its opponents gradually die out, and that the growing generation is familiarized with the ideas from the beginning: another instance of the fact that the future lies with the youth."[21]

In recent decades hundreds of congregations have been doing creative experimentation with adults, especially young adults. But often, while the adults are singing new songs, praying new prayers, hearing new insights in sermons or study groups, and engaging in new (and ancient) spiritual practices, the children are being taught the same old curriculum. The methodology may be innovative, using videos and computer screens rather than flannelgraph and chalkboards, for example. But the theology kids are taught is too often framed in old assumptions that have yet to be challenged; namely, an evacuation Gospel and an elevator theology, a system of belief centered on a view of God that needs to be enlarged and matured. The same goes for youth and college ministry. It's time for parents to refuse to comply with Sunday school and youth curricula that simply rehash old formulas and fail to address our deep need for a great spiritual migration.

That's why we're encouraging collaborations among forward-thinking curriculum developers, Christian educators, youth workers, and campus ministers.[22] One new generation of children and youth can bring about a new day in Christian faith. The process of developing resources and mobilizing leaders can't be rushed—but it can't be delayed either.

I'm reminded of a visit I took to an Eastern European country back in the 1990s, shortly after the Iron Curtain fell. I spent an unforgettable evening with some youth workers, a married couple, who were building a completely unexpected movement of teenagers—the "punks" and "Goths" of that era. Each new teenager who arrived at the gathering seemed more spiked, dyed, pierced, tattooed, and wildly costumed than the last. (Christians in traditions where clergy wear strange and countercultural robes, headgear, special jewelry, and so on shouldn't be too scandalized by any of this!) These teenagers had been raised on repressive communism and now were being inundated with capitalism in all its sugary excess. But now, through the influence of these youth workers, they were learning a far more radical, life-giving, and liberating way of life as followers of Christ. Although I didn't speak a word of their language, I could tell as they prayed, sang, and dialogued that the Spirit was moving among them.

Late that night, I asked the youth leaders this question: "I know that the churches in your country endured a lot during the communist years. They had to be suspicious of strangers because of the danger of informants, and they developed very rigid and conservative rules about dress and behavior. The churches I've visited don't allow *women* to wear earrings or makeup, much less men!"

They laughed, said that's true, and I continued, "How are these very conservative churches going to handle welcoming these pierced and tattooed kids you're working with? Will they ever be accepted in the churches?"

The wife and husband exchanged a quick glance. "Should we tell him?" she asked. "Go ahead," he replied.

"You're right," she said. "These kids won't be accepted in traditional churches anytime soon unless they cut their hair, wear traditional clothing, cover up their tattoos, and lose their metal. But in our minds, we aren't reaching young people who will fill traditional churches. In our minds, what you witnessed tonight isn't a youth group. It's a seminary. We're training a new generation of young Christian leaders who will lead a very different church of the future. They will respect the courage and suffering of the old churches who survived communism, but they won't submit to their rules and traditions. They'll do something creative and new as outliers from the church of the past and as pioneers of the church of the future."

The diagnosis and prescription of those youth workers is, I believe, more relevant to our situation in the capitalist West than many of us realize. We often forget that Jesus was thirty when he launched his movement—a movement that, if it were happening today, might be called a youth movement by the aging leaders like me who run many religious institutions. In that light, let's dare to propose that Christianity should become a movement of young people again, supported by older mentors who know how to encourage without controlling. That brings us to a third proposal.

3. We call upon Christian communities, movements, and institutions to recruit different leaders and train them differently (and without debt, if possible). Emerging forms of Christianity will need new kinds of congregations to embody them. New kinds of congregations will need new kinds of leaders to guide their development. New kinds of leaders will need new kinds of training and formation to equip them. They will need a course of study centered in a way of life rather than a system of belief. They will need mentors and educators who are personally dedicated to God as the liberating Spirit of justice, joy, and peace embodied in Jesus rather than God as a dominating, exclusive, distant, and violent Supreme Being. They will need a learning community that integrates contemplation and action so they can become architects of a regenerative way of life rather than chaplains to an extractive, destructive, suicidal economy. Some of these new approaches are already being tested, and more experiments are on the way. Some seminaries are involved, along with some creative educational entrepreneurs from outside the traditional seminary community.[23]

Traditional seminary education has much to commend it, but there are unanticipated consequences of requiring students training for spiritual, congregational, and missional leadership to spend a few years away from spiritual, congregational, and missional life. And there are unintended consequences of forming people in academic practices at the expense of spiritual, congregational, and missional practices.[24] Potential leaders who are more contemplative and pastoral activists and less academics may be dissuaded from ministry altogether by the current system.

And potential leaders with an aversion to debt may be dissuaded as well, since a typical master's in divinity today costs from $40,000 to $80,000, often leaving the newly ordained to start their ministries saddled with financial pressure.[25] That debt will require the young minister to find a large and stable congregation that can pay a large enough salary to cover both living expenses and debt repayment, which pretty much guarantees that yet another minister is ineligible to take creative risks in his or her critically important younger years. This debt, we might say, enslaves the next generation to the very economy that needs to be challenged. By the time their debts are paid off, too many gifted young leaders are domesticated, disillusioned, or driven out of ministry entirely.

Not only that, but all too often their $80,000 has bought them training to serve in churches that are quickly dying or slowly fading away. Students master theological systems of belief, liturgical protocols, leadership skills, and ministerial competencies that perfectly prepare them for the Church of Christianity Past. When seminary boards and presidents try to bring about needed changes, they often experience dogged resistance from a cadre of professors who are far removed from the realities of church life (if they attend church at all), and whose loyalties, truth be told, are more to the academy than the local congregation. Or the opposite happens: creative faculty who try to innovate are squelched by inflexible bureaucracies that are in turn held hostage by change-averse donors. Yes, the traditional way of training leaders has much to commend it. But it is not the only way, and when it proves unhelpful, it is time for us to refuse to comply and come up with creative new options.

LEADERSHIP CRISIS AND OPPORTUNITY

In the Catholic Church in America, the leadership crisis is especially acute. For starters, there is a rather limited pool of men eager to join the club of celibate male clergy, especially after this fraternity has been scandalized by decades of sexual secrets. To make matters worse, during the reactionary papacies of John Paul II and Benedict, when many sectors of the Catholic Church rejected their own heritage of social teaching and embraced instead a right-wing agenda, who but the most conservative would want to affiliate with American Catholicism? Pope Francis appears to be swinging the pendulum away from the extremism of recent years, but only time will tell if his example portends a long-term migration or a momentary blip. Resistance to his vision is strong, and it will take a grassroots movement of courageous Catholic Christians to turn his reform into a lasting revolution.

In many parts of Africa, Asia, and Latin America, a very different problem presents itself. With the export of American prosperity gospel televangelists through cable TV, a whole new breed of charismatic (in both senses of the word) religious showmen has glutted the church with smarm, false promises, hype, and corruption. Again, this is the last peer group that our best potential leaders would ever want to join.

But if we redefine the curriculum for leadership in the church of tomorrow, if we combine quality guided online learning with experiential learning, if we collaborate with existing seminaries that are doing good and needed work, if we match emerging leaders with experienced mentors, and if we link them with thousands of emerging models of a just and generous Christianity, then we have the makings of a real revolution indeed. Much of this innovation will be nurtured within existing denominations that create "research and development zones" within their systems. Much of it will emerge within nondenominational churches or faith communities that form networks to fulfill important functions provided previously by denominations. A both/and attitude will be necessary if we wish to support and sustain the great spiritual migration that we so urgently need.

The movement we need is not like a wave whose incoming is inevitable and we just need to catch it. It's more like a ship that can be built from available materials: if we catch the desire for adventure, get organized, and collect and fashion the materials, we can soon set sail.[26]

The journey of salvation and liberation is long, the risks and dangers are many, and the costs are high. Anyone who is tempted to turn back in fear is free to do so. But if there are costs to change, there are also costs to resisting change. Both costs are worth counting, as C. S. Lewis so aptly said:

> *It may be hard for an egg to turn into a bird: it would be a jolly sight harder for it to learn to fly while remaining an egg. We are like eggs at present. And we cannot go on indefinitely being just an ordinary, decent egg. We must be hatched or go bad.*[27]

CONTEMPLATION, CONVERSATION, AND ACTION: CHAPTER 8

Contemplation: This chapter emphasizes, among other things, the importance of children in movement work. In silence, open your heart to ways that you might be of help and encouragement to people younger than you.

Conversation:

1. What one sentence, paragraph, image, or idea from this chapter do you most want to talk about?
2. Summarize the idea of our consumptive economy as an unsustainable "suicide machine."
3. How do the first two migrations—from system of belief to way of life, and from a violent/exclusive view of God to a nonviolent/inclusive view of God—relate to the migration described in this chapter?
4. How might a conference about Christian theology and mission be affected by first spending a few days planting rice, doing rural farmwork, and observing the sex trafficking industry?
5. Summarize the three movement proposals in this chapter, and explain why each is important.
6. Why do you think *proposals, demands,* and *refusals to comply* are so important in the author's mind?
7. What hopes and fears or beliefs and doubts are stirred within you as you reflect on this chapter?

Action: Learn about initiatives in your area relating to these three movement proposals and check out the links offered in the notes.

9

You Are Social Poets

Each generation faces some great work, some heroic challenge that summons its children to courage and creativity. The great work of this generation will be to respond to the quadruple threat inherited from previous generations: an *ecological crisis* that, left unchecked, will lead to catastrophic environmental collapse; an *economic crisis* of obscenely increasing inequality that exploits or excludes the world's poor while dehumanizing the rich as well; a *sociopolitical crisis* of racial, ethnic, class, religious, and political conflict that could lead to catastrophic war; and a *spiritual and religious crisis* in which the religious institutions that should be helping us deal with the first three crises either waste our time or make matters worse.

To face one of these crises would be difficult enough; to face all four simultaneously will require all hands on deck—including the best potential contributions of each of the world's religious communities. To save the world from this quadruple threat is the great work for which all people of faith and goodwill, including Christians, must be mobilized.

Millions of people must be invited into this great work—not through the old so-called evangelism that said, "Join my religion or burn in hell forever," but through a new kind of evangelization, described powerfully by the Catholic priest and missionary Vincent Donovan.[1] Our goal is not to leave others where they are, stuck in a suicidal system. Nor is it to bring them to where we are right now, as beautiful as that place might be for us. Rather, Donovan said, our goal is to invite others to journey together with us toward a new place none of us has ever seen. We must invite them to join a great spiritual migration to a new way of life centered in love, a new regenerative economy, a new ecological civilization characterized by peace, justice, and joy. But how can such a profound migration ever move from dream to reality?

How Change Happens

My colleague Michael-Ray Mathews is a leader in organizing people for meaningful social change. He describes a change process that occurs on four interdependent levels.[2] First, there is *intrapersonal change,* as individuals experience a reorientation of heart and mind. This internal personal conversion is essential to ensure that people's engagement is driven not merely by self-interest or momentary passion, but by a deep and abiding moral conviction.

If enough individuals are full of despair and anger in their hearts, there will be violence in the streets. If enough individuals are full of greed and fear in their hearts, there will be pollution in the rivers and toxins in the air. If enough individuals are full of supremacy and privilege in their hearts, there will be racism and oppression in society. You can't remove the external social symptoms without treating the corresponding internal personal diseases.

But just as it is foolish to avoid the need for personal change of heart, it is equally foolish to ignore the social conditions that turn individual hearts greedy, angry, complacent, or desperate. People often speak of "the invisible hand" of the market, but Pope Francis draws our attention to "the invisible thread" of the market, which he describes as "the mentality of profit at any price, with no concern for social exclusion or the destruction of nature." This mentality generates inequality, which in turn generates "a violence which no police, military, or intelligence resources can control."[3]

That's why intrapersonal change must lead to *interpersonal change.* Changed individuals cross racial, religious, ethnic, class, or political boundaries to build friendships. These friendships work like sutures, healing wounds in the social fabric. They "humanize the other," making it harder for groups to stereotype or scapegoat. They create little zones where the beloved community is manifest—on a front lawn, around a kitchen table, on a sports field, in an office, in a church fellowship hall. They help people envision the common good—a situation where all are safe, free, and able to thrive. As my friend Shane Claiborne says, our problem isn't that rich people don't care about poor people; it's that all too often, rich people don't know any poor people. Knowing one another makes interpersonal change and reconciliation possible.

Intrapersonal change and interpersonal change prepare the way for *structural or institutional change.* As reconciled people work together for the common good, they challenge political, economic, religious, and social structures that harm people they now know and care about. These allies are motivated not simply by ideology, but by conscience, compassion, and solidarity. Through their efforts, laws are passed, policies are changed, and institutions become more just.

But there's another level of change that too many ignore: *cultural change.* I have lived most of my life after the civil rights movement in the United States. Back in the 1960s, national and state governments passed laws guaranteeing equal rights in voting, housing, justice, and education. Change happened on a structural or institutional level. But in many places, racism simply went underground, and segregation, police brutality, and prejudice continued as before. Just because racism was written out of the law didn't mean it had been rooted out of the culture. Similarly, many of us live in communities that mandate recycling, but even so, the culture can remain consumptive. Until we care about equality and ecology as cultural norms that frame our habitual daily decisions as individuals and communities, we have not yet fully experienced the change we need. We need deep change on all levels: intrapersonal, interpersonal, structural, and cultural.

Whom Do You Call?

Now imagine: if you wanted to find an organization well positioned to encourage change on all of these four levels, whom would you call? You would need an organization that was both local and global. It would need to involve people from all sectors of society—agriculture to government, health care to education, for-profit to nonprofit, science to the arts. It would need to specialize in personal development, community building, deployment for mission, and public communication. What organization could fulfill these diverse requirements? As soon as you answer *the church,* you have to ask why so many of our churches remain ineffective and complacent about this potentially transformative role. The gap between the church's potential and actual impact can make you cry.

But far better: the gap can make you *cry out,* determined to see the church fulfill its potential. That's why we need movement-building initiatives that help individual Christians, congregational leaders, and denominational and network leaders come together and work together for intrapersonal, interpersonal, structural, and cultural change. We still have a long way to go, but we've never been closer in my lifetime to seeing this kind of convergence happen than we are right now. We already have many effective mobilizing structures within individual congregations, within midlevel judicatories (like presbyteries, dioceses, conferences, and synods), and within denominations as a whole.

True, these structures are too often stuck in denominational silos, but if we find ways to connect and align these mobilizing structures for larger movement purposes, we will unleash exciting potential. True, from Monday to Saturday, many church members listen to cable news and talk radio stations that present a radically different view of the world, but if we become clearer about our message and mission every Sunday, many of them will change channels and tune in to better messengers. True, many church members work for industries or belong to organizations and parties that are often on the wrong side of that Christian moral vision, but if we were to challenge and equip them to be positive agents of change, they could "trouble the waters" and become change agents in their professions. True, many of our institutions and parachurch organizations are plagued by "institutional ego" and see one another as competitors rather than teammates.[4] But a younger generation of leaders is arising that has grown up in a networked world, and they stand ready to lead and collaborate with a different spirit and style, equipped with new social media technologies.

True, many older progressive Christian leaders were shaped in the antiwar and civil rights struggles of the 1960s, and they don't realize the degree to which the world has changed since then. They don't understand the degree to which superrich individuals and corporations now have far more control over politicians—and therefore public policy—than voters do.[5] But thankfully, new strategies of *economic activism* are arising to augment traditional political activism. Because these new strategies will be so important to our work in the years ahead, they're worth some special attention.

New Kinds of Activism

Economic activism works first through *boycotts* (where customers avoid offensive businesses) and *buycotts* (where customers intentionally patronize businesses who lead the way). In addition, economic activists may engage in *corporate protests and campaigns,* such as the campaign of environmentalists to convince Shell and other oil companies not to drill in the Arctic (a campaign that has, so far, been unsuccessful). Economic activists also work through *social entrepreneurship,* where entrepreneurs start new businesses to maximize social benefit, not simply personal profit.

In addition, economic activism works through *ethical divestment,* as investors withdraw funds from companies that are bringing harm into the world. Divestment helped hasten the end of apartheid in South Africa, and current divestment campaigns aim to end child labor, worker exploitation, human trafficking, the ongoing occupation of Palestine, and global dependence on fossil fuels. Then, through *ethical investment,* investors support companies that demonstrate corporate social responsibility (CSR). CSR has been defined as moving beyond the old single bottom line of profit for shareholders, and seeking a new triple bottom line: *economic benefit,* which includes fair pay to employees as well as fair return for investors; *ecological benefit* so that their products and means of production minimize harm to the environment and, where possible, actually improve the environment; and *social benefit,* by adding to the common good rather than subtracting from it.[6]

There is a new kind of ethical investment strategy in which investors seek a significant or controlling interest in companies that behave badly, the idea being to influence company policy and steer unethical corporations in a positive direction. For example, the Interfaith Council on Corporate Responsibility (ICCR) recently used its leverage to convince a powerful bank to stop lending money to corporations engaged in a particularly disgusting form of coal mining called mountaintop removal.[7]

In southwest Florida where I now live, I've gained some invaluable experience in economic activism. I live near Immokalee, the epicenter for migrant farmworkers in the eastern United States, and have been deeply enriched by my volunteer work with the Coalition of Immokalee Workers (CIW).[8] The CIW seeks to improve the lives of farmworkers, arguably one of the most underappreciated, underpaid, and exploited groups of people worldwide. Appealing to the state or national government for help has been futile, especially since so many farmworkers are caught in the crosshairs of America's polarization over immigration reform.

So the CIW made a bold choice: to deal with a different kind of ballot box—the cash register—through a different kind of ballot—the wallet or credit card. They worked with consumers to put pressure on corporations like McDonald's, Taco Bell, and Walmart to join the Fair Food Program, which improves pay and working conditions for farmworkers. At this writing, a few major corporations like Publix and Wendy's are still refusing to participate, but the list of corporations that have joined the program keeps growing, and we are confident that even the holdouts will eventually come around.

SOCIAL POETS

What might happen if congregations and denominations got more serious about mobilizing both their political power and their economic power for ethical ends? What might happen if congregations and denominations saw themselves as cells in a growing spiritual movement? Imagine, for example, if your congregation decided to install some solar panels on your facility to do your part in fighting climate change. There would be some upfront costs, to be sure, but you would experience a full return on investment in only six or seven years. After that, you'd be saving money for decades. And you'd be modeling a responsible conversion from fossil fuels to solar energy.

Then imagine if five families decided to make a similar switch in their homes. Purchasing equipment in bulk and contracting installers cooperatively would reduce the initial costs. Then imagine if ten more followed their example, and then twenty more. Your congregation might arrange loans so that members would continue to pay their average electricity bill to a lender until their loans were repaid—which, again, would happen in just six or seven years. Soon a majority of your members would be setting an example for their entire neighborhoods, and your congregation could become a prime player in mobilizing your whole city to shift to clean energy. Then imagine what might happen if your congregation became known across your region as a leader in protecting God's beautiful earth, and consider the multiplied impact as other congregations followed your example.

Or imagine if your congregation developed a community garden, started planting trees, launched a watershed protection group, or strengthened recycling practices.[9] Or imagine if your congregation got involved in building cross-racial or multifaith relationships, bringing congregations of different ethnic and religious backgrounds together to build low-income housing or develop a tutoring program at a local public school or stage a public "ethical spectacle" after a hate crime.

The result would be a radical migration from "organized religion" to "organizing religion." Again, Pope Francis describes this migration beautifully:

> *Along this path, popular movements play an essential role, not only by making demands and lodging protests, but even*

more basically by being creative. You are social poets: creators of work, builders of housing, producers of food, above all for people left behind by the world market. . . . The future of humanity does not lie solely in the hands of great leaders, the great powers and the elites. It is fundamentally in the hands of peoples and in their ability to organize. It is in their hands, which can guide with humility and conviction this process of change. I am with you.[10]

NEW QUESTIONS?

As Christian individuals and congregations migrate from organized religion (organized for self-preservation) to organizing religion (organizing for mission and the common good), Christians will ask new questions that have hardly been on our radar in the past. For example: In what ways is the local environment under assault—what streams are being polluted, what forests are being destroyed, and what endangered species must be protected? Where do poor and vulnerable people live, and how can we build relationships and alliances among them to increase opportunity, reduce oppression, expand empowerment, and promote the common good? Where are there current and potential conflicts— racial, religious, socioeconomic, or political—and how can we work for just and lasting peace in the larger "us" of the kingdom or commonwealth of God? Where are elites profiting through fear, violence, exploitation, misinformation, and the plundering of the planet, and how can we expose the greed that drives them? Where must we refuse to comply with these elites? How can we in this Christian faith community build relationships and alliances among other Christian faith communities to expose and oppose injustice, and together seek the common good in our region? And how can Christians organizing for the common good then join with other religious communities in a multifaith movement to restore the planet, empower the poor, and build peace?[11]

Multifaith solutions are necessary because the crises we face cannot be solved by any one religion, just as they cannot be contained by national boundaries. Desmond Tutu, the Dalai Lama, and Pope Francis exemplify a new kind of global religious leadership; they see the need for both intrafaith and multifaith mobilization. Now we need tens of thousands of religious leaders of upcoming generations to follow their lead: to stop functioning as religious bureaucrats trapped within the confining walls of our respective institutions, and to rise together in courageous collaboration to face the fierce and urgent challenges of our generation.

I'm experiencing the beauty of multifaith collaboration in my own life. Over the years, I have been part of several multifaith dialogue communities and found them deeply meaningful. But I am now part of a group that brings people of various traditions together for more than dialogue. We're moving from dialogue to contemplative action, praying in our own authentic ways and then collaborating for shared concerns of social justice and the common good.[12] When Sikh, Jewish, Catholic, Protestant, Muslim, and other voices harmonize in joint projects—not in spite of our spiritual roots but because of them—when we cross lines of race, gender, and religion, we demonstrate the vitality and hope of organizing religion.

As I mentioned earlier, this kind of collaboration leads to a fresh understanding of what it means to evangelize.[13] I was taught that it meant converting people to the one true religion, namely, my own. Now I believe evangelism means inviting people into heart-to-heart communion and collaboration with God and neighbors in the great work of healing the earth, of building the beloved community, of seeking first the kingdom of God and God's justice for all. Members of each tradition bring their unique gifts to the table, ready to share and receive, learn and teach, give and take, in a spirit of generosity and vulnerability. Neither my neighbors nor I are obligated or expected to convert. Nor are we obligated to accept every gift that is offered by our counterparts. After all, something imposed by force, threat, or obligation is not a gift: it is a form of colonization and domination. As we work together for the common good, we are all transformed. Those who haven't experienced this kind of transforming collaboration simply don't know what they're missing, as their occasional criticisms make abundantly clear.

Through multifaith collaborations, I have come to see how the language Paul used about one body with many members (1 Corinthians 12, Romans 12:4–5) applies not only to differing gifts among individual Christians but also to differing gifts among religions. Our religions truly are different: They are not simply saying the same things in different ways. Nor are they saying different things about the same things. They are often saying different things about entirely different things. They have, to use a scientific analogy, different research projects, or to use a medical analogy, different medical specialties. This deep level of difference is exactly why each community has gifts to offer the others. In many ways, on many levels, we need each other—now more than ever.

I believe the Holy Spirit has brought us to this point where, in order to grapple with the threat of ecological, economic, societal, and spiritual self-destruction, we must for the first time in history receive the differing gifts each tradition offers. We must, you might say, evangelize one another again—not to convert others to our religion (although people should be free to cross traditional boundaries if they so desire), but to be converted within our own, experiencing changed hearts in the process, so we can work together as never before for the common good.

BEING MUTUALLY CONVERTED

Could it be that the kind of tensions we experience in Christian faith between the priestly/institutional, mystical/poetic, and prophetic/movement streams run across all of our religious traditions? Could it be that most of the tensions between our faiths arise among priestly/institutional traditionalists, who focus on correctness in belief, taboo, and behavior? And could it be that among mystical/poetic contemplatives and prophetic/movement activists across traditions there is much less tension and in fact growing mutual regard? If that's the case, we could be approaching a new threshold in human religious history. We could be approaching a moment when parallel streams across traditions begin flowing together, not to form a new religion, but to migrate together in exactly the ways we have been considering in this book:

- from systems of correct belief (or behavior) to loving, compassionate ways of life
- from violent and exclusive conceptions of God to reconciling and harmonizing understandings of God
- from competitive institutional organized religions to movement-inspired religions organizing and collaborating as social poets, architects, and builders of a better world

Again, Christianity isn't the only religion in need of a great spiritual migration. I remember speaking in England, sharing the platform with a North African Muslim feminist postcolonial scholar-activist (that's a mouthful, I know). I spoke openly about the problems I've seen and experienced in my tradition and about our need for deep change, as I have done here. At the end of the evening, as my colleague and I were saying good-bye, the young activist said to me, "You surprised me tonight. I have never heard a Christian admit the problems you have admitted. The rest of the world sees them, of course. But it seems that few Christians do." Then she paused. "We Muslims have our issues too," she said. "Maybe, if you Christians start talking openly about your problems, it will make it easier for us to talk about ours."

Each generation has some great work to do, some heroic call that summons its children to greatness. The quadruple threat facing this generation can seem insurmountable. If we don't feel tempted to despair, the chances are we don't see the full magnitude of the problem. That's why faith is so important. That's why we can't give up on Christianity or our other religions. True, our religions are flawed, but would we have more hope if religions were eradicated and all we had left was money, politics, and weapons?

We must admit that we are not ready for the task now. We are carrying so much old baggage, so many "weights that so easily entangle us" (Hebrews 12:1). Preoccupied by our belief systems, held hostage to our violent understandings of God, and mired in institutional inertia that must be turned into movement momentum, our strength is not sufficient for the challenge. But if we simply start moving in faith, what has been impossible can become possible.

The great work before us will be messy and costly. It will demand generosity and sacrifice. It will require creativity and faith to keep moving forward against daunting opposition. We will need the endurance of Paul, who said, "Love bears, believes, hopes, and endures all things. Love never fails" (1 Corinthians 13:7–8). We will need the faith of Jesus, who said that with faith in God, nothing is impossible. And we will need ongoing encouragement and support from one another, because we're in this together, and we can't succeed in isolation.

So Much Right with the World

There is so much right with Christianity. Sunday by Sunday, caring ministers prepare sermons into which they pour their hearts. Week by week they care for their flock, visiting the sick, honoring the dead, welcoming new life, nurturing those in need of counsel, challenge, recovery, or encouragement. Church musicians practice and prepare a weekly feast of beauty. Faithful people show up and generously show kindness to one another, from sharing after-church coffee and baked goods to preparing epic potluck dinners to cooking nourishing meals for the hungry and lonely. Hospitality abounds. Mission flows. People give money, year after year, so staff are supported, buildings are constructed and maintained, and the good news is spread in word and deed.

There is so much right with the world. The sun faithfully does its work, bathing us in life-sustaining energy. The moon faithfully does its work, lifting tides and letting them fall, and no one worries it will fail. Water faithfully does its work, the lifeblood of our planet, circulating from cloud to rain to stream to river to sea to cloud. Creatures do their work as well, filling the earth with life and song, sharing the gift of life through death and birth, through nesting and migration, through pollination and germination, each specimen a living miracle if we have eyes to see. Your body, a civilization of cells more sophisticated than any megacity, works amazingly well amazingly often, your heart beating, your lungs breathing, your eyes seeing, your mind aware.

There is so much right in humanity. Children play. Adolescents fall in love. Young couples marry. Lovers entangle their limbs, breath, and dreams. Babies are conceived and born and nurtured, through their smiles and cries teaching their parents to love in ways they never knew they were capable of. Friends laugh, plan adventures, throw parties, stick together, weep at gravesides after a lifetime of shared joy. Farmers grow, harvesters pick, transporters transport, grocers distribute, and meals of unimaginable variety and delight are prepared and eaten. Entrepreneurs plan and launch new ventures. Colleagues work side by side as managers seek to steer their companies toward success. Researchers seek cures, discoveries, solutions, understanding. Teachers teach and children catch the gift of curiosity. People are honest. They make promises they keep. People take vacations. They watch the surf, ride horses, cast lines, take hikes, swim, ski, bike, sail, and slow down so they can remember they are alive. Grandparents and elders watch all this, their eyes brimming with tears of joy.

There is so much right in the church, in the world, in humanity. There is so much good. And so much beauty. When we see it, even a tiny glimmer of how precious it is, our hearts swell in gratitude and awe.

And we feel in those moments why it matters for forward-leaning Christians to embark on this great spiritual migration: to support the wild goodness, rightness, beauty, and aliveness that surround us so that they can ever grow, ever thrive, ever diversify and deepen.

The Spirit of goodness, rightness, beauty, and aliveness, Jesus said, is always moving. Like wind, like breath, like water, the Spirit is in motion, inviting us to enter the current and flow.

The problem is that we often stop moving. We resist the flow. We get stuck. The word *institution* itself means something that stands rather than moves. When our institutions lack movements to propel them forward, the Spirit, I believe, simply moves around them, like a current flowing around a rock in a stream. But when the priestly/institutional and prophetic/movement impulses work together, institutions provide stability and continuity and movements provide direction and dynamism. Like skeleton and muscles, the two are meant to work together.

For that to happen, we need a common spirituality to infuse

both our priestly/institutional– and our prophetic/movement–
oriented wings. This spirituality will often be derived from the
mystical/poetic/contemplative streams within our traditions.
Without that shared spirituality, without that soul work that
teaches us to open our deepest selves to God and ground our souls
in love, no movement will succeed and no institution will stand.
Father Richard Rohr says it perfectly when he describes the Center for Action and Contemplation, which he founded: "The most
important word in our name is *and*." It is the linking of action *and*
contemplation, great work *and* deep spirituality, that keeps the
goodness, rightness, beauty, and aliveness flowing.

So, the great spiritual migration we need cannot simply be
a matter of strategies and structures, as important as they are.
Rather, as Pope Francis has said, this moment calls for *social poets*:
sincere and creative people who will rise on the wings of faith to
catch the wind of the Spirit, the wind of justice, joy, and peace.
The season is changing, and it is time for us to rise.

CONTEMPLATION, CONVERSATION, AND ACTION: CHAPTER 9

Contemplation: Ponder the quotation attributed to Gandhi: "First, they ignore you. Then they laugh at you. Then they fight you. And then you win." Let this simple quotation stimulate quiet reflection and a simple prayer.

Conversation:

1. What one sentence, paragraph, image, or idea from this chapter do you most want to talk about?
2. Put "this great work" and "the quadruple threat" into your own words.
3. Respond to the "So Much Right" section of this chapter.
4. The concept of "evangelism" or "evangelization" comes up in this chapter. How do you respond to the way that term is defined traditionally—and here?
5. Summarize the four levels of change outlined in this chapter, and the role you have seen or can imagine churches playing in each.
6. What is "economic activism" and why is it so important now?
7. Have you ever worked closely with another religious community for the common good? If not, why not, and if so, what was the experience like?

Action: Pick one or two ideas from this chapter to share with someone from your own church or denomination, and with someone from another church, denomination, or religion. Listen with curiosity and without judgment to their responses.

10

THE BROKEN-OPEN HEART

TRANSFORMATIVE SPIRITUAL MOVEMENTS ARE EXCITING. But they are also dangerous and difficult. They require a profound change of heart, a profound change in character, a radical shift in the "level of consciousness" of their participants.[1] Those who join the great work for deep change almost always face great suffering (and you can almost certainly drop the *almost*).

NECESSARY OBSTACLES

I wish that danger, difficulty, and suffering weren't a necessary part of this great journey. I wish we could get where we need to be simply by saying (or writing) the right words. But the capacity to endure and suffer—generously, without bitterness, without revenge, without fail—will be absolutely essential. In his groundbreaking book from the 1970s, *The Road Less Traveled,* M. Scott Peck said exactly what we need to hear today:

> *Life is difficult. This is a great truth, one of the greatest truths. It is a great truth because once we truly see this truth, we transcend it. Once we truly know that life is difficult—once we truly understand and accept it—then life is no longer difficult. Because once it is accepted, the fact that life is difficult no longer matters.*[2]

Spiritual migration is difficult, start to finish, from the intra-personal level to the interpersonal level to the institutional level to the cultural level. It's difficult to doubt, deconstruct, or decenter the system of beliefs you've worked so hard to perfect. It's difficult to change your vision of God from the tribal deity of a "little we" to the mysterious and majestic Holy Spirit who calls all into the union of communion. It's difficult to make love for neighbor, self, the earth, and God your life's highest ambition. It's difficult to cancel your nostalgic vacation into the past or awaken from your fanciful speculations about the future so you can engage passionately with the fierce urgency of now. It's difficult to retool our churches from service providers, museums of religious lore, or climate-controlled spiritual warehouses or country clubs into schools or studios of love. It's difficult to stop complaining and start organizing, especially when complaining is so enjoyable and costs us so little. None of this is easy, and we will surely be worn down if we don't know how to tap into a liberating and sustaining spiritual power beyond ourselves.

Ask any mother whether love is easy. From pregnancy to delivery to nursing to dirty diapers to sleepless nights to early mornings to battles over homework to navigating puberty to college tuitions and beyond, love demands heroism that lasts for decades. The same is true for marriage; all that "in sickness and in health, for richer, for poorer, for better, for worse, until death do us part" language is telling us that love demands toughness, resilience, and determination—for a lifetime! That's simply the nature of love:

> *You can't learn to love people without being around actual people—including people who infuriate, exasperate, annoy, offend, frustrate, encroach upon, resist, reject, and hurt you, thus tempting you not to love them.*
> *You can't learn the patience that love requires without experiencing delay and disappointment.*

*You can't learn the kindness that love requires without rendering
yourself vulnerable to unkindness.*

*You can't learn the generosity that love requires outside the
presence of heartbreaking and unquenchable need.*

*You can't learn the peaceableness that love requires without being
enmeshed in seemingly unresolvable conflict.*

*You can't learn the humility that love requires without moments
of acute humiliation.*

*You can't learn the determination that love requires without
opposition and frustration.*

*You can't learn the endurance that love requires without
experiencing unrelenting seduction to give up.*

The way of love, then, is the way of annoyance, frustration, disappointment, unkindness, need, conflict, humiliation, opposition, and exhaustion. No one would choose it if love weren't, in the end, its own reward. This difficult way, this way of love and suffering, this way of Christ is unavoidably the way of the cross.

Broken Apart, Broken Open

Christianity in its current form loves crosses—as architectural elements and personal jewelry. But beyond that, we Christians are not so fond of the cross. I include myself in this indictment. When I face unfair criticism, attack, and mistreatment, even on a minor scale, I whine. Forget about nails and spears: even small sacrifices evoke complaints and self-pity. I am among those who prefer Jesus to do all the cross-work of suffering and dying. But we who dare to lead must bear the cross, not on a gold chain around our necks, but in our deepest heart, in nonretaliatory suffering, as a way of life lived in what the educator and spiritual sage Parker Palmer calls "the tragic gap."

This tragic gap stretches between what is and what should be, between what life demands of us and what we can currently offer. The stress of holding that gap can break our hearts, he says, but there are "at least two ways for the heart to break."[3] First

the heart can be broken into a thousand shards, sharp-edged fragments that sometimes become shrapnel aimed at the source of our pain. Every day, untold numbers of people try without success to "pick up the pieces," some of them taking grim satisfaction in the way the heart's explosion has injured their enemies. Here the broken heart is an unresolved wound that we carry with us for a long time, sometimes tucking it away and feeding it as a hidden wound, sometimes trying to "resolve it" by inflicting the same wound on others.

In contrast, Palmer says, we can imagine the heart as a "small, clenched fist" that can be "'broken open' into largeness of life, into greater capacity to hold one's own and the world's pain and joy." In this way, our heartbreak can actually *increase* our empathy for others, which leads us not to acts of revenge but rather to acts of compassion and reconciliation. He quotes the Sufi master Hazrat Inayat Khan: "God breaks the heart again and again and again until it stays open." Palmer explains:

In Christian tradition, the broken-open heart is virtually indistinguishable from the image of the cross. It was on the cross that God's heart was broken for the sake of humankind, broken open into a love that Christ's followers are called to emulate. In its simple physical form, the cross embodies the notion that tension can pull the heart open. Its cross-beams stretch out four ways, pulling against each other left and right, up and down. But those arms converge in a center, a heart, that can be pulled open by that stretching, by the tensions of life—a heart that can be opened so fully it can hold everything from despair to ecstasy. And that, of course, is how Jesus held his excruciating experience, as an opening into the heart of God.

If we Christians want to contribute to the healing of the world's wounds rather than to the next round of wounding—and we have a long history of doing both—we must understand and inhabit the cruciform way of life that is at the heart of our tradition.

My wise friend Richard Rohr says, "Pain that isn't processed is passed on," or "Pain that isn't transformed is transmitted." By denying our pain, by minimizing it, by doing anything other than actually feeling it, processing it, and transforming it into fuel for love, we increase the likelihood that we will pass it on—projecting it sideways, camouflaged, twisted, indirectly perhaps, but dangerously, like shards of shrapnel. I recently heard someone say, "We will respond to trauma either by praying for God to punish those who hurt us, or by praying, 'Lord, make me an instrument of your peace.'" If we dare pray to be made instruments of divine peace, we must walk the way of the cross, the way of the broken-open heart, the way of suffering and nonviolence, the way of responding to hurt not with more hurt, but with healing. Again, here's how Richard Rohr expresses it: "Jesus' wounds were not necessary to convince God that we were loveable (atonement theory); his wounds are to convince *us* of the path and the price of transformation."[4]

Dr. King explained the process perfectly:

I've seen too much hate to want to hate, myself, and . . . every time I see it, I say to myself, hate is too great a burden to bear. Somehow we must be able to stand up before our most bitter opponents and say: "We shall match your capacity to inflict suffering by our capacity to endure suffering. We will meet your physical force with soul force. Do to us what you will and we will still love you. . . . But be assured that we'll wear you down by our capacity to suffer, and one day we will win our freedom. We will not only win freedom for ourselves; we will so appeal to your heart and conscience that we will win you in the process, and our victory will be a double victory."[5]

Elsewhere, Dr. King spoke of "generously endured suffering for the sake of the other" and its "educational and transforming possibilities."[6] Here he echoes Paul, who compares the holy and creative work of ministry to the labor pains of childbirth (Galatians 4:19). For a new and better world to be born, for our faith to experience a deep change of heart, for the great spiritual migration we need to become a reality, someone must be willing to suffer birth pains, and those pains will often come in the form of criticism and personal attack.

WHAT DID I EXPECT?

Years ago, when I first started venturing into these waters and the first waves of criticism starting crashing on me, I was terribly naive. What did I expect when I wrote about "a new kind of Christian" or "a new kind of Christianity" or "a generous orthodoxy"—a standing ovation? Of course many readers would interpret a call to deep change as a personal and institutional insult. Of course they would see anyone issuing such a call as a traitor, a threat, an outsider, a compromiser, an apostate, a revisionist, a heretic, and an infidel. Of course they would do all they could to marginalize, bypass, reject, discredit, and defund anyone advocating such radical change. Of course!

Pretty quickly, I realized that the reactions of my critics were not my greatest danger, nor were my critics my greatest enemies.

My greatest danger lay in how I would react to my critics, and my greatest enemies were the immaturity, pride, fear, and insecurity within me. If I chose to fight fire with fire, condemnation with condemnation, insult with insult, excommunication with excommunication, then I would spiral down into contentious defeat.[7] If I were driven by the need to be right—or to be *thought* right by others—I would show how little I had experienced the liberation to which I was calling others!

Even more than the temptation to be defensive, I felt tempted to side with the criticism, to surrender to it, to "sell the store" and give up, to look for some rock to crawl under and hide, or to walk away feeling defeated or disgusted. But if I yielded to that temptation and allowed myself to be intimidated, I would surrender my integrity and slip into self-hatred, leading to depression and paralysis. And it wouldn't be my critics who made this self-defeating choice: it would be me.

Unexpected Gifts

So I had no good option left but to learn to work with the criticism, to find whatever value I could in it. If there was something valid in a critique, I had to admit it, learn from it, and even say thanks for it. If the criticism was expressed crudely and uncharitably, I had to separate the chaff from the grain. Sometimes I failed in these attempts: when I read some of my responses to criticism from fifteen or twenty years ago, I wince at the transparent passive-aggressiveness and ego. But gradually I made a little progress, through trial and many errors. With God's help and the help of many friends, I broke some old habits and developed some new strengths.

I came to understand that even if what they said about me was completely false, unfair, or inaccurate, my critics were giving me true information about their own fears, biases, assumptions, and concerns. They were giving me a gift, if only I could receive it that way. I could use this information to better understand them and perhaps better communicate with them in the future. Even if what they had written was harsh and unloving in tone, I could use each criticism as an opportunity to learn to love them—to see them as fellow human beings, to truly forgive them, and in so doing, become more Christlike. Another gift! Even if their criticism distorted my actual message, I could treat every criticism as an opportunity to graciously clarify my message—yet another gift! And even if my critics succeeded in harming my reputation, they would be my allies in disguise, helping to liberate me from the need to be approved of or be thought right.[8]

Early on in this learning process, one of my mentors gave me a sheet of paper. As he handed it to me, he said, "I have a feeling you're going to need this." He was right. On the sheet was the prayer of a Serbian Orthodox bishop, Nikolai Velimirovich, who spoke out against the Nazis and was arrested and held at Dachau. As I understand the story, he suspected one or more of his priests of turning him in to the Nazis, and while in prison, he felt anger at his betrayers burning like acid in his soul. The prayer was his way of processing the pain and neutralizing the corrosive acid of hate.

In the years since receiving that simple sheet of paper, each time a new book comes out—and with it, new waves of criticism—I go back to that precious prayer. Here are some of the phrases of the prayer that have helped me the most:

Bless my enemies, O Lord. Even I bless them and do not curse them. Enemies have driven me into your embrace more than friends have. . . . Just as a hunted animal finds safer shelter than an unhunted animal does, so have I, persecuted by enemies, found the safest sanctuary, having ensconced myself beneath

Your tabernacle, where neither friends nor enemies can slay my
soul. Bless my enemies, O Lord. Even I bless and do not curse
them.[9]

One section of the prayer seems far beyond me, but I pray it
anyway, hoping I will become worthy of it:

Bless them and multiply them; multiply them and make them
even more bitterly against me: So that my fleeing will have no
return; So that all my hope in men may be scattered like cob-
webs; So that absolute serenity may begin to reign in my soul;
So that my heart may become the grave of my two evil twins:
arrogance and anger; So that I might amass all my treasure in
heaven; Ah, so that I may for once be freed from self-deception,
which has entangled me in the dreadful web of illusory life.

The prayer concludes:

Enemies have taught me to know what hardly anyone knows,
that a person has no enemies in the world except himself. One
hates his enemies only when he fails to realize that they are not
enemies, but cruel friends. It is truly difficult for me to say who
has done me more good and who has done me more evil in the
world: friends or enemies. Therefore bless, O Lord, both my
friends and my enemies. A slave curses enemies, for he does not
understand. But a son blesses them, for he understands. For a
son knows that his enemies cannot touch his life. Therefore he
freely steps among them and prays to God for them. Bless my
enemies, O Lord. Even I bless them and do not curse them.

This is the way of the cross. This is the way of nonviolence.
This is the way of liberation. And this is the necessary opening
to a great spiritual migration. The pains and difficulties we will

suffer on the path of migration will burn bridges behind us and allow us no return, thus driving us forward. They will serve as purifying fires, burning away unworthy motives and insecurities, freeing us from old patterns and cycles of conflict. Our struggles and sufferings will disrupt the spirituality of comfort and privilege that bind us with golden chains. Our struggles are a gift nobody would choose, but they are a gift indeed: a blessed disruption.[10]

DISRUPTIVE SPIRITUALITY

Speaking of disruption, in chapter 1 we began looking at a powerful story at the beginning of John's Gospel: Jesus's protest in the Temple, when he drove out the merchants of sacrifice and appeasement and then made two outrageous statements. First, he said that God intended the Temple to be a house of prayer for all people (no exceptions), and second, he said that the corrupted Temple would be destroyed and replaced by something new, which would be resurrected in its place.

Jesus was introducing what, in today's parlance, might be called a disruptive technology. Where sustaining technologies stimulate incremental improvements, like, say, going from a rotary phone to a touch-tone or keypad phone, or even from a landline to a wireless phone, a disruptive technology displaces established assumptions, as in, say, combining a phone, a camera, a computer, a music library and player, a GPS device, and a mobile Internet portal.[11] The old status quo is disrupted, the game changes, and old technologies become irrelevant.

In the next two chapters of John's Gospel, Jesus continues to use the imagery of disruption (John 3–4). First he tells a man that in spite of all his learning, in spite of all his status, he needs to go back and start over, to be *born again*—perhaps the most apt

image for disruption ever. Then he tells a woman that the location of worship doesn't matter at all—which in their day meant
that temples were irrelevant. What matters, Jesus says, is the attitude (or spirit) and authenticity (or truth) of the worshipper.
Jesus was calling for a radical disruption in his religion, a great
spiritual migration, and a similar disruption and migration are
needed no less today in the religion that names itself after him.

A later New Testament writer repeated and expanded upon
the disruption and migration Jesus was calling for (1 Peter 2:5).
The way of life centered in the Temple must be disrupted because God wanted to dwell not in buildings of bricks or stones
cemented together by mortar, but rather *in human beings—living
stones,* he called them—cemented together by mutual love, honor,
and respect. Paul made a similar point, trading the static imagery
of an immovable building for the dynamic imagery of a living,
breathing, moving human body. Each one of us, he said, is like a
cell, a limb, or an organ in a larger body, the vital and dynamic
body or embodiment of Christ (Romans 12; 1 Corinthians 12–
13). When we are filled and guided by the Spirit, we work together. We honor each member. We value diversity. We function
as one. And we move.

The old way of life centered in the Temple, with all its assumptions about a violent God needing appeasement, can now
be left behind, the New Testament teaches us. The old sacrifices
are gone, once and for all. Now the only sacrifice we need is what
Paul calls a "living sacrifice"—our bodies given as a gift to a loving God, so that we, individually and together, may be like movable temples, carrying the loving presence of the Spirit into the
world: every nation and neighborhood, every profession and political system, every family and friendship.

This theme resonates in Luke's account of the day of Pentecost (Acts 2). The "tongues of fire" that descended upon the individuals present evoked the glorious *shekinah* that had descended upon Solomon's original temple (2 Chronicles 7). The meaning was clear for anyone with eyes to see: rather than keeping the holy fire of the Spirit in one physical temple that was located in one culture and language, God was on the move, spreading like wildfire through human bodies across human cultures to set the whole world ablaze. God was ready to call people on a great spiritual migration from a static organized religion to a movement-building organizing religion, from buildings to bodies, we might say, from temples to people, from stone to flesh, from inertia to momentum.[12] It remains for us to get moving.

The Hindu mystic and poet Basava captured this vision back in the twelfth century:

> The rich will make temples for Shiva.
> What shall I, a poor man, do?
> My legs are pillars, the body the shrine,
> the head a cupola of gold.
> Listen, O lord of the meeting rivers,
> things standing shall fall,
> but the moving ever shall stay.[13]

This disruptive revolution, this liberation, this great spiritual migration begins with each of us presenting ourselves, with all of our doubts and imperfections, all of our failures, fears, and flaws, to the Spirit, our legs as pillars, our bodies as temples, our heads as cupolas, as Basava said. You. Me. Everyone. No exceptions.

"The moving ever shall stay," Basava said. Those words contradict so much of our inherited religious sensibility. "Stay the same. Don't move. Hold on. Survival depends on resistance to change," we were told again and again. "Foment change. Keep moving. Evolve. Survival depends on mobility," the Spirit persistently says. That prompting tells us that the migration we seek is not merely from one static location to another. It is, rather, from one static location to a journey of endless growth.

If you want to see the future of Christianity as a great spiritual migration, don't look at a church building. Go look in the mirror and look at your neighbor. God's message of love is sent into the world in human envelopes. If you want to see a great spiritual migration begin, then let it start right in your body. Let your life be a foothold of liberation.

LIBERATION, INNER AND OUTER

One of the most important theological movements of the mid-twentieth century was liberation theology.[14] It built upon the Social Gospel movement of the early twentieth century, but it went further, with unique nonviolent expressions around the world, including the civil rights movement of North America, the base community movement in Latin America, and the antiapartheid movement of South Africa. At its best, it wasn't just a *theology* about liberating the poor and oppressed externally; it was also a *spirituality* that helped set people free internally.

The rich might run the show, liberation spirituality taught, but we can rejoice because we know God loves us and God believes in our dignity, even if the rich don't. The careless and greedy may plunder, liberation spirituality taught, but we can refuse to comply; we can plant beautiful gardens and create alternative economies in our neighborhoods and churches. We don't have to wait until some future day when oppressors stop oppressing, liberation spirituality taught; we can start living today as if we are already free, walking tall, singing with exuberance, dignity intact. When liberation spirituality frees the poor from the dehumanizing scripts of the oppressed, they can help the rich be liberated from their dehumanizing scripts of oppression. When poor and rich are liberated together from those old scripts, we become protagonists in a movement of mutual liberation that challenges every individual, community, movement, and institution.

It's odd that we have to label this stream of Christian theology and spirituality with a term like *liberation,* as if it's something eccentric and odd. Shouldn't liberation be normative for a way of life centered in Jesus and his good news for the poor and oppressed? Perhaps we should call traditional approaches *oppression theology* or *supremacist spirituality,* and let liberation theology and spirituality be, for us going forward, simply *Christian* and normative.

Oppression theology and supremacist spirituality developed in the belief ecosystem of an angry God who needed appeasement in order to dispense grace, who favored some and disfavored others, and who welcomed the favored into religious institutions that accumulated and hoarded privilege and protected the status quo. In spite of their great flaws, much that was good and beautiful coexisted with these forms of spirituality. But like primary school, they have done their job. Repeating sixth grade six more times won't teach you what you'll learn in seventh through twelfth grades, so it's time now to grow up and move on in liberation.

AT PLAY WITH GOD

But what does liberation spirituality look like? We're so used to seeing people advocate something they don't actually embody that when we meet someone who authentically embodies liberation spirituality, the experience is profoundly moving. That's how I felt recently when I saw an old friend whom I hadn't seen in a long time.

Back in the 1990s, Dieter Zander was to many of us young pastors what rock stars are to kids jamming on guitars and drums in their basement. He pastored a big church. He was good-looking and ultratalented, both as a speaker and as a musician. He spoke and led worship at the best conferences. He wrote popular books. He was a genuinely good guy, giving his all to bless and inspire others.

Then in 2008, one night while he was asleep, Dieter had a stroke.

When he awoke, his right hand was useless. He couldn't speak. Music and preaching were gone overnight. A ministry career and all that went with it ended. Dieter was alone in a body that once served him, but now seemed to imprison him.[15]

A friend, knowing that Dieter's creative personality must still be alive in his limited body, gave him a camera. Soon he learned to let his photographs speak and tell stories in shape, light, shadow, and color rather than words. To pay the bills, he eventually got a job working as a crossing guard, and then at a grocery store, cleaning toilets, collapsing cardboard boxes, packing up expired but still-good food and sending it to food pantries. When I was with him recently, I was impressed by how much of his speech he has been able to regain, through long years and great struggle.[16]

"Before stroke, I working for God," he said. "German man. Working, working, working!" Then he smiled. "Now, I playing with God. Playing, playing, playing. Much better!"

After all he had lost, it would have been easy for Dieter to be bitter, and I don't doubt that he had seasons of adjustment and grief that were painful in ways I can't imagine. His old life, his glorious and successful and prestigious life, was over, and now he found himself scrubbing toilets in a grocery store. Surely that kind of work doesn't matter, doesn't amount to much. Surely.

But one day, as he cleaned out a urinal, Dieter felt a voice speaking deep within him. "Urinal holy," the voice said. "Toilet holy. Bathroom holy. Grocery store holy. Everything holy."

The words came to him as a revelation, a revelation from God, and a liberation as well.

Everything holy. Dieter learned something too few of us know. If a urinal is holy, then our bodies are holy. If our bodies are holy, then our marriages and nuclear families and extended families are holy—these beautiful collections of bodies related by genes and promise. So are the networks of families that we call congregations, denominations, communities, and nations. So are the farms and fields that produce the food that keeps all these families alive and thriving. So are the breezes that blow fresh air for their lungs to breathe, and so are the forests that continually refresh the air, and so are the wild places where all living things, plant and animal, coexist in the earth community of God.

THE WEIGHT OF THE WORLD, LIFTED

How many of us find ourselves taking the weight of the world on our shoulders? *We* need to solve climate change. *We* need to stop nuclear war. *We* need to end racial and religious bigotry. Before long, *we* collapse under the weight. We become embittered and break down. We burn out. But then comes the liberating word. I can't clean up everything. But I can clean out this urinal. I can love this little neighborhood, and these few neighbors. I can give this little talk, write this little book, take this little photograph, make this little meal, do this little thing. And if enough of us are freed from the unbearable weight of doing everything and do the one little thing that is ours to do now, then, we can trust, God can get done through all of us what none of us can do alone. And suddenly, it's not burdensome work. It's aliveness. It's joy. It's freedom. Instead of playing God, I'm playing with God, at play in God's good world, where everything is holy.

Everything holy and *playing with God,* taken together, define as well as any words ever could the liberation spirituality that emerges when we pass through disruptive difficulty and suffering as part of the great spiritual migration.

We might say that our old systems of belief, understandings of God, and institutional religions were perfectly suited to keeping us in captivity, working, working, working for the competing civilizations and extractive economies of our past. But now, because our competing civilizations and extractive economies have turned suicidal, we need to be liberated from them. To rise to the occasion of this great work, we must descend in humility, to see what Dieter now sees: that we are but children at play with God, living in a world where everything is holy.[17] That is liberation spirituality.

Through his great suffering and disruption, Dieter has come to know liberation at a depth that I at present only faintly grasp. But his example inspires me, and through my own small struggles, little by little, step by step, I keep growing toward the simple aliveness that I saw in Dieter's face and felt in the bear hug he gave me when we last parted.

To relax in play, in God's limitless grace. To be who we are, where we are, doing what is ours to do. Through suffering and loss, through disruption and grief, through the way of the cross, to finally see that everything is holy. And in this way, to be alive and free.

CONTEMPLATION, CONVERSATION, AND ACTION: CHAPTER 10

Contemplation: "Playing with God" . . . hold this thought in a spirit of contemplation and prayer for a few minutes.

Conversation:

1. What one sentence, paragraph, image, or idea from this chapter do you most want to talk about?

2. Reread the section that begins, "You can't learn to love people without being around actual people." Which of those statements feels most relevant to you right now, and why?

3. Respond to this quotation: "If you want to see the future of Christianity as a great spiritual migration, don't look at a church building. Go look in the mirror and look at your neighbor."

4. Contrast the "broken apart heart" with the "broken-open heart," as described by Parker Palmer. What does "the way of the cross" mean to you after reading this chapter?

5. What did you learn from this chapter about responding to criticism? What role has criticism played in your life? What gifts can come to us wrapped in criticism? What part of the Serbian Orthodox bishop's prayer most touched you, and why?

6. Why, after talking about such serious and important subjects, do you think the author concludes this chapter with the idea of "playing, playing, playing" with God? Contrast the idea of "playing with God" to the idea of "playing God."

7. As we near the end of this book, what emotions are you feeling, and why?

Action: This chapter speaks of presenting ourselves to the Spirit. Practice presenting yourself to God—once, three times, five times, or as many times as possible per day—until it becomes a constant internal habit.

AFTERWORD

We Stepped Forth.
The Waters Parted.

I AM FLYING THROUGH THUNDERSTORMS AS I WRITE THESE
words, returning from a retreat that brought together the
multifaith group of contemplative activists I mentioned earlier:
two creative young rabbis, three dynamic African American
Christians, a Latina Methodist bishop, an inspiring Sikh leader,
the world's first openly gay Episcopal bishop, a Unitarian human
rights organizer, a bold white Evangelical theologian and justice
activist, a Catholic nun dedicated to changing the game for poor
people, and me. (Our group also includes a dedicated Muslim
activist who couldn't be present because she was participating in
a march for justice on the other side of the country.) This un-
likely assemblage, brought together by the Auburn Senior Fellows program, spent a few days in the Arizona mountains. There
we shared stories, cried, laughed, dreamed, prayed, planned, and
even danced together.[1]

The thunderstorm outside my window is nothing compared
to the energy that flowed among this group of spiritual leaders.

We each came into this circle with a shared commitment to be
true to our own deep religious convictions, to treat our differences
as assets, not liabilities. We each came fully convinced that our
faiths contain unique treasures, resources, empowerments, and
insights that can help us, in the words of Bono, to tear a little corner off the world's darkness so a little more light can stream in.

You might say that we represent parallel migrations within each of our faith communities.

Among our little group is a gifted young rabbi named Stephanie Kolin. During a time of prayer the other day, Rabbi Stephanie offered a prayer that touched me deeply:

> *God Who Creates, God Who Redeems,*
> *God of shalom—of peace, God of sh'leimut—of wholeness,*
> *We remember standing at the shore of the sea, afraid,*
> *Our enslavers in hot pursuit, ready to take us back to captivity.*
> *We remember the tumultuous sea before us that showed no signs*
>   *of parting.*
> *And we remember you told us:* v'yisa'u—*go forward.*
> *We stepped forth. The waters parted.*
> *We moved our bodies from slavery to freedom.*
> *You moved our souls from oppression to redemption.*
> *God who Creates, God who Redeems,*
> *If it can happen once, it can happen over and over and over.*
> *V'yisa'u.*
> *Let us cross the sea with all who are enslaved, with captors on*
>   *their heels.*
> *And together, let us make those waters part!*[2]

The image won't let me go: the Hebrew children standing in the tragic gap between an approaching army and a "tumultuous sea . . . that showed no sign of parting," about to embark upon a bold migration of faith.

Talk about a predicament! They can't see any way forward, they can't turn back, and they can't stay where they are. In that impossible context, in that stressful zone, in that tragic gap, the call comes: *V'yisa'u!* The Hebrew is often translated as "Go forward!" but it could also be translated as "Get going!" or "Let the migration begin!"

As I reflect on Rabbi Stephanie's prayer and the meaning of *v'yisa'u,* I realize that in the place of uncertainty, it is tempting to freeze in paralysis or flee in fear. In the thick of criticism and controversy, it's tempting to turn back to our pursuers to fight them—or to surrender to them. We may want to defend ourselves, to convince them we aren't so bad or so wrong, to persuade them to think as highly of us as we do. But no: we have new places to go. We have a great work to do. Our calling is forward; we can't turn back. In that impossible moment, in that tragic gap when our hearts break open, in that agonizing place where there is no way ahead, God makes a way. We step forth and the waters part. *V'yisa'u!*

I recall the message I heard deep in my heart many years ago in front of a palo verde tree, when I first felt that my old system of beliefs was crumbling and I was being driven out into a spiritual wilderness—the same message from Rabbi Stephanie's prayer: *V'yisa'u! Go farther! Go forward!*

And suddenly, the core message of faith becomes clear to me afresh: We hear the call to go forward not after the sea has opened, but before. The call to get moving comes not after the way is clear, but while it still seems impassable. The call to join in a great migration away from the old toward the new comes not when we have everything figured and settled and made certain, and not when all obstacles have been removed, but before, when chaos, uncertainty, and turmoil prevail, and when the tumultuous sea shows no sign of parting. Only in that impossible, uncertain, disruptive place, when finger by finger, the fist of our little hearts is pulled open—only in that impossible agonizing place— does a new depth of naked, essential faith in God mysteriously become possible.

The word of God comes to us: *Get going! Go farther! Go forward!*

A way opening in the tumultuous sea: first a few, then a

dozen, a thousand, a million human hearts breaking open with divine love that can heal the world, rising as one like birds on the wing, migrating toward a better way to be Christian and a better way to be human.

If it happened once, it can happen over and over. Yes, even now.

CONTEMPLATION, CONVERSATION, AND ACTION:
AFTERWORD

Contemplation: Ponder that word *V'yisa'u!* and its meanings: *Get going! Get moving! Go farther! Migrate!* Picture yourself hearing that word before a "sea that shows no signs of parting."

Conversation:

1. What one sentence, paragraph, image, or idea from this afterword do you most want to talk about?
2. What part of the rabbi's prayer most touched you, and why?
3. Respond to this quotation: "Only in that impossible, uncertain, disruptive place, when finger by finger, the fist of our little hearts is pulled open—only in that impossible agonizing place—does a new depth of naked, essential faith in God mysteriously become possible."
4. In what ways could you say that faith is "a matter of life and death"?
5. What in your life could be represented by a "sea that shows no signs of parting"?
6. As we reach the end of this book, what is your deepest wish or prayer?
7. Use question 1 above to discuss the three appendices.

Action: Recommend this book to three or four friends, or better, make plans to invite them over to read and discuss it together.

CHARTER FOR A JUST AND GENEROUS CHRISTIANITY

The following is adapted from the October 2013 Mesa Document and the Charter for a Just and Generous Christianity of the Convergence Network, in which I am an enthusiastic participant.[1]

Growing numbers of Christian leaders from many traditions—traditional Protestant, progressive Catholic, progressive Evangelical and charismatic, and others—are coming to shared convictions that are both radical and exciting:

> the future of the church will not simply be a replication of the past, and
> it is time for vital, new expressions of just and generous Christian faith to emerge.

We have often felt marginalized and alone in these convictions. But when we voice them, we soon discover that we are not alone. Many others resonate with the restlessness we feel, and speak of . . .

> a deep thirst for a more authentic, honest, and sustaining spiritual life

a compelling hunger to do justice, to show compassion, to
   walk humbly with God
a powerful desire to understand and engage with the critical
   problems of our world
a profound need for space to grapple honestly with our questions of theology and practice
an impatient readiness to move beyond narratives of decline to
   narratives of hope and empowerment
a growing loneliness for a sense of shared identity and belonging that transcend institutional affiliation.

We agree with the Charter of Compassion, that "at the heart
of all religious, ethical and spiritual traditions" lies the principle
of compassion, which calls us "always to treat all others as we
wish to be treated ourselves." Compassion "impels us to work
tirelessly to alleviate the suffering of our fellow creatures, to de-
throne ourselves from the centre of our world and put another
there, and to honour the inviolable sanctity of every single human
being, treating everybody, without exception, with absolute justice, equity and respect." Compassion "is essential to human relationships and to a fulfilled humanity . . . [and is] indispensable to
the creation of a just economy and a peaceful global community."
This emphasis on compassion, we believe, echoes Jesus' one great
commandment to love.

And so in that spirit, we affirm together these ten commitments:

We love *Jesus* and have confidence in his good news of the
   reign, commonwealth, or ecosystem of God, and we seek
   for God's will to be done on earth as it is in heaven by
   making love our highest aim—love for God and neighbor, for outsider and enemy, for ourselves and the good
   earth.

We affirm God's preferential option for *the poor* and *the young* in the struggle for justice and freedom ... through advocacy, relationships, organizing, and action.

We seek to honor, interpret, and apply *the Bible* in fresh and healing ways, aware of the damaging ways the Bible has been used in the past.

We seek to reconnect with *the earth,* to understand the harm human beings are doing to it, and to embody more responsible, regenerative ways of life in and with it.

We seek the common good, locally and globally, through *churches* of many diverse forms, contexts, and traditions, and we imagine fresh ways for churches to form Christlike people who join God in the healing of the world.

We build inclusive *partnerships* across gaps between the powerful and vulnerable—including disparities based on wealth, gender, race and ethnic identity, education, religion, sexuality, age, politics, and physical ability.

We propose new ways of *encountering the other* in today's pluralistic world through the creative and nonviolent wisdom of peacemaking, and we collaborate with other religious and secular groups in alliances for the common good.

We host safe space for *constructive theological conversation,* rooting our practice in theological reflection, and translating our reflection into practical action.

We value *the arts* for their unique role in nurturing, challenging, and transforming our humanity.

We emphasize *spiritual and relational practices* to strengthen our inner life with God, to build healthy families, and to deepen our relationships with one another.

We have set an inspiring goal together: to identify first 100, and then 1000, and then 10,000 vital faith communities in North America who share these commitments. We invite these

communities to stand tall and stand together so we can synergize and organize concerted efforts.

In faith and hope, we raise our sails to be filled by the wind
of the Spirit, so a just and generous Christian faith will thrive as
never before in our world, to the glory of God and for the joyful
freedom of all God's creatures.

FOURTEEN PRECEPTS OF JUST AND GENEROUS CHRISTIANITY

Christianity isn't the only religion that loses its way from time to time. That's why every religious community has prophetic voices who arise and call for spiritual migration. Thich Nhat Hanh has been such a voice in his tradition, calling for Buddhists to embrace an "engaged Buddhism."[1] I've taken his "Fourteen Precepts of Engaged Buddhism" and adapted them for "Just and Generous Christianity."

1. **Humility:** Do not be idolatrous about any doctrine, theory, belief, or ideology, even Christian ones. Christian systems of thought or belief are guiding means, a pathway rather than a destination.

2. **Lifelong Learning:** Do not think the knowledge you presently possess is changeless, complete, and absolute truth. Avoid being narrow-minded and bound to present views. Be open to the Holy Spirit and practice childlike humility, demonstrating curiosity about others' viewpoints. Truth is found in life and not merely in conceptual knowledge. Be ready to learn throughout your entire life and to observe reality in yourself and in the world at all times.

3. **Gentleness:** Do not force others, including children, by any means whatsoever, to adopt your views, whether by authority, threat, money, propaganda, or even education. However, through

compassionate dialogue, help others renounce fanaticism and narrow-mindedness, and be ready to gently and humbly share what gives you life whenever it is appropriate.

4. **Compassion:** Do not avoid suffering or close your eyes before suffering. Do not lose awareness of the existence of suffering in the life of the world. Find ways to be with those who are suffering and to be an agent of comfort and healing. Awaken yourself and others to the reality of suffering in the world. And do the same regarding joy, so you can weep with those who weep and rejoice with those who rejoice.

5. **Generosity:** Do not accumulate wealth while millions are hungry. Do not take as the aim of your life fame, profit, wealth, or sensual pleasure. Live simply and share time, energy, opportunity, and material resources with those who are in need.

6. **Love:** Do not maintain anger or hatred. Learn to penetrate and transform them when they are still seeds in your consciousness. As soon as they arise, turn your heart toward God in order to see and understand the nature of your hatred, so it will not be translated into word or deed. Make love your highest goal.

7. **Serenity:** Do not lose yourself in dispersion and in your surroundings. Dwell in the presence and peace of God to come back to what is happening in the present moment. Be in touch with what is wondrous, refreshing, and healing both inside and around you. Plant seeds of joy, peace, and understanding in yourself in order to facilitate the work of transformation in the depths of your consciousness.

8. **Reconciliation:** Be careful with your words. Do not utter words that can create discord and cause the community to

break. Make every effort to reconcile and resolve all conflicts, however small.

9. **Communication:** Do not say untruthful things for the sake of personal interest or to impress people. Do not utter words that cause division and hatred. Do not spread news that you do not know to be certain. Do not criticize or condemn things of which you are not sure. Always speak truthfully and constructively. Have the courage to speak out about situations of injustice, even when doing so may threaten your own safety.

10. **Justice:** Do not use your faith community for personal gain or profit, or politicize it for partisan ends. A faith community, however, should take a clear stand against oppression and injustice and should strive to change unjust and unhealthy situations without being manipulated or controlled by outside forces or interests.

11. **Vocation:** Do not live with a vocation that is harmful to humans and nature. Do not invest in companies that deprive others of their chance to live. Select a vocation that helps realize your ideal of compassion.

12. **Nonviolence:** Do not kill and do no harm, and do not stand by when others seek to do so. Find creative, just, and nonviolent ways to prevent or end conflicts and to promote and strengthen peace.

13. **Property:** Possess nothing that should belong to others. Respect the property of others, but prevent others from profiting from human suffering or the suffering of other species on Earth.

14. **Body:** Do not mistreat your body. Learn to treat it with respect. Practice self-control. Sexual expression should not take

place without love and corresponding commitment. In sexual relations, be aware of future suffering that may be caused. To preserve the happiness of others, respect the rights and commitments of others. Be fully aware of the responsibility of bringing new lives into the world. Be aware of the ways your body connects you to all creation, and be grateful for every meal, every heartbeat, and every breath.

More on Beliefs

If your beliefs are working fine for you, and if holding them is a life-giving and enriching dimension of your life, then feel free to skip this appendix. Keep in mind, though, that at some point in the future, if your system of beliefs begins undermining your integrity and well-being, this appendix might be helpful for you. And it might be helpful right now for someone you know who is struggling with his or her beliefs.

The concept of belief, like the concept of time, is much clearer the less one thinks about it. Even defining the word is harder than it seems.

One line of definition focuses on the acceptance of a statement or claim that something is real, true, or in existence. In this sense, you might have a belief in aliens, climate change, superstring theory, evolution, or God—meaning you believe that they exist. These *notional* or *conceptual beliefs* can easily be expressed as statements or propositions, and your belief can easily be expressed in a sentence containing *that*: I believe *that* aliens are real, *that* evolution is a valid theory, *that* miracles can happen, and so on.

In contrast, *relational beliefs* are usually followed by the preposition *in,* and they suggest personal confidence, trust, or loyalty: I believe *in* peace, *in* you, *in* our team, *in* democracy, *in* fidelity in marriage, *in* the Bible, *in* my wife, or *in* some other person, value, or institution. The issue in relational faith isn't whether these objects of belief exist. (My belief in peace, for example, may matter most precisely when peace is nowhere to be found.) The issue is whether I am loyal and faithfully committed to these objects of belief. In other words, *relational beliefs* say less about the object of belief and more about the subject. To say "I believe" is to say, "I am committed, I am loyal, I am bound by affection and dedication" to the object of my belief.

The situation becomes more complex when an object of *relational belief*—like a religion or a church, for example—demands statements of *conceptual belief* as a proof of loyalty or requirement for belonging. The situation is even more highly charged when an object of relational belief provides rewards and punishments based on conceptual beliefs: honor or shame, acceptance or rejection, tolerance or torture, employment or unemployment, marriageability or unmarriageability, life or death, heaven or hell.

It's easy to see how, in the presence of rewards and punishments like these, you could be pressured, even subconsciously, to uphold your community's required conceptual beliefs, whether or not you actually believe them. In addition, you might continue to claim adherence to a belief even after you have stopped believing it simply to avoid having to admit you were wrong. Some people feel these tensions most acutely when they go off to college and are exposed to new information, while at the same time being physically removed from the community back home that enforces belief maintenance. Others face these tensions in the second half of life, a period when many of us rethink or redefine not only what we believe, but how we believe.[1] We easily find ourselves caught between relational belief and conceptual belief, between personal loyalty to a community and personal intellectual integrity.

The situation is especially conflicted for clergy, whose way of making a living depends upon upholding the conceptual beliefs of the community in which they have a relational belief. It's no wonder that conceptual beliefs can become "make believe" or pretend; it's no wonder that believers can be tempted to hold "right beliefs" in "bad faith." And it's no wonder that sometimes, when they are forced to make false confessions of conceptual beliefs, people lose relational belief in the community that exerted that pressure. Why should you believe relationally in a group that pressures you to be conceptually dishonest?

The Catholic philosopher John Caputo suggests that this "bad faith/make believe" situation can continue for centuries, "until . . . religious beliefs become, well, unbelievable and incur mass incredulity."[2]

One response to this predicament has been to throw barrels of old conceptual beliefs overboard, like excess ballast or baggage that threatens to sink a ship in a storm. Taken to an extreme, this ejection of beliefs indeed saves the ship from sinking, only to leave it without any meaningful cargo and therefore reason to exist after the storm.[3]

Still, the tradition of distinguishing "essential" beliefs from "nonessential" beliefs goes back to Jesus (who warned his hearers about straining out gnats while swallowing camels) and Paul (who urged his readers to "approve the things which are excellent" and who repeatedly warned them not to argue over matters of little importance).[4] One recalls the old maxim (falsely attributed to Augustine, probably coming from a seventeenth-century German Reformer named Rupertus Meldenius): "In essentials, unity; in nonessentials, liberty; in all things, charity." In our day, Philip Clayton and Steven Knapp have addressed the question of "essential beliefs" with extraordinary intelligence, honesty, and due caution in *The Predicament of Belief*.[5] They ask, "What might hold a Christian community together when fixed creedal boundaries no longer define it?" And then they offer this concern: "Clearly, if what its members believe plays *no* role at all, nothing will distinguish this community from others that engage in charitable actions and encourage the spiritual or moral growth of their participants" (2818).[6]

Clayton and Knapp propose a kind of Christian minimalism, where Christian identity is related to how one answers this set of questions about Jesus:

> *Was this an ordinary human life that, thanks to the vivid imagination of early witnesses and later interpreters, took on a false aura of religious significance? Or is there a reason to think that, in the case of Jesus, "something happened"—something, that is, of enduring religious importance? More precisely, is there reason to think that the events of Jesus' life and death made the nature and the core dispositions, the ultimate values, of God present to human beings in a way that, perhaps, they had never been before, in a way that would have decisive consequences for the relationship between that divine reality and human beings? (1605)*

Strong Christians would answer this set of questions by affirming a seminal conceptual belief that they call "the Christian proposition": "that the infinite grace and compassion of the Ultimate Reality itself were present, and in some sense continue to be present, in a particular human being, namely, Jesus of Nazareth" (1610). This minimal conceptual belief serves, we might say, to reduce emphasis on conceptual beliefs about Jesus and to shift the focus to relational belief in Jesus, his message, and his mission.

Clayton and Knapp acknowledge that Christians will believe even this minimalist claim in different ways, and with more and less strength, over time. In that light, they offer six levels of belief, which I name and simplify as follows:

1. **Universally Compelling Belief:** We believe this claim because of compelling logical arguments that should convince any rational person in any community. Anyone who does not accept this belief has made a conceptual error.

2. **Rationally Defensible Belief:** Some strong voices in today's world, perhaps even the majority, do not judge this proposition to be true, but I have good reasons to explain why the majority is wrong to reject this belief, and why I am right to hold it.

3. **Personalized Belief:** I do not have good reasons to expect all people to believe this proposition to be true, but I have personal reasons—experiences, intuitions, assumptions, and needs—that lead me to believe it. My community of faith generally shares these reasons and experiences.

4. **Vacillating Belief:** Sometimes I have personal reasons to believe that this proposition may be true, but at other times the reasons don't seem compelling to me. Although I often doubt, I frequently find myself believing nonetheless.

5. **Wishful Belief:** I do not believe this claim is true, but I consistently wish it were true or hope it will turn out to be true, and I try to live as if it were true.

6. **Metaphorical Belief:** I do not believe this claim to be true, but I believe it is a metaphor for something else that I do judge to be true.

The Christian community should, they argue, make room for people at each of these levels of belief, especially because someone who is at level 5 this week might be at level 2 next week, and vice versa. But they offer this warning:

> When church leaders can no longer presuppose a securely shared
> fabric of beliefs, they rely increasingly on extrinsic motivations:
> professional musicians, high-tech services, attractive social pro-
> grams, and the like. The trouble is that reflective persons recog-
> nize that such initiatives are no longer tied to compelling and
> persuasive beliefs about what is ultimately the case. When those
> beliefs become merely *metaphorical* or *poetic*—or worse, when
> one finds oneself using language one no longer believes but
> vaguely feels that one *ought to believe*—one begins to wonder
> about the raison d'etre of the entire institution and its practices.
> (2931)

To manage the tension between believing Christian beliefs in
good faith and make-believing them in bad faith, they speak of
focus and *attraction*: a "shared focus on this core proposition is
sufficient to define a community of Christian life and worship . . .
the community can and should be open to all who are attracted to
Jesus, so understood, even when they do not stand in a position of
continuous and undoubting belief in the Christian proposition"
(2822) In other words, whatever one's level of conceptual belief
on any given Sunday, if one remains relationally focused on and
attracted to Jesus, one belongs.

By acknowledging these complexities in the experience of
holding beliefs, Clayton and Knapp hope that we will "prepare
the way for the possible emergence of a deeper consensus that will
once again provide a basis of concerted thought and action" (2947).

What possibilities other than conceptual beliefs might sustain
that "deeper consensus . . . of concerted thought and action"? Or
to put the question slightly differently, *Can Christianity of the future convene around something other than a list of conceptual beliefs?*

As I've pondered this question for over twenty years now,
a fourfold alternative to the centrality of conceptual beliefs has
emerged for me. This alternative could be pictured as a conven-

ing table with four legs: a compelling story, inspiring saints and elders, a meaningful practice, and a vision of the future.[7]

Leg 1: A Story

The story, of course, is an emerging understanding of the biblical story. The conventional version many of us inherited has been reduced to what I have called "the six-line narrative," a story of (1) perfect creation, (2) "the fall," (3) human history in a sinful and damned world, (4) salvation defined as repairing "the fall," and a conclusion in one of two eternal states—(5) perfect redemption in heaven or (6) perfect damnation in hell.[8] This version of the story has become highly problematic, and it is also terribly hard to square with the actual texts in the biblical library.

For these and other reasons, more and more of us are telling the story in fresh ways. First and foremost, we are letting Jesus and his good news of the kingdom of God be the focus or central attraction of the story (to use Knapp and Clayton's terms)—the tabletop, if you will. And rather than sealing the biblical story off from our other ways of knowing—such as astronomy, physics, biology, sociology, psychology, and the arts—we are integrating our reading of the Bible with all our other sources of understanding. We might call this an integral or evidential approach to revelation.[9]

When we tell the story in this integral way, we begin with a universe that appeared 14.7 billion years ago, that constantly expands and evolves, and that has proven hospitable on at least one planet to the development of human beings and all they have created—from Bach to Bob Dylan, from petroglyphs to Picasso, from aqueducts to airplanes. In this approach, our understanding of science isn't in competition with God; rather, as we better understand the logic and language of creation, we better understand the logic and language of the Creator or Source.

God is both *in* this story, as we are telling it, and the hospitable setting or presence in which the story unfolds. In other words, rather than conceiving of God as outside of time and space—either above it as a machine operator pulling levers, or behind it as a prime mover or divine watchmaker who sets it in motion—we tell the story of God present with creation, present to every event, in deep solidarity. Each pain and each joy is shared by God, and God is the compassionate witness to every outrage and every act of grace and heroism. Where a choice is to be made, God is the inherent voice calling people to justice, joy, love, wisdom, and peace. Where evil happens, God is the compassionate presence of acknowledgment, healing, repentance, and restoration. From before the Big Bang, God is the presence in whom the universe unfolds, and God's wisdom and love are the logic on which the universe operates.[10]

Many of us are learning that within this great liberating and reconciling story, smaller stories must be told in conversation with one another.[11] For example, if we only tell the biblical story of Jacob being God's beloved and Esau being rejected (Genesis 25–28), we set the stage for the kind of exclusivity we need to reject. But if we pair the early stories of Jacob competing with and disgracing Esau with the later stories of Jacob encountering the face of God in his supposedly rejected brother (Genesis 33), we see the stories move from exclusivity to inclusivity—all the more when we realize that in the Parable of the Lost Son, Jesus models the father on Esau (Luke 15:11–32).[12] If we only tell the story of Elijah confronting the prophets of Baal in a literal death match, we unintentionally affirm violence in the name of God (1 Kings 18). But if we put that story in conversation with the story of Jesus rebuking his disciples for suggesting a repeat performance of Elijah's triumph, we see how these stories lead from violence to peace (Luke 9:53–55). This way of engaging with story is supported by what we called (in chapter 6) an integral/literary way of reading the Bible.

All stories have heroes, but the true protagonist of a liberating, reconciling story of good news is better named a *saint,* as Francis J. Ambrosio explains:

> *For the hero the meaning of life is honor. For the saint the meaning of life is love. For the hero the goal of living is self-fulfillment, the achievement of personal excellence, and the recognition and admiration that making a signal contribution to one's society through one's achievements carries with it. For the saint, life does not so much have a goal, as a purpose, for which each human being is responsible, and that purpose is love, and the bonds of concern and care that responsibility for one's fellow human beings carry with it. These two paradigms, the hero and the saint, and the way of life that descends from each, are really two fundamentally distinct and genuinely different visions of human society as a whole, and even of what it means to be a human being. They are two distinct and different ways of asking the question of the meaning of life.*[13]

Leg 2: Saints

Saints embody a different set of values than heroes, and although saints play a prominent role in Christian history, they typically play second fiddle to heroic figures, especially among Protestants. We tend to convene around institutional leaders who carry titles like apostles, bishops, popes, priests, and preachers (and today, flashy televangelists, eloquent speakers, and even some authors). These "heroes of faith" have often distinguished themselves by vanquishing those with faulty belief systems and by articulating or defending the correct beliefs, meaning those shared by their successors. These kinds of heroic leaders will remain important to many, no doubt, as we move forward, but as willing sectors of Christian faith experience the great spiritual migration we have explored together in this book, I believe we will find ourselves gravitating increasingly toward saints, "attractors" whose gravitas derives from moral authority, Christlike character, authentic spirituality, and self-giving service. I would put these conveners or attractors in two categories—*saints* for those of past generations, and *elders* for those who are alive today.

If you visit St. Gregory of Nyssa Episcopal Church in San Francisco, you'll see a vivid example of what I'm talking about. In their rotunda, a beautiful mural depicting ninety of their saints encircles the congregation.[14] The saints (with a few animals thrown in) are not sitting on thrones of authority as they do in much ancient iconography; rather, they are dancing together, suggesting that they are inviting us today to join them in the dance of justice, joy, and peace in the Holy Spirit. Some are "official" saints of the church, like Thomas Aquinas, Francis of Assisi, Patrick, and Teresa of Ávila. Many are not "official" saints, but they are the kinds of people around whose creative example the people of St. Gregory's are convened, from Charles Darwin and Gandhi to Lady Godiva and John Muir, from John Coltrane and Anne Frank to Cesar Chavez and Thurgood Marshall.

Alongside these inspiring examples from the past, we can be convened by living elders. These are tried and tested people whose words are backed up by their way of life, and whose example challenges us to grow in faith, hope, and love. They are contemporaries we can observe in action and consult for guidance.

Our saints from the past and elders from the present don't need their weaknesses or failures to be whitewashed. We're looking for growth and authenticity, not perfection. Nor do our saints and elders need to all hold the same beliefs. We're looking for a harmony of values, not a uniformity of opinions. As a New Testament writer put it, we "consider the outcome of their way of life, and imitate their faith" (Hebrews 13:7). In this way, their lives form a dancing choir that beckons us to dance and sing along with them. Convened in this great company, we are ready to be spiritually formed to extend the story and to extend the good example and great work of our saints and elders, which brings us to the third leg: a practice.

Leg 3: A Practice

By a practice, I mean a set of shared rituals, habits, and behaviors by which we bond to meaning and joy. A community of football fans bonds to the meaning and joy provided by the game of football. Their rituals, habits, and behaviors might include attending games in person, watching them on TV, keeping track of scores and team standings, talking with friends about great plays, gossiping about the personal lives of players, wearing team colors, giving gifts with team themes, reading books and magazines about the game, and so on. We can easily imagine the parallel practices of birders, photographers, painters, and wine connoisseurs. Sadly, many of us seem to be less clear about the essential practices that naturally go along with following Jesus, and we may not even be clear about what the meaning and joy of that way of life should be.

When we lose sight of the meaning and joy of our faith, our rituals, habits, and behaviors descend into ritualism and people lose interest in the community, as the Jewish sage Abraham Joshua Heschel so powerfully described:

> *It is customary to blame secular science and anti-religious philosophy for the eclipse of religion in modern society. It would be more honest to blame religion for its own defeats. Religion declined not because it was refuted, but because it became*

*irrelevant, dull, oppressive, insipid. When faith is completely
replaced by creed, worship by discipline, love by habit; when
the crisis of today is ignored because of the splendor of the past;
when faith becomes an heirloom rather than a living fountain;
when religion speaks only in the name of authority rather than
with the voice of compassion—its message becomes meaning-
less.*[15]

One of our greatest challenges—and opportunities—as we
move forward is to rediscover and rearticulate what meaning and
joy matter most to us. Then we can experiment with how that
meaning and joy can be best captured in practices including liturgy, song, confession, sermon, holiday, pilgrimage, retreat, daily
devotion, feast, fast, and mission.

This rediscovery and rearticulation are necessary because so
many elements of our Christian practice have lost their meaning and joy for us. For example, I can no longer sing "Onward
Christian Soldiers" or other militant Christian hymns, knowing
the harm done by the fusion of militaristic Christianity and colonialism.[16] Similarly, some traditional hymns uphold a theory of
atonement that I now find unhelpful, and some use exclusively
masculine imagery and pronouns for God that I find distracting
or disturbing. And although I still affirm and love the creeds, I
suspect that saying them today has a very different meaning than
it did when they were originally articulated, and I do not want to
use the creeds as lists of conceptual beliefs that define Christianity. I can't help but wonder what it would mean to write creeds or
confessions that are as relevant to issues today as our traditional
creeds were to their context.[17]

Thankfully, creative and theologically rooted Christians are
working on these elements of practice, including adapting ancient
practices with contemporary technology, and I am enthusiastic
about what the future holds. Speaking of the future, if we are

rooted in a great story, inspired by great saints and elders, and spiritually formed through a wise practice, we will be well positioned to develop and work toward a brighter future, but not within the parameters of traditional eschatology.

Leg 4: A Vision of the Future

Traditional eschatology is, of course, alive and well, selling millions of books and movie tickets by (mis)using Bible passages to predict the future—complete with timetables and charts about the Rapture, the Tribulation, the Antichrist, and so on. Sadly, this approach to the future is based on many misguided assumptions, among them the notion that a controlling Supreme Being has already written the script of the universe and so we're just playing our prescribed parts in a predestined show. This predetermined-future project has many ugly and dangerous side effects, and it's time to replace it with a better approach.

Rather than using the Bible to foretell a predetermined future, I suggest we use it to deepen our moral imagination so we can, with the Spirit's guidance and empowerment, envision and cocreate a desirable future. One way to imagine such a future is to look at things we as a human civilization have left behind, or are in the process of leaving behind: human sacrifice, slavery, domestic violence, killing of those deemed witches, apartheid/segregation, inequality of women and girls, homophobia, and so on. Then we can ask what current elements of human society we would like to leave behind next, such as nuclear war, war in general, unsustainable economies, ecological destruction, terrorism, global warming, religious discrimination, extreme poverty, overpopulation, drug addiction, racism, and government corruption. This vision has enormous convening power—all the more when the community that proclaims it is actually equipping and organizing people to make it so.

A Convening Table

Traditional Christianity has focused on a clear list of prescribed conceptual beliefs, while its story, saints, practice, and vision of the future have been present, but secondary and far less clear. I propose that it is now time to reverse that emphasis, and come together around a sturdy table upheld by four legs, with bread and wine in the center, speaking to us of Jesus.

Around this table we will celebrate the meaning and joy of *the loving way of life* embodied by Jesus. Around this table, we will commune and be filled with *the nonviolent, liberating Spirit of God* embodied by Jesus. And around this table, we will *organize people* for mission so more and more of us can become embodiments of Christ in our world, *working for the common good*.

This is good news of great joy for all people—good news to believe in, good news to share, good news to launch a great spiritual migration.

Notes

Preface

1. For more on the Plymouth Brethren, see Nathan DeLynn Smith, *Roots, Renewal, and the Brethren* (Pasadena, CA: Hope, 1986), and F. Roy Coad, *A History of the Brethren Movement* (Vancouver, BC: Regent College Publishing, 2001).
2. Something similar might be said about liberals or progressives and Evangelicals.
3. Stanley Grenz described this cyclical process in *Renewing the Center* (Grand Rapids, MI: Baker, 2006). For an interesting analysis of different types of Evangelicals in America in 2016, see http://www.cnn.com/2016/01/22/politics/seven-types-of-evangelicals-and-the-primaries/index.html. For an intelligent critical analysis of my work by an Evangelical scholar, see Scott Burson, *Brian McLaren in Focus: A New Kind of Apologetics* (Abiline, TX: Abilene Christian University Press, 2016).
4. John Stott and Dave Tomlinson are two other Christian thinkers and writers with a deep love for birds.

Introduction

1. Readers of the Gospels will recognize this parable as an adaptation of Jesus's words about cups and graves in Matthew 23.
2. Obviously, the word *Christianity* is an important word in this book. In several of my earlier books, I avoided the term, wary of an abstraction that was too big and diverse to define. Some people speak of *Christianities,* suggesting that very different and even contradictory projects are included under the same name. That is no doubt true.

For our purposes here, *Christianity* simply means the family of diverse religious traditions based or centered on the life and teachings of Jesus. Many Christian traditions will prefer, no doubt, to remain right where they are, resolutely resisting the migration explored in this book, but others will hear in this call to migration an invitation to be more truly Christian.

3. In "Recasting Inerrancy: The Bible as Witness to Missional Plurality," John Franke helpfully describes what I mean by "system of beliefs": "a series of systematically arranged assertions" that "codify" the meaning of Christian faith and "then function as the only proper interpretive grid through which we read the Bible" (*Five Views on Biblical Inerrancy* [Grand Rapids, MI: Zondervan, 2013], pp. 259–87).

4. For more on the authoritarian father versus nurturing parent, see the work of George Lakoff, starting here: http://georgelakoff .com/2011/02/19/what-conservatives-really-want/.

5. Rev. Otis Moss III made a related observation in *Blue Note Preaching in a Post-Soul World* (Louisville, KY: Westminster John Knox, 2015, p. 4): "The church is becoming a place where Christianity is nothing more than capitalism in drag."

6. As I was writing this book, a new study reported the latest data on American religious life: http://www.pewforum.org/2015/05/12/ americas-changing-religious-landscape/.

7. Many thanks to Diana Butler Bass for this apt turn of phrase.

8. *A New Kind of Christian, A New Kind of Christianity, A Generous Orthodoxy, Finding Our Way Again, Naked Spirituality, We Make the Road by Walking.* The titles of books by my colleagues tell a similar story: *The Great Emergence, Flipped, Jesus Wants to Save Christians, The New Christians, Post-Traumatic Church Syndrome, The Future of Faith, Searching for Sunday, Christianity After Religion, Christianity for the Rest of Us,* and *Water to Wine,* by Phyllis Tickle, Doug Pagitt, Rob Bell and Don Golden, Tony Jones, Reba Riley, Harvey Cox, Rachel Held Evans, Diana Butler Bass (two titles), and Brian Zahnd, respectively.

9. Much of what I've written so far resonates, nearly a hundred years later, with a sermon preached by Harry Emerson Fosdick at Manhattan's Riverside Church, *Shall the Fundamentalists Win?,* http:// baptiststudiesonline.com/wp-content/uploads/2007/01/shall-the

-fundamentalists-win.pdf. What Fosdick said then I believe is still true today: "We should not identify the Fundamentalists with the conservatives. All Fundamentalists are conservatives, but not all conservatives are Fundamentalists. The best conservatives can often give lessons to the liberals in true liberality of spirit, but the Fundamentalist program is essentially illiberal and intolerant." A century of hard work by passionately committed fundamentalists has made our situation even more ugly and dire, and the need for a more vigorous, constructive response even more urgent. We might say that in many sectors of both Protestantism and Catholicism, the fundamentalists have indeed won, or very nearly so, which creates the need for a book like this.

10. It's worth noting that Jude did not say, "Contend for the belief system once delivered to the saints." *Faith* and *belief systems,* it turns out, are quite different things, as we'll see in chapters 1 and 2, and in appendix III.

11. For a balanced assessment of Constantine, see Justo González, *The Story of Christianity* (Peabody, MA: Prince Press, 2001), chapter 13. See also Diarmaid MacCulloch, *Christianity: The First Three Thousand Years* (New York: Viking, 2010), chapter 6.

12. For more on Christian anti-Semitism, see James Carroll, *Constantine's Sword* (New York: Mariner, 2002). For more on the Crusades, see MacCulloch, *Christianity,* chapter 14.

13. See Toby Green, *Inquisition* (New York: Thomas Dunne, 2009). For details on the use of torture, including graphic images of torture devices used by inquisitors, see Kenneth Gambin, *Torture and the Roman Inquisition* (Santa Venera, Malta: Midsea, 2004).

14. Surprisingly little theological scholarship has been solely devoted to the Doctrine of Discovery and its global impact, although several books address the doctrine's impact on Native American rights in the United States. Several groups are currently asking the pope to rescind and apologize for the doctrine. For more on this subject, see chapter 4, along with https://en.wikipedia.org/wiki/Discovery_doctrine and http://wirelesshogan.blogspot.com/2014/12/doctrine-of-discovery.html.

15. For a contemporary critique of ways the Bible has been used for these ugly purposes, see Mae Elise Cannon, Lisa Sharon Harper, Troy Jackson, and Soong-Chan Rah, *Forgive Us* (Grand Rapids, MI:

Zondervan, 2014); Derek Flood, *Disarming Scripture* (San Francisco: Metanoia, 2014); Peter Enns, *The Bible Tells Me So* (San Francisco: HarperOne, 2014); Brian Zahnd, *Water to Wine* (Spello, 2016); and my book *A New Kind of Christianity* (New York: HarperOne, 2011).

16. The quotation continues: "All conversion implies a break: 'Whoever loves father or mother more than me is not worthy of me' (Matt. 10:37). To wish to accomplish it without conflict is to deceive oneself and others. . . . We have to break with our mental categories, with the way we relate to others, with our way of identifying with the Lord, with our cultural milieu, with our social class, in other words, with all that can stand in the way of a real, profound solidarity with those who suffer, in the first place, from misery and injustice. Only through this, and not through purely interior and spiritual attitudes, will the 'new person' arise from the ashes of the 'old'" (*Gustavo Gutiérrez: Spiritual Writings* [Maryknoll, NY: Orbis, 2011], p. 48).

17. Here is Thesis 1: "When our Lord and Master, Jesus Christ, said 'Repent', He called for the entire life of believers to be one of repentance." On the close relationship between repentance and conversion, see Acts 3:19.

18. Maajid Nawaz, *Radical: My Journey Out of Islamist Extremism* (Guilford, CT: Lyons Press, 2013).

19. I should clarify that I do not believe belief-system Christianity will collapse. If anything, I expect a robust resurgence of fundamentalist streams within Catholicism, Protestantism, and Eastern Orthodoxy in the coming decades. (Times of rapid and ambiguous change frequently energize fundamentalist movements.) But I believe that millions of Christians across these traditions will experience a collapse of their own internal form of belief-system Christianity, along the lines of my own experience described here. Belief-system Christianity will, in other words, no longer be a viable personal option *for them*.

CHAPTER 1: CRISIS BY THE PALO VERDE TREE

1. See Matthew 7:16; John 15:12; John 13:34–35. Unless otherwise noted, the New Revised Standard Version (NRSV) is quoted in the text.

2. See 1 Corinthians 13:1–3.

3. See James 1:27.

4. See 1 John 4:8.
5. See appendix III for more on beliefs.
6. It's important to note that I do not believe "enter the kingdom of God" means "go to heaven when you die." We will explore "kingdom of God" in more detail in chapter 7.
7. *A New Kind of Christianity* (New York: HarperOne, 2011).
8. For more on beliefs, see appendix III.
9. Doug Pagitt uses the apt word *flipped* to describe this kind of unexpected paradigm shift; see *Flipped* (New York: Convergent Books, 2015).
10. Reba Riley uses similar language in *Post-Traumatic Church Syndrome* (New York: Howard, 2015): "Did the beliefs my parents taught me about God, the ones that were stacked one on top of another Jenga-style, have to be destroyed so something stronger could take their place?"
11. This willingness of Gospel writers to creatively relocate and adapt events shows why literalistic readings of the Bible are so inappropriate. They try to reduce the ancient tradition of spiritual storytelling to the modern constraints of journalism or historiography. I address this subject in my book *We Make the Road by Walking* (New York: Jericho, 2014) and we'll come back to it in greater depth in chapter 6.
12. On this subject of sacrifice, see chapters 13 and 23 of my book *Why Did Jesus, Moses, the Buddha, and Mohammed Cross the Road?* (New York: Jericho, 2012). There I reference the seminal anthropological work of René Girard, which is being theologically interpreted in highly provocative ways by James Alison, Suzanne Ross, Paul Nuechterlein, Michael Hardin, Dorothy Winston, Sharon Putt, and others.
13. For many people, *prophetic* means being preoccupied with predictions about the future. But prophets in the Scriptures are actually focused on telling the truth about injustice in the present, often through stories about the past or warnings about the future.
14. Father Richard Rohr explains, "Ironically, a prophet must be educated inside the system in order to have the freedom to critique that very system. You have to know the rules of any tradition, and you have to respect those rules enough to know why they do exist—and thus *how to break them properly, for the sake of a larger and more essential value.* This is what Martin Luther King Jr. taught America and

what Gandhi taught the British. Here is the key: you can only un-
lock systems from the inside. A prophet critiques a system by quoting
its own documents, constitutions, heroes, and Scriptures against its
present practice. That's why they eventually win, but at a huge price
to themselves" ("Prophets Then, Prophets Now" and "Scripture
as Liberation," http://store.cac.org/Prophets-Then-Prophets-Now
-CD_p_113.html).

15. For an example of Jesus pitting the prophetic tradition against the
scholastic/priestly tradition, see Matthew 23.

16. It's important for this section not to be read as a rejection of the
scholastic/priestly tradition. The pastoral care of hundreds of millions of human beings is in the hands of priests and scholars, and
their work as institutional leaders is absolutely essential. But for their
work to remain vital over time, they need to be in a productive relationship with the mystical/poetic and prophetic traditions, as will be
explained in some detail in chapters 7–10.

17. For decades, Father Richard Rohr has been a prime evangelist calling for a great spiritual migration in Christianity. His daily e-mails
articulate and encourage this migration in many ways. The following piece, published on January 8, 2015, articulates the Franciscan
concept of alternative orthodoxy:

> Most Christian churches have spent an awful lot of time con-
> cerned about maintaining verbal and ritual orthodoxy—the of-
> ficial doctrines and liturgies. . . . We must be honest and admit
> that it has focused much less on the practicals of the Sermon on
> the Mount or what Jesus spent most of his time doing: touching
> and healing people, doing acts of justice and inclusion, teaching
> and living ways of compassion and non-violence.
>
> Franciscanism, insofar as it actually imitated Francis of Assisi,
> emphasized . . . a different view on what really matters, which
> had much more to do with orthopraxy (right practice) than
> merely believing the right words. (Read Jesus' parable about the
> two sons where he makes this same point in Luke 21:28–32.)
> While not rejecting the traditional orthodoxy of the church, the
> Franciscan "alternative orthodoxy" was a parachurch viewpoint
> on the edge of the inside of organized Christianity. It often seems
> this is where wisdom has to hide, as Proverbs says, "Wisdom

builds herself a house" (9:1). . . . Franciscanism's offering, similar to the Quakers, Shakers, Amish, and Mennonites, was a simple return to *lifestyle itself*.

Rohr even quotes Thomas Aquinas, the paragon of traditional orthodoxy, to make the point: "The alternative orthodoxy is a phrase that the Franciscan tradition has applied to itself. At its core, the alternative orthodoxy is an 'orthopraxy' believing that lifestyle and practice are much more important than mere verbal orthodoxy. (*Prius vita quam doctrina,* 'life is more important than doctrine,' says Thomas Aquinas, *Summa Theologica,* 'De Anima', II, 37.)" See https://cac.org/rohr-inst/ls-introduction/ls-orthodoxy and https://cac .org/living-school/program-details/the-franciscan-alternative -orthodoxy/. For more, see https://www.youtube.com/watch? v=A9Azd93Luko.

18. Adapted from Richard Rohr, *Eager to Love: The Alternative Way of Francis of Assisi* (Cincinnati, OH: Franciscan Media, 2014), pp. 52–53, 81, 86–87. See also "The Franciscan Way: Just Do It," June 25, 2015, http://myemail.constantcontact.com/Richard-Rohr-s-Meditation-- Just-Do-It.html?soid=110309866861&aid=EaWLHfqvA4l.

19. Harvey Cox, *The Future of Faith* (New York: HarperOne, 2010).

20. For more on human evolution, biological and cultural, see Robert Wright, *Nonzero: The Logic of Human Destiny* (New York: Vintage, 2001).

21. Even compliance tests that focus on practice and ritual—infant baptism versus believers' baptism, for example—derive their power from beliefs about the meaning and purpose of the ritual or practice.

Chapter 2: A Deeper Loyalty

1. Writer, comedian, and actor John Cleese captured this idea in a tweet: "I would like 2016 to be the year when people remembered that science is a method of investigation, and NOT a belief system" (@JohnCleese, 1/3/16).

2. This traditional method is defined succinctly by Father William G. Most: "A 'theologian' who would claim he needs to be able to ignore the Magisterium in order to find the truth is strangely perverse: the teaching of the Magisterium is the prime, God-given means of finding the truth. Nor could he claim academic freedom lets him

contradict the Church. In any field of knowledge, academic freedom belongs only to a properly qualified professor teaching in his own field. But one is not properly qualified if he does not use the correct method of working in his field, e.g., a science professor who would want to go back to medieval methods would be laughed off campus, not protected. Now in Catholic theology, the correct method is to study the sources of revelation, but then give the final word to the Church. He who does not follow that method is not a qualified Catholic theologian" (https://www.ewtn.com/faith/teachings/chura4.htm).

3. In late 2015, a group of Catholic activists published *The Telling Takes Us Home* (Catholic Committee of Appalachia), http://www.ccappal.org/thetellingtakesushome2015.pdf. One section is entitled "The Magisterium of the Poor and of the Earth," suggesting a migration among some Catholics regarding what I here call "the Catholic method." They explain, "Official pronouncements and projects have not always helped us to hear these voices [of the poor and of the earth]. But we remember the deep, Biblical truth that the voice of God does not come from high places and halls of power but rather in the still, small voices of the least of our sisters and brothers" (pp. 7–8).

4. Although Martin Luther wrote *On the Freedom of a Christian* in 1520, his tolerance for the questioning of authority decreased markedly the longer he was the one in authority.

5. Ironically, to defend the doctrine of the inerrancy of the Bible, its defenders have very little data in the Bible to draw upon, and they must ignore mountains of biblical evidence to the contrary, as Derek Flood and Peter Enns have made so clear in their recent books *Disarming Scripture* (San Francisco: Metanoia, 2014) and *The Bible Tells Me So* (San Francisco: HarperOne, 2014). I addressed this subject as well in my book *A New Kind of Christianity* (New York: HarperOne, 2010), chapters 4–9.

6. Such claims seem all the more ludicrous when those making them have been involved in cover-ups of pedophilia, for example, or thinly veiled defenses of bigotry.

7. Just as religion can be corrupted through money, political pressure, and personal and institutional ego, so too, of course, can science.

8. The exception, of course, is in conservative religious communities. Because a long series of scientific findings have called many religious

beliefs into question over the last few centuries, many conservative believers have responded with skepticism about science, seeing it as a threat to their faith. As a result, 37 to 42 percent of Americans don't believe in the theory of evolution (see http://www.theatlantic.com/national/archive/2014/11/you-cant-educate-people-into-believing-in-evolution/382983/), and conservative Christians are among the most resistant to scientific data about global warming (see http://www.slate.com/articles/health_and_science/climate_desk/2014/05/conservative_christians_and_climate_change_five_arguments_for_why_one_should.html).

9. Dalai Lama XIV, *The Universe in a Single Atom: The Convergence of Science and Spirituality* (New York: Harmony, 2006), p. 3. Interestingly, in September 2012, the Dalai Lama sent this message to his Facebook followers: "All the world's major religions, with their emphasis on love, compassion, patience, tolerance, and forgiveness can and do promote inner values. But the reality of the world today is that grounding ethics in religion is no longer adequate. This is why I am increasingly convinced that the time has come to find a way of thinking about spirituality and ethics beyond religion altogether." The Dalai Lama may have been grappling with exactly the problem of religious credibility we are addressing in this chapter.

10. I should add here that I know some people who have created strong and sustainable families in this context. But I know others who found such an arrangement impossible and destructive to sustain, as the next paragraph illustrates.

11. The word *perfect* could be better translated as *mature* or *fully formed*.

12. On nonviolence, see John Dear, *The Nonviolent Life* (Athens, OH: Pace e Bene Press, 2013).

13. Today, many of us focus more on rules about belief than rules about diet, Sabbath, or clothing.

14. Again, while many Christians today would focus on correctness of *beliefs* in conformity to the demands of their religion (often using Paul's writings as their standard), Paul in the first half of his life focused on correctness of *behavior* in conformity to the demands of his religion (Philippians 3:4–7). For many Christians, the good news is that it's easier to achieve and maintain correct beliefs than correct behavior, and God is willing to let correct beliefs trump incorrect behavior by making grace contingent on the former rather than

the latter. Belief-based grace may indeed be easier for some than behavior-based grace, but for others, consenting to beliefs to earn a blessing feels like hypocrisy and dishonesty. Not only that, but I would argue that whenever grace is conditional or based on a requirement, whether a requirement of behavior or belief, it is no longer grace.

15. For more on this subject, see Peter Enns, *The Sin of Certainty* (San Francisco: HarperOne, 2016).

16. See appendix III for more on beliefs.

17. On faith, hope, and charity as conviction, confidence, and love, see Alain Badiou, *Saint Paul: The Foundation of Universalism* (Stanford, CA: Stanford University Press, 2003), p. 15.

18. Although creation should be cherished for its essential and inherent value, it also must be loved as a by-product of loving your neighbor. If you love your neighbor, you don't pollute the stream from which she drinks. If you love your neighbor, you don't heat up the climate in which she lives. If you love your neighbor, you don't rob from her children and grandchildren the beauty and companionship of diverse ecosystems and endangered species.

Chapter 3: Learning How to Love

1. For more, see http://www.stmarksmarco.org/ and http://www.campable.org/.

2. In early 2016, they replaced this description with one that begins, "EastLake is an inclusive Christian community where faith is less about a story to be believed as it is a life to be lived." They then identify love as their "supreme value," along the lines advocated in this chapter.

3. See, for example, the Certificate in Engaged Compassion offered by Triptykos, http://www.triptykos.com/events-and-courses. Or see Gary Chapman's highly practical guidance in *The 5 Love Languages* (Chicago: Northfield, 2004) and *Love as a Way of Life* (WaterBrook, 2009). See also Susie Albert Miller's *Listen, Learn, Love* (Dunham Books, 2015) and the work of David Kyuman Kim and the Love-Driven Politics Collective, starting with http://meaningoflife.tv/programs/love-driven-politics/.

4. The new presiding bishop of the Episcopal Church in the United

States repeatedly speaks of his denomination as "the Episcopal branch of the Jesus Movement." This linking of a church institution with a larger movement will be discussed in more detail in chapters 7–9.

5. For more on "just and generous communities," see the Convergence Network, http://www.convergenceus.org.

6. For more on the church as a school or dojo of love, see Mark Scandrette, *Practicing the Way of Jesus* (Downers Grove, IL: IVP, 2011) and *Soul Graffiti* (San Francisco: Jossey-Bass, 2007). See also Roger D. Joslin's *School of Love: Planting a Church in the Shadow of Empire* (New York: Morehouse, 2015). Like Mark's books, *School of Love* beautifully embodies the spirit I am trying to convey in these pages.

7. Gustavo Gutiérrez said it like this: "Bonhoeffer was right when he said that the only credible God is the God of the mystics. But this is not a God unrelated to human history. On the contrary, if it is true that one must go through humankind to reach God, it is equally certain that the 'passing through' to that gratuitous God strips me, leaves me naked, universalizes my love for others, and makes it gratuitous. Both movements need each other dialectically and move toward a synthesis. This synthesis is found in Christ; in the God-Man we encounter God and humankind. In Christ humankind gives God a human countenance and God gives it a divine countenance. Only in this perspective will we be able to understand that the 'union with the Lord,' which all spirituality proclaims, is not a separation from others; to attain this union, I must go through others, and the union, in turn, enables me to encounter others more fully" (*Spiritual Writings* [Maryknoll, NY: Orbis, 2011], p. 50).

8. Gary Chapman, most famous for his practical and helpful book *The 5 Love Languages,* has articulated seven key components of love in *Love as a Way of Life*: kindness, patience, forgiveness, courtesy, humility, generosity, and honesty.

9. Again, Gutiérrez powerfully captures this conversion to solidarity: "A spirituality of liberation will center on a *conversion* to the neighbor, the oppressed person, the exploited social class, the despised ethnic group, the dominated country. Our conversion to the Lord implies this conversion to the neighbor.... To be converted is to commit oneself lucidly, realistically, and concretely to the process of the liberation of the poor and oppressed.... To be converted is to know and experience the fact that, contrary to the laws of physics, we

can stand straight, according to the Gospel, only when our center of gravity is outside ourselves" (*Spiritual Writings,* p. 48).

10. Bernard of Clairvaux described a process whereby we begin loving self for self's sake, then we love God for self's sake, then love God for God's sake, and then love self for God's sake. For more, see http://www.soulshepherding.org/2013/08/bernard-of-clairvauxs-four-degrees-of-love/.

11. A quotation attributed to Albert Einstein captures this sense of connection to all creation: "A human being is a part of the whole called by us universe, a part limited in time and space. He experiences himself, his thoughts and feeling as something separated from the rest, a kind of optical delusion of his consciousness. This delusion is a kind of prison for us, restricting us to our personal desires and to affection for a few persons nearest to us. Our task must be to free ourselves from this prison by widening our circle of compassion to embrace all living creatures and the whole of nature in its beauty."

12. See https://www.facebook.com/permalink.php?story_fbid=1015373 9834242990&id=65814657989.

13. Fyodor Dostoevsky, *The Brothers Karamazov,* trans. Richard Pevear and Larissa Volokhonsky (New York: North Point Press, 1990), p. 319.

14. See appendices I and II for examples of ways that congregations can announce this intention. Becoming one of the ten thousand congregations in the Convergence Network is another way to make this kind of announcement; see http://www.convergenceus.org.

15. I define *ritual* as using a repeatable bodily action to bond to meaning and joy, and I define *ritualism* as repeating the action without the meaning and joy.

16. During the contentious 2016 campaign for the presidency of the United States, Presbyterian pastor Rev. Robert Cunningham wrote perceptively about the relative power of beliefs and love in forming people spiritually and politically: ". . . what if evangelicals (or any tribe, for that matter) aren't primarily compelled by what they believe but instead by what they love? In fact, what if every one of us will gladly repudiate what we believe before we would ever repudiate what we love? . . . What happens when the liturgies of our greedy culture train evangelicals to love money and power? What happens when the liturgies of talk radio train evangelicals to love anger and paranoia? What happens when the liturgies of social media train

evangelicals to love sensational sound bites more than thoughtful discourse? What happens when the liturgies of modern worship services train evangelicals to love novel, flashy, and glib emotional experiences that feel more like a rally than corporate worship? What happens when the conference culture of the church trains evangelicals to love the big celebrity leader? What happens when preaching that prioritizes relevant, shocking, and brash sermons trains evangelicals to love 'tell it like it is' ranting? What happens when the liturgies from the days of the Moral Majority train evangelicals to love America as much as Jesus, which then leads to an incessant longing within churches to 'make America great again!' What happens? Evangelicals in love with Donald Trump happens." The whole article is available here: http://tcpca.org/2016/03/17/in-love-with-donald -trump/.

17. The "five fundamentals" and "thirty-nine articles" are statements of the core beliefs of fundamentalism and the Church of England, respectively. The fourteen qualities of love listed in 1 Corinthians 13 include

1. Love is essential: without it, nothing else matters.

2. Love is patient.

3. Love is kind.

4. Love is generous, not envious.

5. Love is appreciative of others, not boastful of self.

6. Love is humble, not arrogant.

7. Love is courteous, not rude.

8. Love is flexible; it does not insist on its own way.

9. Love is gracious, not irritable.

10. Love is merciful, not resentful.

11. Love is positive: it does not rejoice in wrongdoing, but rejoices in the truth.

12. Love is resilient: bearing, believing, hoping, and enduring all things.

13. Love is perpetual: it never ends and never goes out of style.

14. Love is supreme, even greater than faith and hope.

18. Bryan Sirchio, in the song "Follow Me (87 Times)"; see http://sirchio .com.

19. Progressive mainline Protestants are often perplexed by the growth of their conservative Evangelical counterparts over the last several

decades. Evangelicals often attribute this growth to their conservative theology, but I suspect their growth had other primary sources, including this: many Evangelical pastors focused their messages on the practical skills and daily practices of love, especially in the family, but also in the Christian community. Progressive critics may complain that Evangelicals didn't sufficiently emphasize love of the stranger, alien, refugee, racially and sexually other, or enemy. That was often the case, but instead of complaining about the omission, these critics would be wiser to imitate and expand upon their Evangelical counterparts' positive though incomplete example of teaching the practical how-tos of Christian love.

20. One good source for consultants working in this framework would be the Center for Progressive Renewal (www.progressiverenewal .org). Church leaders developing love curricula will ask questions like these: What does a loving person look like in today's world? How does love manifest differently in different personality types, different cultures, different economies, different political systems, and at different stages in life? How do parents teach their children the habits, skills, and practices of love? What love lessons are appropriate for toddlers, young children, preteens, teenagers, young adults, engaged couples, married couples, young parents, parents of teens, parents of adults, grandparents, widows and widowers? How do we help people learn the special skills of love evoked by people with diverse abilities and special needs, from autistic children to elderly folk with dementia? What does it mean to love strangers, outsiders, outcasts, and enemies in our specific context? What is the state of the art in compassion and nonviolence training, and how can these trainings be more widely disseminated? How does one process feelings of anger, prejudice, revenge, fear, resentment, or exhaustion—and move toward love? How do we develop appropriate love for animals, plants, and inanimate creation? What music, rituals, prayers, creeds, and daily contemplative and other spiritual practices would contribute to the development of loving people? When people wander from the ways of love, how do we most effectively bring them back? What kind of training—in or out of seminaries—would equip people to become great principals or master teachers in schools of love around the world?

CHAPTER 4: THE GENOCIDE CARD IN YOUR BACK POCKET

1. See his book *Why Christianity Must Change or Die* (New York: HarperOne, 1999).

2. I detailed several Christian beliefs that have been used to harm and kill others in *Why Did Jesus, Moses, the Buddha, and Mohammed Cross the Road?* (New York: Jericho, 2012). I also explored ways in which those doctrines (including original sin, the Trinity, election) could be disarmed and converted into "healing teachings."

3. For more on this subject, see my book *Why Did Jesus, Moses, the Buddha, and Mohammed Cross the Road?* and these websites: http://www .journeywithjesus.net/Essays/20120709JJ.shtml, http://www.patheos .com/blogs/rogereolson/2013/07/every-known-theistic-approach-to -old-testament-texts-of-terror/, and http://www.girardianlectionary .net.

4. See the work of Sharon Putt, Michael Hardin, Derek Flood, Peter Enns, John Dominic Crossan, Brad Jersak, John Dear, and Brian Zahnd, among others, for important contributions on Christian non-violence and the disarming of Scripture.

5. Edited by Steve Heinrichs (Harrisonburg, VA: Herald Press, 2013).

6. Used with the author's permission. In later drafts, this paragraph was softened. In fact, I understand that the editor had to fight to keep the chapter in at all because of fears that even in its softened form it was too critical of Christianity. You can hear Waziyatawin online in several places, including https://www.youtube.com/watch?v=S -EhBOmOvRs.

7. See James Carroll, *Constantine's Sword* (New York: Mariner, 2002).

8. On this and other areas of Christian failure, see Mae Elise Cannon, Lisa Sharon Harper, Troy Jackson, and Soong-Chan Rah, *Forgive Us: Confessions of a Compromised Faith* (Grand Rapids, MI: Zondervan, 2014). This powerful and needed book explores in greater detail subjects that I am only mentioning in this chapter.

9. See Harvey Cox, *The Future of Faith* (New York: HarperOne, 2010). It would be better said that Constantine converted Christianity to the values and mission of the Roman Empire than to say the reverse.

10. See Brian Zahnd, *A Farewell to Mars* (Colorado Springs, CO: David C. Cook, 2014); Brad Jersak, *A More Christlike God* (Printed

by CreateSpace, 2015); and Derek Flood, *Disarming Scripture* (San Francisco: Metanoia, 2014).

11. I first addressed this subject in chapter 18 of *A Generous Orthodoxy* (Grand Rapids, MI: Zondervan, 2005) and later in chapter 9 of *Why Did Jesus, Moses, the Buddha, and Mohammed Cross the Road?* Much more needs to be said and done regarding this catastrophic age of atrocities in the history of Christianity.

12. To read the entire papal proclamation, see http://self.gutenberg.org/articles/romanus_pontifex. The original statement was addressed specifically to King Afonso V of Portugal, but taken in concert with other papal proclamations (especially Dum Diversas and Inter Caetera), it legitimized an age of atrocities for all the Christian kings of Europe during the so-called Age of Discovery.

13. For more, see http://archive.adl.org/education/curriculum_connections/doctrine_of_discovery.html.

14. In places like Rwanda and Burundi, nonwhites imitated their white Christian colonial oppressors and learned to use the card as well in intertribal conflict. In places like Uganda, it is still being used against sexual minorities.

15. For more on the untold story of Columbus, see Thom Hartmann, *The Last Hours of Ancient Sunlight* (New York: Broadway Books, 2004), pp. 50ff. See also my *Why Did Jesus, Moses, the Buddha, and Mohammed Cross the Road?* (New York: Jericho, 2012), chapters 9–11.

16. Bartolomé de las Casas, *The Devastation of the Indies: A Brief Account,* trans. Herma Briffault (Baltimore: Johns Hopkins University Press, 1992), p. 117. The document is also available here: https://www.asdk12.org/staff/bivins_rick/HOMEWORK/216236_Las Casas_TheDevast.pdf, and period illustrations are available here: http://nationalhumanitiescenter.org/pds/amerbegin/contact/text7/casas_destruction.pdf.

17. Ibid., pp. 33–34. The resonances with contemporary terrorism among groups like ISIS or Daesh, al-Qaeda, and Boko Haram are chilling indeed.

18. Ibid., p. 31.

19. Ibid., p. 30. Of his own motivations, Bartolomé explained, "Seeing all of this, I was moved, not because I was a better Christian than anyone else, but by a natural feeling of compassion which I had at seeing a people suffer terrible oppression and injustice, who did not

deserve it." See Paul Vickery, *Bartolomé de las Casas: Great Prophet of the Americas* (Newman Press, 2006). *Bartolomé*'s reference to a "natural feeling of compassion" resonates with the primacy of love we considered in chapters 1 through 3. His biographers call his decision to stand for the indigenous peoples his "second conversion." For more, see Vickery.

20. The full text of the Requerimiento is available in English translation here: https://en.wikipedia.org/wiki/Requerimiento.

21. Waziyatawin, in *Buffalo Shout, Salmon Cry,* edited by Steve Heinrichs (Harrisonburg, VA: Herald Press, 2013), p. 211. My response to Waziyatawin's chapter, written in the form of a prayer of lament, can be found on pp. 225–28.

22. I am deeply indebted to Mark Charles for educating me on the Doctrine of Discovery. An account of our relationship can be found here: http://wirelesshogan.blogspot.com/2016/03/an-invitation-to-risk.html. For more on Mark Charles and his important work, see http://wirelesshogan.com.

23. People of the Navajo, Chickasaw, Shawnee, Lenape, Osage, Kickapoo, Choctaw, Seminole, Creek, Sauk, Fox, and Dakota tribes suffered similarly horrific atrocities.

24. Ned Blackhawk, "Remember the Sand Creek Massacre," http://www.nytimes.com/2014/11/28/opinion/remember-the-sand-creek-massacre.html?_r=0.

25. See, for example, https://www.americanprogress.org/issues/civil-liberties/news/2015/09/02/120437/voting-rights-advocates-turn-to-north-carolina-courts-stacked-by-campaign-cash/.

26. For more on this subject, see James W. Loewen, *Lies My Teacher Told Me: Everything Your American History Textbook Got Wrong* (New York: New Press, 2008).

27. Yolanda Pierce, "When Our Truths Are Ignored: Proslavery Theology's Legacy," *Religion & Politics,* August 10, 2015, http://religionandpolitics.org/2015/08/10/when-our-truths-are-ignored-proslavery-theologys-legacy/.

28. See chapter 6 for more on this important subject.

29. The Mason-Dixon Line became the symbolic dividing line between the North and South during the Civil War.

30. See the papal encyclical *Laudato Si,* https://laudatosi.com/watch. In speaking of "the cry of the earth and cry of the poor," Pope Francis

is echoing the brilliant Brazilian theologian Leonardo Boff, who was silenced by Francis's predecessor.

CHAPTER 5: GOD 5.0

1. It's worth noting that many scholars agree this passage is actually the lyric of our earliest extant Christian hymn, a proposal that, if true, highlights its importance even more.

2. The donkey is especially significant because of its allusion to Zechariah 9:9–10, where it is contrasted to the warhorse.

3. See Luke 22:25–27.

4. As "homebrewed theologian" Tripp Fuller playfully says, it doesn't matter whether cooties literally exist. If they define the terms of engagement on the playground, they are real enough. See http://home brewedchristianity.com.

5. This 1.0–5.0 schema is offered here as a playful rhetorical device, not a serious developmental theory. For a more sophisticated understanding of moral, intellectual, and spiritual development, see the work of Lawrence Kohlberg, William G. Perry Jr., and James W. Fowler III. See also Jonathan Haidt's *The Righteous Mind* (New York: Pantheon, 2012); the work of integral theory and cultural evolution associated with Ken Wilber, Don Beck, Steve McIntosh, and others; and Joshua Greene's *Moral Tribes* (New York: Penguin Press, 2013). I offer a synthesis of developmental theory in a four-stage schema (simplicity, complexity, perplexity, and harmony) in my book *Naked Spirituality* (New York: HarperOne, 2012). And for a related schema for stages of development in the Christian church, see John Dorhauer, *Beyond Resistance* (Chicago: Exploration Press, 2015).

6. Some people think South Africa was our evolutionary "garden of Eden," and others think it was somewhere in modern Ethiopia.

7. This accounting of our ancestral past emphasizes intertribal violence. Intragroup rivalry, anxiety, and hostility were also a significant factor in our social development, a subject explored in great depth by René Girard and other advocates of *mimetic theory*. For an introduction to Girard's theory, see James Warren's *Compassion or Apocalypse?* (Christian Alternative, 2013).

8. For a fuller macrohistorical perspective, see Jared Diamond's *Guns,*

Germs, and Steel (New York: Norton, 1999) and Robert Wright's *Nonzero: The Logic of Human Destiny* (New York: Vintage, 2001).

9. About twelve thousand years ago has been the agreed-upon date for the birth of agriculture until recently, when evidence arose of primitive agriculture over twenty thousand years ago.

10. James Finley, *Jesus and Buddha: Paths to Awakening* (Center for Action and Contemplation, 2008), disc 2 (CD, DVD, MP3 download).

11. She is working on a book entitled "Go Deep, Get Naked, and Come Clean: Getting a Grown Up God."

12. The Lakota phrase *mitakuye oyasin* beautifully captures this sense of connectedness. It is also celebrated in Saint Francis's prayer *Laudato Si*.

13. In *Naked Spirituality,* I described four stages of the spiritual life: *simplicity, complexity, perplexity,* and *harmony.* God 1.0 and 2.0 roughly correspond with *simplicity,* and God 3.0 and 4.0 correspond with *complexity.* A loss of confidence in a belief system based on Gods 1.0 through 4.0 would correspond with *perplexity.* God 5.0, as described here, would be the God of *harmony.*

14. Many conservative churches tend to reject a proposal like God 5.0 before even considering it, simply on the basis of the proposal being deemed progressive rather than conservative. More liberal churches may appear to embrace such an idea, but their liturgies frequently encode 3.0 and 4.0 understandings in prayers, hymns, creeds, and rituals, thus undercutting their apparent openness. That's why I believe that new church developers, supported by songwriters and liturgists, along with developers of curricula for kids and youth, will have a primary role in making the actual emergence of God 5.0 possible. We need bold and creative experimenters to do research and development, along with rigorous evaluation to improve the effectiveness of our theological and spiritual formation endeavors.

CHAPTER 6: THE BIBLE IN LABOR

1. You'll notice that Lucy's short sermon contains one statement followed by six questions—a wise ratio to "make you think."

2. Contrary to what is often said, the situation isn't simply a tension between the "Old Testament God" being violent and the "New Testament God" being nonviolent. One can find support for both views of

God throughout both testaments. In fact, the whole Bible can be seen as a library containing documents that show different views of God interacting and evolving together, serving as an invaluable record of human theological development. In this light, the Bible should not be seen as a ceiling or road block inhibiting further progress, but rather as a launch pad or an open road from the past from which each generation launches into the future.

3. The theological term for my inherited orientation to the Bible is *biblicism,* defined by the theologian Peter Enns as follows: "the tendency to appeal to individual biblical verses, or collections of (apparently) uniform verses from various parts of the Bible, to give the appearance of clear, authoritative, and final resolutions to what are in fact complex interpretive and theological issues generated by the fact that we have a complex and diverse Bible." It is expressed in "a tendency to prooftext—where the 'plain sense' of verses are put forth as final and incontrovertible 'proof' of a given theological position." See http://www.patheos.com/blogs/peterenns/2015/06/what-biblicism -is-and-why-it-makes-baby-jesus-cry/.

4. Theologically astute readers will sense a resonance between my use of the word *literary* and the word *poetic* in the term *theopoetics.* For more on theopoetics, see http://theopoetics.net/what-is-theopoetics/ definitions/.

5. In my *A New Kind of Christian* trilogy (San Francisco: Jossey-Bass, 2001; *The Story We Find Ourselves In,* 2003; and *The Last Word and the Word After That,* 2005), I simply wrote of operating "above the line."

6. The term *second naïveté* is often associated with the twentieth-century philosopher Paul Ricoeur. See Dan Stiver's *Theology After Ricoeur* (Louisville, KY: Westiminster John Knox, 2001) for a helpful introduction to his work. Before Ricoeur, the American sage Oliver Wendell Holmes Jr. spoke of the *second simplicity* beyond complexity. And before Holmes, the Romantic poet William Blake spoke of a state of innocence followed by experience, after which one may encounter a state of second innocence or higher experience.

7. The monastic practice of *Lectio Divina* guides people into an innocent/literary approach to the text, and for this reason has been useful in helping many innocent literalists explore possibilities outside their accustomed box. I would also put preachers from the "positive thinking" genre, from Norman Vincent Peale to Joel Osteen, in this

innocent/literary zone. Strange bedfellows, perhaps, but they share the goal of personal inspiration rather than objective explanation.

8. Frederick Buechner has served many of us in a similar way. Like Lewis, he writes both nonfiction and fiction, demonstrating both critical and postcritical sensibilities. This quotation on the virgin birth beautifully illustrates Buechner's integral/literary approach: "The earliest of the four Gospels makes no reference to the virgin birth, and neither does Paul, who wrote earlier still. On later evidence, however, many Christians have made it an article of faith that it was the Holy Spirit rather than Joseph who got Mary pregnant. If you believe God was somehow in Christ, it shouldn't make much difference to you how he got there. If you don't believe, it should make less difference still. In either case, life is complicated enough without confusing theology and gynecology" (*Wishful Thinking* and *Beyond Words,* http://www.frederickbuechner.com/content/virgin-birth-0).

9. The term *texts in travail* is often associated with René Girard, and it may have originated with him. The Girardian theologian Paul Nuechterlein helpfully explains the term at http://girardianlectionary .net/learn/nuechterlein-bible-sacrifice/.

10. This language, of course, evokes the wisdom of Proverbs (11:14, 15:22). John Franke describes this approach in his helpful book, *Manifold Wisdom: The Plurality of Truth* (Nashville, TN: Abingdon, 2009).

11. In *We Make the Road by Walking* (New York: Jericho, 2014), I offer an integral/literary reading of the whole Bible in line with the insights of this chapter.

12. For more on this important subject, see Tony Jones, *Did God Kill Jesus?* (New York: HarperOne, 2015), and my book *A New Kind of Christianity* (New York: HarperOne, 2011), chapters 12–13.

13. See Derek Flood, *Disarming Scripture* (San Francisco: Metanoia, 2014).

CHAPTER 7: THAT BEAUTIFUL ROMANCE

1. I encountered this quotation through Diana Butler Bass, *Christianity After Religion* (New York: HarperOne, 2012) and *Grounded* (New York: HarperOne, 2015). It comes from David Buchdahl's 1974 doctoral dissertation, "American Realities: Anthropological Reflections

from the 'Counterculture,'" which is no longer in print. The quotation also appears in William G. McLoughlin's *Revivals, Awakenings, and Reform* (Chicago: University of Chicago Press, 1978), p. 215.

2. Gregory P. Leffel, *Faith Seeking Action* (Lanham, MD: Scarecrow Press, 2007).

3. Greg's fellow Kentuckian Wendell Berry defines a community as "the mental and spiritual condition of knowing that the place is shared, and that the people who share the place define and limit the possibilities of each other's lives. It is the knowledge that people have of each other, their concern for each other, their trust in each other, the freedom with which they come and go among themselves" ("The Loss of the Future," http://www.manasjournal.org/pdf_library/VolumeXXI_1968/XXI-47.pdf, p. 4).

4. Just as institutions can go awry, so can movements, as Wendell Berry explains in "In Distrust of Movements," http://www.arvindgupta toys.com/arvindgupta/WBerry.pdf. Social sickness also resides in communities, requiring movements and institutions to respond.

5. Here's how Greg explained the process in *Faith Seeking Action*: "Social movements are non-institutionally organized human collectives, that put meaningful ideas into play in public settings, that actively confront existing powers through the strength of their numbers and the influence of their ideas, and that grow in size and power by inspiring others to act, in order to create or resist change" (p. 48).

6. Ibid., p. 49.

7. For more on these dimensions of institutions and movements, see Hildy Gottlieb's article "Movements vs. Organizations," http://blogs.creatingthefuture.org/walkingthetalk/wp-content/uploads/2015/07/Movement-or-Organization-chart-form-07-24-15.pdf.

8. A pastor named Jim Dethmer proposed a similar three-part schema over twenty years ago: *community, cause* (movement dimension), and *corporation* (institutional dimension). For more see http://www.mark howelllive.com/community-cause-and-corporation/.

9. It comes as a surprise to many that the political polarization between liberal and conservative generally belies a deeper shared commitment to a civilization that is driven by the quest for maximum financial profit (corporate), dependent upon war (militaristic), dedicated to the rapid transformation of natural resources into waste (extractive/consumeristic), and aided by the complicity of the masses through

stage-managed elections that typically avoid the deepest and most consequential issues (democratic).

10. Its vulnerabilities include terrorist attacks (as occurred in 2001), economic bubbles and collapses (as occurred in 2008), social uprisings (such as the Arab Spring and Occupy movements in 2010 and 2011), political manipulation by economic elites (supported by the US Supreme Court's *Citizens United* ruling of 2010), cybercrime and hacking (frequently in the headlines), epidemics (like Ebola in 2014), and mass migrations of refugees (as seen in 2015). Movements that arise in response to these vulnerabilities may be creative and constructive; they may also be reactive and destructive.

11. The spiritual, theological, and missional migrations advocated in this book clearly represent "cosmopolitan" sensibilities. See the work of Namsoon Kang, especially *Cosmopolitan Theology* (Chalice Press, 2013).

12. See Jonathan Haidt's eighteen-minute lecture on moral argument at https://www.ted.com/talks/jonathan_haidt_on_the_moral_mind?language=en.

13. For example, if the Jesus Movement demanded that more churches add guitars and drums to worship, or allow more people to wear jeans and other casual clothing to services, it achieved great success. But was that all the movement stood for?

14. We spoke of eight levels of movement affiliation: *leaders* guide the movement by word and example; *core members* advise and support the leaders; *activists* work to achieve movement goals; *supporters* get behind the movement with financial and other resources; *listeners* are open to the movement's message and may eventually become more actively involved; *the opposition* speaks or organizes against the movement; *the indirectly impacted* include all who will be affected positively or negatively by the movement's success or failure; and *the unaware* do not yet know the movement exists.

15. For more on wounds suffered in religious organizations, see Teresa Pasquale, *Sacred Wounds* (St. Louis, MO: Chalice, 2015).

16. See Ezekiel 4 and Hosea 1–2.

17. See 1 Samuel 19 and http://www.educationanddemocracy.org/ED_FSC.html.

18. While I was completing this book, many observers were engaging in a new round of critical assessment of the religious right as

the presidential campaign of Donald Trump disrupted the co-alitions it developed over decades. For two especially insightful analyses of this disruption, see http://tcpca.org/2016/03/17/in-love -with-donald-trump/ and http://www.vox.com/2016/3/1/11127424/ trump-authoritarianism.

19. http://www.huffingtonpost.com/fr-richard-rohr/reflections-on-a -new-face_b_2885215.html.

20. American Christianity is not the only source of a right-wing agenda. I've encountered right-wing Korean Christianity, right-wing Ni-gerian Christianity, and other right-wing versions of Christianity as well, each a reflection of issues we have addressed in previous chapters—a boxed-in version of God, a priestly "law and order" spirit that is opposed to a prophetic "peace and justice" spirit, a weak-ness for demagoguery, and so on.

CHAPTER 8: SALVATION FROM THE SUICIDE MACHINE

1. Paraphrased from Matthew 16:25.

2. Brian D. McLaren, *Everything Must Change* (Nashville, TN: Thomas Nelson, 2009), p. 130.

3. Herman E. Daly, *Steady-State Economics* (Washington, DC: Island Press, 1991), p. 248.

4. It has been said that we Americans write "In God We Trust" upon the god in whom we actually trust: the Almighty Dollar.

5. For a powerful analysis of educational institutions in this light, see Peter McLaren (no relation), *Pedagogy of Insurrection* (New York: Peter Lang Publishing, 2015).

6. Mark Anspach, "Desired Possessions," http://static1.squarespace .com/static/55a55b50e4b08015467323fc/t/565f46c9e4b0aca7d4243290 /1449084617531/Anspach-2004.pdf, p. 187.

7. It has been unfashionable in economics circles to acknowledge lim-its to growth, including limits to available fossil fuels. Thomas Mal-thus, who originated the idea of limits to growth in 1798, is often mocked. But as Herman Daly has said, "Malthus has been buried many times ... but ... anyone who has to be reburied so often can-not be entirely dead" (*Steady-State Economics,* p. 43).

8. See *Laudato Si,* his encyclical on the environment, https://laudatosi .com/watch.

9. See *Christianity After Religion* (New York: HarperOne, 2012) and *Grounded* (New York: HarperOne, 2015).

10. In the United States, we would add "American (over non-American)." The long-standing tradition of American exceptionalism should, in this light, be seen for what it actually is: a euphemism for a nationalistic version of white supremacy.

11. Thanks to Carolyn and Fuzz Kitto from Australia for their work in organizing this international gathering. For more on their work, see http://spirited.com.au/. Thanks also to Ash and Angi Barker who led our adventures in Thailand. For more on their current work in the UK, see http://www.urbanlifetogether.org/.

12. See www.mesa-friends.org.

13. See appendix I.

14. For example, conservatives bring high confidence in business as a solution to human problems. Liberals bring high confidence in democratic government as a solution to human problems. The problems we face are so significant that we will need both ethical business and democratic government solutions, inviting both conservatives and liberals to bring their energies not to compete (business versus government as the solution), but to collaborate (both ethical business and responsible government in collaboration as solutions).

15. You'll find two charters in this book; see appendices I and II.

16. See http://www.convergenceus.org for a US-based network and http://www.oasisuk.org for a British network. See http://mesa-friends.org for links to other national or regional networks.

17. See http://www.convergenceus.org/common-good-news.html for links regarding news, advocacy, and action.

18. See http://www.convergenceus.org.

19. One promising new initiative in this regard is the OPEN Network: www.theopennetworkus.org.

20. William G. McLoughlin, *Revivals, Awakenings, and Reform* (Chicago: University of Chicago Press, 1978), p. 216. Thanks to Diana Butler Bass for this quotation.

21. Max Planck, *Scientific Autobiography and Other Papers,* trans. Frank Gaynor (New York: Philosophical Library, 1949), p. 97. In another paper in the same collection, Planck expressed the same thought in a slightly different way: "A new scientific truth does not triumph by convincing its opponents and making them see the light, but rather

because its opponents eventually die and a new generation grows up that is familiar with it" (p. 33).

22. See www.faith-forward.net.

23. See http://www.theoedu.org/ for the important project in this regard led by Philip Clayton.

24. This is not intended to devalue academic practices, which can play a pivotal role in helping people grow in the skills of critical and post-critical thinking described in chapter 6. For more on changes in seminary education, see http://www.christianitytoday.com/parse/2013/october/does-mdiv-have-future.html?start=1.

25. The average United Methodist master of divinity graduate, for example, has accumulated over $49,000 in debt. See http://www.gbhem.org/article/average-debt-united-methodist-mdiv-graduate-reaches-49303.

26. One thinks of a quotation often attributed to Antoine de Saint-Exupéry: "If you want to build a ship, don't drum up the people to gather wood, divide the work, and give orders. Instead, teach them to yearn for the vast and endless sea."

27. C. S. Lewis, *Mere Christianity* (1952; repr., New York: HarperOne, 2001), 198–99.

CHAPTER 9: YOU ARE SOCIAL POETS

1. See Vincent Donovan, *Christianity Rediscovered* (Orbis, 2003). I am paraphrasing this quotation: "Do not try to call them back to where they were, and do not try to call them to where you are, as beautiful as that place might seem to you. You must have the courage to go with them to a place that neither you nor they have ever been before" (p. xix).

2. From a personal conversation in 2015. To learn more about Michael-Ray Mathews, see http://faithsource.org/faithsource_voices/michael-ray-mathews. And for more on this change model, see http://visions-inc.org/what-we-offer/. For a highly readable and helpful field book on helping your congregation put the concepts of this chapter into practice, see Tim Conder and Daniel Rhodes, *Organizing Church* (St. Louis, MO: Chalice Press, 2017).

3. From his "Land, Lodging, and Labor" speech delivered in Santa Cruz de la Sierra, Bolivia, July 9, 2015: http://time.com/3952885/pope-francis-bolivia-poverty-speech-transcript/.

4. For more on "institutional ego," see the Res Publica report "The Progressive and Social Justice Faith Movement: Portrait and Prospects" by Sheila Greeve Davaney, http://www.resourcelibrary.gcyf .org/sites/gcyf.org/files/resources/2014/davaneysheila_2014_the_ progressive_and_social_justice_faith_movement-_portrait_and_ prospects.pdf.

5. If corporations now rule the world, as David Korten rightly asserts, we need a new agenda and a new vision of what engagement looks like. See especially Korten's *The Great Turning* (San Francisco: Berrett-Koehler, 2006), *When Corporations Rule the World* (San Francisco: Berrett-Koehler, 1995), *Agenda for a New Economy* (San Francisco: Berrett-Koehler, 2010), and *Change the Story, Change the Future* (Oakland, CA: Berrett-Koehler, 2015).

6. Pamela Wilhelms is a theologically articulate and passionate Christian leader working in this space; see especially her Soul of the Next Economy initiative: http://wcgsite.weebly.com/about.html.

7. See http://www.iccr.org/investors-convince-pnc-stop-financing -mountaintop-removal-mining.

8. For more information, see http://ciw-online.org.

9. For wise guidance in this kind of congregational activism, see http:// watersheddiscipleship.org/, http://blessedtomorrow.org/, and http:// www.interfaithpowerandlight.org/.

10. Pope Francis, "Land, Lodging, and Labor."

11. One ecumenical Christian movement-building organization in which I am involved is Convergence; see http://www.convergenceus .org. One multifaith movement-building organization in which I am involved is the Auburn Senior Fellows program; see http://www .auburnseminary.org/seniorfellows.

12. See http://www.auburnseminary.org/seniorfellows for more information.

13. For more on evangelism in a postmodern and postcolonial context, see my book *More Ready Than You Realize* (Grand Rapids, MI: Zondervan, 2002).

Chapter 10: The Broken-Open Heart

1. For more on levels of consciousness, see the work of Steve McIntosh (http://www.stevemcintosh.com), beginning with *Integral Con-*

sciousness and the Future of Evolution (St. Paul, MN: Paragon, 2007). Richard Rohr offers one of the best one-page summaries of levels of consciousness, available via link at http://brianmclaren.net/archives/ blog/politics-and-consciousness.html. I also addressed this subject in some detail in my book *A New Kind of Christianity* (New York: HarperOne, 2010), chapters 20–22.

2. M. Scott Peck, *The Road Less Traveled* (New York: Touchstone, 1978), p. 15.

3. See http://www.couragerenewal.org/PDFs/PJP-WeavingsArticle -Broken-OpenHeart.pdf. Quotations appear on pp. 6–7.

4. See http://myemail.constantcontact.com/Richard-Rohr-s-Meditation --The-Sacred-Wound.html?soid=1103098668616&aid=EPrl0ZQ H1C8.

5. Martin Luther King Jr., "A Christmas Sermon on Peace," 1967, http:// www.ecoflourish.com/Primers/education/Christmas_Sermon.html.

6. Martin Luther King Jr., "An Experiment in Love," in *A Testament of Hope,* ed. James Melvin Washington (San Francisco: Harper & Row, 1986), p. 18.

7. Shane Claiborne wisely says that if you fight fire with fire, you get a bigger fire.

8. One of my mentors said most of us care about being *thought* right much more than we care about actually being right.

9. You'll find the whole prayer at http://brianmclaren.net/archives/blog /prayer-for-enemies.html. It was published in *Prayers by the Lake,* 2nd ed. (Serbian Orthodox Metropolitanate of New Gracanica, 1999), which is now out of print.

10. Rev. Dr. William Barber, leader of the Moral Mondays movement, gave a sermon about the necessity of disruption; see https://www .youtube.com/watch?v=YAhiQdHBSWo.

11. For more on disruptive innovation, see Clayton Christensen's *The Innovator's Dilemma* (Boston: Harvard Business Review Press, 2016).

12. You could make a case that the book of Genesis begins with a temple-reversal story. Temples were ubiquitous in the ancient Near East. And they were expensive to build and maintain. As a result, they were associated with wealth, kings, empires, power, and domination. Imagine the effect of telling poor and oppressed people seeking relief from domination that all creation is God's temple, and that human beings can simply "walk with God in the cool of the day" (Genesis

3:8)—no temple needed. Even more striking, the main purpose of ancient Near Eastern temples was to house an idol or image of a god. According to Genesis, in the temple of creation, at the center of creation is not a stone idol, but two naked and unashamed human beings who are the image or icon of God.

13. For more on Basava, see Alistair McIntosh and Matt Carmichael, *Spiritual Activism* (Cambridge, UK: UIT Cambridge Ltd, 2015), pp. 79–80.

14. Key to the development of liberation theology was the rediscovery of the Exodus story as the primary biblical narrative. For an accessible introduction to this rediscovery, see Rob Bell and Don Golden, *Jesus Wants to Save Christians* (Grand Rapids, MI: Zondervan, 2008).

15. You can see Dieter's photographs and read his story in a beautiful artisan book, *A Stroke of Grace,* by Dieter Zander and LaDonna Witmer, available at https://www.etsy.com. To learn more about Dieter, see http://www.dieterzander.com.

16. I'm thrilled that Dieter has begun accepting speaking engagements again. You can contact him here: dieter@dieterzander.com.

17. For a serious philosophical reflection on play, see Johan Huizinga, *Homo Ludens: A Study of the Play-Element in Culture* (Martino Fine Books, 2014). Thanks to the ever-playful Rev. Kyle Bennett for this book.

Afterword

1. For more on this group, see http://www.auburnseminary.org/senior fellows.

2. To learn more about Rabbi Stephanie Kolin, see http://blogs.rj.org/blog/2015/01/15/building-a-new-model-of-political-leadership-how-a-rabbi-stephanie-kolin-changed-our-community/.

Appendix I

1. See http://www.convergenceus.org. Also see http://www.mesa-friends.org and http://charterforcompassion.org. For another helpful and positive expression of progressive Christian faith, see the Phoenix Affirmations here: https://phoenixaffirmations.wordpress.com/. Rev. Eric Elnes, the thought leader behind the affirmations, introduces them here: https://www.youtube.com/watch?v=V_-laPEnmqA/.

APPENDIX II

1. See http://viewonbuddhism.org/resources/14_precepts.html. See also Thich Nhat Hanh, *Interbeing: Fourteen Guidelines for Engaged Buddhism,* rev. ed. (Berkeley, CA: Parallax, 1993).

APPENDIX III

1. See Richard Rohr's *Falling Upward* (San Francisco: Jossey-Bass, 2011) and my book *Naked Spirituality* (New York: HarperOne, 2012) for two compatible schema of first and second halves of the spiritual life.
2. John D. Caputo, *The Folly of God* (Polebridge, 2015), p. 76.
3. In *Why Did Jesus, Moses, the Buddha, and Mohammed Cross the Road?* (New York: Jericho, 2012), I describe a "weak" Christian identity that ejects its distinguishing features so as to be less different from, and therefore more tolerant of, other faiths. In the process, it risks losing its essential vision, unique gifts, and reason for existence.
4. See Matthew 23:24 and Philippians 1:10. Fundamentalism can be seen as an attempt to clearly define essentials. American fundamentalism of the early twentieth century, for example, concentrated on five fundamental conceptual beliefs: the inspiration and inerrancy of Scripture; the deity of Christ; Christ's virgin birth; penal substitutionary atonement; the physical resurrection and the personal bodily return of Christ. One wonders what could have happened if they had concentrated with equal fervency on five relational beliefs, such as belief in the justice, compassion, humility, reconciliation, and wisdom embodied in Jesus.
5. Citations are listed in the text as locations in the Kindle e-book of the 2013 Oxford University Press edition.
6. Actually, if one group becomes more effective at encouraging desired charitable actions and moral or spiritual growth, its effectiveness would, in fact, distinguish it even without distinctive beliefs. In this case, factors other than superior beliefs would account for the difference—such as compelling stories, inspiring examples, engaging practices, and a beautiful vision of the desired future, which we will address shortly.
7. These four legs could be seen as a contemporary alternative to the

single foundation of *sola scriptura* and to John Wesley's famous quad-rilateral of Scripture, tradition, reason, and experience. For reasons explained in chapters 1 and 2, what is needed today is not an indubi-table or incorrigible conceptual foundation, but rather a center suf-ficiently dynamic to convene people for what Clayton and Knapp call "concerted thought and action." For those who don't like the table image, we could say (following the work of the philosopher W. V. Quine) it is a web suspended by four anchor points.

8. See my book *A New Kind of Christianity* (New York: HarperOne, 2011), chapters 4–6.

9. The evolutionary theologian Michael Dowd gives one important take on this approach in his books, videos, and articles; see http://michaeldowd .org. See also Brian Thomas Swimme and Mary Evelyn Tucker, *Journey of the Universe* (New Haven, CT: Yale University Press, 2014).

10. This understanding of God is frequently associated with terms like *process or relational theology* and *panentheism,* in contrast to conventional supernatural theism that conceives of God as apart from nature or creation. For an accessible introduction to these matters, see Thomas Oord, *The Uncontrolling Love of God* (Downers Grove, IL: IVP, 2015).

11. A metanarrative (or imperial narrative) colonizes, conquers, replaces, reduces, assimilates, or eliminates all competing stories, and in this way, it becomes totalizing and often employs violence in achieving absolute compliance. In contrast, a liberating and reconciling story is a proclamation of good news. Good news (as articulated by the Cath-olic novelist and thinker Walker Percy) means a story that points a way out of our predicament. If one dimension of our predicament is violence, then good news must be nonviolent—otherwise, it will more deeply entangle us in our predicament rather than lead us out of it. For this reason, a message of good news must always challenge metanarratives because it refuses to comply with their violent ends and means. And messengers of good news must remain nonviolently vulnerable to being ignored, mocked, rejected, or even persecuted and killed by adherents of other stories. For this reason (as I am using the terms), the great liberating and reconciling story of good news can never function as a metanarrative, but rather must expose metanarratives and proclaim an alternative, a way out.

12. See my book *We Make the Road by Walking* (New York: Jericho, 2014), chapter 8.

13. Thanks to Brian Zahnd for this quotation from Ambrosio, found here, http://brianzahnd.com/2013/06/hero-or-saint/. Francis J. Ambrosio, *Philosophy, Religion, and the Meaning of Life* (Chantilly, VA: Teaching Company, 2009).

14. To read about why they were chosen, see http://www.saintgregorys.org/Resources_pdfs/Dancing_Saints_Bios2.pdf.

15. Abraham Joshua Heschel, *God in Search of Man* (New York: Farrar, Straus and Giroux, 1976), p. 3. Elsewhere, in an essay called "The Spirit of Jewish Prayer" (reprinted in *Moral Grandeur and Spiritual Audacity* (New York: Farrar, Straus, and Giroux, 1996, pp. 100–101), Heschel wrote: "Our services are conducted with pomp and precision. The rendition of the liturgy is smooth. Everything is present: decorum, voice, ceremony. But one thing is missing: *life*. One knows in advance what will ensue. There will be no surprise, no adventure of the soul; there will be no sudden burst of devotion. Nothing is going to happen to the soul. Nothing unpredictable must happen to the person who prays. He will attain no insight into the words he reads; he will attain no new perspective for the life he lives. Our motto is monotony. . . . There is nothing new in the synagogue. The fire has gone out of our worship. It is cold, stiff, and dead. Inorganic Judaism. . . . Yes, the edifices are growing. Yet worship is decaying. Has the synagogue become the graveyard where prayer is buried?" Thanks to Rabbi Sharon Brous for this quotation.

16. I ended up stirring up some productive controversy recently when I offered an alternative set of lyrics for the old hymn: http://brianmclaren.net/archives/blog/q-r-what-do-you-say-to-russell-m.html/.

17. For more on practice, see my book *Finding Our Way Again* (Nashville, TN: Thomas Nelson, 2010). In that book, I speak at length of *missional practices*. Some may wonder where mission fits into this table image. Here, it is an essential and natural practice that flows from our story; it is modeled by our saints and elders, and it helps make real in the present our vision of the future. We might say it is the life and work to which we arise from the table.

ACKNOWLEDGMENTS

1. John O'Donohue, "For the Time of Necessary Decision" in *To Bless the Space Between Us* (New York: Doubleday, 2008), p. 143.

ACKNOWLEDGMENTS

In one of his beautiful blessings, the Irish sage John O'Donohue wrote,

> May we have the courage to take the step
> Into the unknown that beckons us;
> Trust that a richer life awaits us there,
> That we will lose nothing
> But what has already died;
> Feel the deeper knowing in us sure
> Of all that is about to be born beyond
> The pale frames where we stayed confined,
> Not realizing how such vacant endurance
> Was bleaching our soul's desire.[1]

I would like to acknowledge all my colleagues in this great work, too many to name, some I know as dearest friends and even more who would be dearest friends if only we had met. Thank you for refusing to settle for "vacant endurance" and thank you for having the courage to step into the beckoning unknown. Many of you are named in this book and even more are not, but each of you deserves great respect for your leadership and example. When you read these words, I trust you recognize yourself.

As always, I want to thank my friend and agent, Kathryn

Helmers, who has been a most excellent professional companion, not to mention a fellow kayaker and lover of birds.

I asked my new editor, David Kopp, to be hard on me. He and fellow editor Derek Reed didn't disappoint, and if this book has helped you, David and Derek deserve great thanks from both of us. It is an incomparably better book than it would have been without their guidance and skill.

I thank all the groups who have had me speak, and all the wonderful people who asked incisive questions and made intriguing comments in our Q&R sessions. I especially thank Ring Lake Ranch in Dubois, Wyoming, for a delightful setting in which to finish the first draft of this project.

Of course, I must thank the birds: swallow-tailed kites, snowy plovers, white and brown pelicans, house and Carolina wrens, common robins, wood thrushes, ospreys, white-eyed vireos, goldfinches, hooded warblers, loons, ibises, egrets, herons, mergansers, hawks, hummingbirds, red knots, Canada geese, and so many more, whose songs, colors, graceful movements, and intriguing habits delight me every day, and whose instinct for migration inspired the title for this book.

I thank Grace, my wife and friend, for her constant love and commitment to keep growing more alive as we grow older.

Finally and most important, thanks be to God, who calls us to rise in a great spiritual migration.

INDEX

Campbell, Simone, 88

Caputo, John, 106, 217

Catholics, 12, 23, 64, 101–2, 166,
175, 201, 207, 217, 231*n,* 259*n*
beliefs and, 36–37, 39, 232*n,*
235*n*–36*n*
and frustration with
Christianity, 3–5
leadership crisis in, 163
movements and, 143, 145, 155,
157
violence and, 77, 81–82

Center for Action and
Contemplation, 181

change, xi–xii, 3, 5, 8–12, 16, 20,
28–29, 32, 41–42, 51, 152,
167–71, 174, 182, 194, 232*n*
Bible and, 112, 114–15
conversion and, 10, 167
cultural, 168–69
God and, 93, 95, 98, 103, 108,
112, 127
heart and, 8, 10, 167, 176, 188
how it happens, 167–69
integral, 103, 109
interpersonal, 168–69
intrapersonal, 167–69
levels of, 167–69, 182
love and, 59, 64, 168
movements and, 130–37, 139,
141–42, 146, 162–64, 169–70,
183, 250*n*
science and, 34, 36–37
social, 167
structural or institutional,
168–69
violence and, 71, 75, 167–68
wholesale rejection vs., 103, 109
and whom to call, 169–70

your little inner fundamentalist
and, 11–12

Charles, Mark, 82

Charter for a Just and Generous
Christianity, 155, 207–10

Christians, Christianity:
birth of, 13
competing traditions in, 28–29,
33, 234*n*–35*n*
core ethos and mission of, 3, 77,
154–55, 165
definitions of, 229*n*–30*n*
elevator, 152
in embracing new
understandings of itself,
41–42
frustration with, 3–6
in future, 195, 200, 220
history of, 3, 12, 71–72, 74–85,
87, 89–90, 92–93, 129, 132,
143–44, 244*n*
leaving, xiii, 5, 8, 16
of McLaren, x–xi, xiii, 7, 12, 14–
15, 27–28, 40, 42, 71, 75–76,
85, 93–94, 111–12, 188
and migration to better way of
being, xiii
need for systemic shift in, 31–32
numerical decline of, 5, 148
saving of, 7–11, 74–75, 88–89
as spiritual journey, xi, 8
things right with, 179
treasures of, 4, 8, 10–12, 16, 75
unintended consequences of, 2
weak, 258*n*

churches, xi, 4, 6, 8, 12, 14–15,
24, 26, 61–67, 85, 110, 154,
179–80, 184, 195, 197, 200,
207, 209, 224, 247*n*